Grades 6–8

Lessons for Algebraic Thinking

Grades 6–8

Ann Lawrence

Charlie Hennessy

Lessons for Algebraic Thinking

$$y = 2x + 3$$

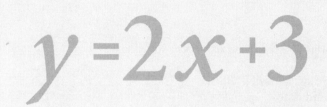

Math Solutions Publications
Sausalito, CA

Math Solutions Publications
A division of
Marilyn Burns Education Associates
150 Gate 5 Road, Suite 101
Sausalito, CA 94965
www.mathsolutions.com

The illustration on pages 158 and 245 is adapted from "Using Hooke's Law to Explore Linear Equations," *Mathematics Teacher* 93(5): 392.

Library of Congress Cataloging-in-Publication Data

Lawrence, Ann, 1946–

    Lessons for algebraic thinking. Grades 6–8 / Ann Lawrence, Charlie Hennessy.
       p.   cm.—(The lessons for algebraic thinking series)
    Includes bibliographical references and index.
     ISBN 0-941355-49-7 (alk. paper)
    1. Algebra—Study and teaching (Middle school)   I. Hennessy, Charlie.
II. Title. III. Series.
    QA159 .L38   2002
    512'.0071'2—dc21

                                           2002009288

Editor: Toby Gordon
Production: Melissa L. Inglis
Cover and interior design: Catherine Hawkes/Cat & Mouse Design
Composition: Cape Cod Compositors, Inc.

Printed in the United States of America on acid-free paper
06 05 04 03 02   ML   1 2 3 4 5

A Message from Marilyn Burns

We at Marilyn Burns Education Associates believe that teaching mathematics well calls for increasing our understanding of the math we teach, seeking greater insight into how children learn mathematics, and refining lessons to best promote children's learning. Math Solutions helps teachers achieve these goals by providing professional development through inservice courses and publications.

Our publications include a wide range of choices, from books in our new Teaching Arithmetic and Lessons for Algebraic Thinking series to resources that link math and literacy; from books to help teachers understand mathematics more deeply to children's books that help students develop an appreciation for math while learning basic concepts.

Our inservice offers five-day courses, one-day workshops, and series of school-year sessions throughout the country, working in partnership with school districts to help implement and sustain long-term improvement in mathematics instruction in all classrooms.

To find a complete listing of our publications and workshops, please visit our Web site at *www.mathsolutions.com*. Or contact us by calling (800) 868-9092 or sending an e-mail to *info@mathsolutions.com*.

We're eager for your feedback and interested in learning about your particular needs. We look forward to hearing from you.

A DIVISION OF MARILYN BURNS EDUCATION ASSOCIATES

This book is dedicated to our parents,
Kate and Tom Hennessy
Louise and George Lawrence

Contents

Foreword

Most professionals in the field of mathematics education believe that we are at a critical juncture. We recognize that the changes in our world and what research tells us about how students learn dictate concomitant changes in what we teach and how we teach it. To function in everyday life and in the workplace, every student needs the thought processes and the mathematical skills that are the results of a rigorous but sensible study of algebra. Thus, it has become a nationwide goal for every student to successfully complete, at a minimum, one course in algebra.

To reach this goal, we must place the emphasis on student learning. As succinctly stated in *Principles and Standards for School Mathematics* (NCTM 2000, 20), "Students must learn mathematics with understanding, actively building new knowledge from experience and prior knowledge."

In no area of mathematics are changes needed more than in preparation for algebra. At the same time that there is increasing societal pressure to achieve "algebra for all," the overall success rate of students in our algebra courses remains dismal. Classroom teachers and researchers alike assign much of the blame for the failure rates in algebra to the huge conceptual difference between the primarily concrete arithmetic procedures involving known numbers that are studied in pre-algebra and the abstractions of variables, functions, and equations that are studied in algebra. The transition from pre-algebra to algebra should not be so stark. Instead, as stated in *Principles and Standards for School Mathematics* (37), "By viewing algebra as a strand in the curriculum from pre-kindergarten on, teachers can help students build a solid foundation of understanding and experience as a preparation for the more sophisticated work of algebra." Moreover, we believe that attention to algebraic thinking should be incorporated into all the strands of the mathematics curriculum. It has been our experience that students can be effectively prepared for algebra when the middle school curriculum makes the development of algebraic thinking a key goal. This is true regardless of the students' previous mathematical experiences.

It is critical to note that the development of algebraic thinking, like the development of number sense or spatial reasoning, is not accomplished haphazardly or quickly. Key understandings are built upon facility with concrete materials that form the foundation for working with pictorial, tabular, graphic, and, eventually, symbolic representations. Students need many varied experiences in meaningful contexts with each of these representations before they can truly understand the symbolic expressions and rules of formal algebra.

We believe *all* students can attain the kind of thinking required by a formal algebra course. More important, they can learn to use mathematics to make sense of the world—to look at the world through a mathematical lens that allows them to explain and predict phenomena. By having a series of experiences through the middle school years that help them make connections between arithmetic and algebra, our students can progress gradually toward the view that algebra is a natural extension of their previous mathematical experiences.

Thus, the goals of this book are the following:

- To help teachers establish a classroom atmosphere conducive to maximizing student discovery and expression/sharing of ideas

- To provide sample lessons that help teachers get a feel for how to focus on algebraic thinking in a range of contexts

- To provide sample lessons that help teachers see how certain methods foster the development of algebraic thinking

- To provide examples of the kind of questioning and other techniques teachers can use to increase student understanding

- To provide examples of student work to help teachers see a variety of student solutions that reflect algebraic thinking

In short, this book is offered as a set of lessons to stimulate thought about how mathematics instruction during the middle school years can maximize the acquisition of algebraic thinking.

Finally, we would like to acknowledge how much we've learned while writing this book. We highly recommend that all teachers take the time and the challenge to reflect in detail upon their own philosophies and methods of teaching and learning—for their students and themselves. We are confident that all will benefit. We assure you it is both a rewarding and a humbling experience. Enjoy!

Introduction: Developing Algebraic Reasoning

What Do We Mean by Algebraic Thinking?

In the broadest sense, algebraic thinking encompasses the set of understandings that are needed to interpret the world by translating information or events into the language of mathematics in order to explain and predict phenomena. Also, algebraic thinking leads to the abstract thinking required for success in textbook algebra. Applying these understandings effectively often requires the following components:

- Using or setting up a mathematical model, if needed
- Gathering and recording data, if needed
- Organizing data and looking for patterns
- Describing and extending those patterns
- Generalizing findings, often into a rule
- Using findings, including any rules, to make predictions

To develop true understanding, students must work with problem situations that arise throughout the strands of mathematics and in various contexts that are familiar or make sense to them. While students are solving engaging, meaningful problems, we teachers must focus the students' attention on the concepts vital for success in formal algebra. These concepts include the following:

- Analyzing change, especially rates of change
- Understanding functions, especially linear functions
- Understanding and using variables in different ways
- Interpreting, creating, and moving fluently between multiple representations for data sets

How Is This Approach Implemented?

Emphasizing algebraic thinking does not require a new middle school curriculum. It does not require a huge add-on component to the curriculum. Instead, maximizing the development of algebraic thinking can be accomplished by simple shifts in emphasis and teaching methods.

How, then, do we foster the development of algebraic thinking among our students? First, the chances for success with any lesson are greatly increased in a nurturing classroom environment. A safe environment with clear values and high expectations sets the stage for student growth: we work to help each class develop into a community of learners by repeatedly stating and showing that there must be respect for every learner. We consistently demonstrate that we value risk taking, independent thinking, and work of high quality. As teachers, we primarily facilitate learning as opposed to merely dispensing knowledge. Students often work with partners or in small groups; however, we make sure students understand that, while collaboration leads to more learning for everyone, each student is ultimately responsible for his or her own learning.

Learning by doing lies at the heart of these lessons. The approach we use focuses on genuine student understanding. We believe such understanding grows out of personal inquiry and discovery, not through being told what and how to think. Such learning is promoted by problem solving in authentic contexts, collaboration among students, probing questions, and thoughtful processing. These methods are grounded in research that tells us students achieve understanding of concepts and develop new ways of thinking only when they build on previous experience and knowledge. These principles of learning are embodied in the NCTM *Principles and Standards for School Mathematics* (2000).

It is essential to start slowly. At first, we focus on recognizing, extending, describing, and generalizing patterns as the primary targeted algebraic thinking skills. The first few lessons, like *Surprising Squares*, must be carefully structured and may seem to require an inordinate amount of time. This is largely true because each student must develop understanding based on his or her own prior knowledge and experience. This often means that several different ways of thinking must be explored for each pattern. Different learning modalities should be accommodated. With these first investigations, we carefully choose problems and guide the students to progress from concrete objects to abstract ideas, from numerical examples to generalizations.

During these lessons we begin to expand students' ways of viewing patterns. Most middle school students come to us still thinking iteratively to a great extent. Thus, they would express the rule for the pattern 1, 3, 5, 7 . . . as, "Each term is two larger than the term before it" or "To get the next term, add two to the previous term." Often it takes a lot of hard work for students to be able to view changes in patterns as being related to the stage or term number, as in the *Go Figure!* lesson. Even then, they may be able to express the rule only by using specific examples. Expressing the rule for the pattern listed above, for example, a student thinking in this way might say, "The tenth term of the pattern is nineteen because you can multiply the ten times two (the amount of change from one term to the next) and then subtract one." Only after several more guided experiences are most students able to independently generalize and state the rule for this pattern using a variable, as, for example, "Each term follows the rule $2n - 1$ when n represents the stage number." This learning sequence is complicated by the fact that other students in the same class are likely to view the pattern in such a way that the explicit rule is expressed as $2(n - 1) + 1$ or some other equivalent form of the rule.

Additionally, of course, students do not progress from concrete to abstract understanding and expression of ideas at the same pace. Therefore, we must be especially artful in how we structure the initial experiences that focus on the development of algebraic thinking so that all students have opportunities to increase their levels of understanding. To help students make the transition from the concrete world of arithmetic to that of algebra with its abstract symbols and rules, we structure these lessons using small conceptual steps.

As we move beyond the most basic introductory lessons (like those in Part One), one of our focuses is to offer a wide variety of experiences. We choose explorations that both involve significant mathematics and allow us to emphasize components of algebraic thinking. We often use problems that can be solved using several different strategies and/or have multiple solutions. The *Condo Challenge* and *Who Finishes When?* lessons are particularly rich in these ways. For some problems we ask small groups of students to investigate different variations of a particular situation, as in the *Stretching Slinkies* lesson, in order for students to consider the effects of those variations. In all these lessons students are encouraged to use various representations for data—to become familiar and comfortable with models, drawings, tables, graphs, words, and symbols as problem-solving tools. After many such lessons, the students are able to move comfortably among the different representations. Ultimately, we believe it is the mental processes required to connect these representations that enable students to analyze and understand rates of change, uses of variables, and the concept of function—that is, to develop algebraic thinking.

Spreading these experiences throughout the middle school mathematics curriculum gives students many opportunities to absorb and develop the understandings they need. This slow and steady exposure to concepts and skills provides spiraled learning opportunities for all students—another chance at initial understanding for those who were not ready on the "last round," a chance to strengthen concepts, and/or the challenge to gain a deeper understanding for others. For example, either *Personalized Patterns* or *Stretching Slinkies* can serve as another opportunity to grasp the basics of finding explicit rules for patterns for some students while it gives other students a chance to begin internalizing the meaning of such concepts as function, intercept, and slope. During *The Window Problem*, while some students will primarily be strengthening their understanding of linear functions, others will be able to focus on comparing linear with nonlinear functions. Through this kind of repeated exposure, students experience success and develop confidence in their ability to do mathematics and in themselves.

In all these lessons our pedagogical and content goals are tightly interwoven. For example, in trying to help students learn to express explicit rules for patterns, we are also mindful of which questions we want to ask, how to best word those questions, and how to respond to student answers. We encourage and require, in varying degrees, both oral and written expression by students of their mathematical thinking. We use a variety of assessment techniques. Observing, questioning, and having students share their thinking and their work all provide opportunities for ongoing assessment during the lessons. Individual or group reports or summaries serve as endpoint assessments of student learning. There are multiple conceptual and pedagogical objectives for each lesson, some designed for every student and many others aimed at students who are at a different level of understanding in one or more ways than most of those in the class.

Additionally, during these lessons the vocabulary of algebra begins to take on meaning for students. Before we give the mathematical definition for a concept, we first try to have students develop understanding of that concept within one or more contexts that make sense to them. For example, the meaning of the steepness of a line is examined in the *Stretching Slinkies* lesson when students are asked to examine the line of points that represents the length of a Slinky plus a cup when quarters are added to the cup one at a time. They are then asked to compare the steepness of a similar line of points when dimes are added to the cup to the steepness of the original line of points and explain how the difference makes sense in the context of their investigation. After the students have several experiences that focus, at least in part, on the real-world meaning of the slope of a line, we ask our students to express their understanding of the concept using their own words. At that time, the word *slope* may or may not be introduced. Over time, we push for student definitions that are more and more mathematically precise. However, evidence of a student's understanding of a concept remains more important than using the mathematical term for it throughout the middle school years.

We also feel compelled to mention the use of technology. We strongly believe that appropriate uses of technology can enhance student learning in many ways. Calculators and computers, when used appropriately, can help students discover mathematical concepts and/or understand them more completely. These tools can be used to help students produce and interpret multiple representations. Perhaps most important, they can help students develop understanding of the connections among such representations. There are many other benefits that can be achieved through using technology.

That said, most of the lessons described in this book were carried out without the use of technology. We are all too aware that many teachers do not have access to such tools at the present time, and, therefore, we opted to design lessons that we believe can help students develop algebraic thinking without the use of technology. However, we have included technology connections for each lesson—connections that we have used with our students before, during, or after these same lessons. It is our hope that every teacher reading this book will have the opportunity to incorporate at least some of these suggested uses of technology. Our experience has been that using technology as an integral part of our teaching has greatly enhanced learning for our middle school students.

Finally, we pose and encourage students to ask "What if . . . ?" questions and invite them to offer ideas for extensions to the lessons, as in the *Who Finishes When?* lesson. Such follow-up investigations add an extra dimension of excitement for the students and model the importance of life-long inquiry and learning, which we want to cultivate in our students.

More specifically, they demonstrate the power of algebraic thinking to solve new problems and explain or predict phenomena to make sense of the world.

What Else Should You Know About These Lessons?

For most of the lessons presented in this book, the central problem or question in the lesson is not our own invention. Some (e.g., *Condo Challenge*) are "old chestnuts," long-used problems that offer a plethora of opportunities for multiple interpretations. Some lessons are based on investigations included in inquiry-based curricula (e.g., *Who Finishes When?* and *Surprising Squares*), while others grew out of problems gleaned from an article or presentation by a colleague (e.g., *Stretching Slinkies* and *The Window Problem*). But each of the lessons was adapted, altered, and/or expanded in important ways—that is, each lesson was developed and carried out in ways designed to stimulate the development of algebraic thinking among students. Our objective is to present the lessons as they occurred, along with our motivations, reactions, and interpretations of what went on in the classroom, in order to demonstrate the flavor and detail of such lessons.

We think it is important to note that none of these "lesson accounts" is based on the first attempt to use a particular problem or investigation with a class of students. Details ranging from the way we worded the problem to the way we posed questions to the way we used procedures in these versions of the lessons were developed and refined through many "practice rounds" with classes at different grade levels and in different schools, often over several years. Also, for each write-up, one of us was the teacher, the other an observer. Use of "I" in the manuscript was chosen because each lesson was taught by one of us with the other present. However, both the lessons and the book are truly a collaborative effort and the opinions are ones we share.

Further, the lessons are not offered as models or finished products: there are details that change every time we go through the lessons with a new class of students. Even after many attempts, we try something slightly different or students take the class down a different learning path, and we learn something new each time we offer the same problem to a different group of students. What we hope is that these lessons offer other teachers a chance to reflect upon the numerous components of planning, implementing, and assessing instruction that can help maximize the development of algebraic thinking in students.

To help you teach the lessons, each is organized into the following sections:

Overview   This is a nutshell description of the mathematical focus of the lesson and what the students will be doing.

Background   This section addresses the mathematics underlying the lesson and at times provides information about prior experiences or knowledge students need.

Prerequisite Concepts or Skills   This section lists experiences students need prior to doing the lesson.

Vocabulary   The algebraic terminology used in the lesson is listed alphabetically.

Time   The number of class periods required is indicated, sometimes with a range allowing for different-length periods and for differences among classes. Most lessons call for more than one class period.

Materials   This section lists the materials needed, along with quantities. Not included are regular classroom supplies such as paper and pencils. Activity sheets required are included in the Blackline Masters section at the back of the book.

The Lesson   This section presents the heart of the lesson with a vignette that describes what occurred when the lesson was taught, providing the details needed for planning and teaching the lesson. Samples of student work are included.

Similar Problem   This problem is appropriate for a follow-up lesson.

Extension Problem   This section suggests further experiences that expand upon the chapter's primary lesson.

Technology Connections   This section suggests uses of technology either before, during, or after the lesson.

These lessons are not designed for any particular grade level. The grade level mentioned in each lesson only indicates the level of the students with whom that lesson was carried out in the vignette presented in this book. We have done most of the lessons with students at other grade levels as well. Students' prior experiences and understandings about algebraic thinking are far more important indicators of whether the lesson is appropriate for a given class than their grade level is. For example, students will be unlikely to compare and contrast linear with nonlinear functions in *The Window Problem* unless they have at least a basic understanding of linear functions. Any particular lesson is appropriate for some classes at grade 6, 7, or 8. In general, the lessons are presented in a roughly sequential order, aligned with the complexity of the concepts involved, according to what we have observed in our middle school students through the years.

Some of the lessons (e.g., *Personalized Patterns*, *Stretching Slinkies*, and *Condo Challenge*) were not completed in a single class session. They were done during double periods or spread out over several days. Sometimes the extra time was needed to allow the students time for thoughtful application of what they had learned. For example, as a part of the *Personalized Patterns* lesson, students were given several days to extend the concepts dealt with in the first part of the lesson by creating their own patterns that followed explicit function rules before they presented those patterns to their classmates for investigation. In other cases, as with *Stretching Slinkies*, there simply was not enough time available to complete the investigation and adequately carry out the sharing and analysis of the results in a single class period. We have provided some guidelines to help teachers select appropriate lessons for their classes in the table in Figure 1. This table indicates the content and process goals for students for each lesson in this book.

FIGURE 1 Checklist of content goals for students

Understanding, knowledge, or skill related to the development and use of algebraic thinking	Surprising Squares	Personalized Patterns	Go Figure!	Bulging Backpacks	Who Finishes When?	Stretching Slinkies	Condo Challenge	The Window Problem
Explore patterns using multiple representations (models, drawings, tables, graphs, words, and/or symbolic rules).	X	X	X	X	X	X	X	X
Describe, extend, and generalize patterns.	X	X	X	X	X	X	X	X
Use observations, tables, graphs, and/or rules to analyze change in quantities.	X	X	X	X	X	X	X	
Build understanding of linear functions.		X		X	X	X		X
Identify functions as linear or nonlinear; compare and contrast their properties.								X
Use function rules to make predictions.	X	X			X	X		X
Model and solve contextual problems using algebraic thinking.		X	X	X	X	X	X	X
Explore conceptual meaning for slope and/or intercept in the context of a problem situation.				X	X	X		X
Explore and develop understanding of use(s) of variables.	X	X	X	X	X	X	X	X
Gather real-world data to find relationship(s) between variables.				X		X		
Investigate how changes in one variable relate to changes in a second variable.				X	X	X		X
Recognize, generate, and evaluate equivalent forms for simple algebraic expressions.	X	X	X		X	X	X	X
Apply algebraic thinking to solve problems across the other mathematics curriculum strands.			X	X		X	X	X

In all lessons, the following are process goals for students:

- Employ a variety of appropriate strategies to solve a problem
- Make and investigate mathematical conjectures
- Develop and express mathematical arguments verbally and in writing
- Use and examine various types of reasoning
- Communicate mathematical thinking orally and in writing

- Use mathematical terms, language, and notation appropriately
- Recognize and use connections between/among mathematical ideas
- Apply mathematics in a wide variety of contexts
- Use and move comfortably among mathematical representations to solve problems
- Use representations to model, interpret, and predict phenomena

PART ONE

Getting Students Ready

As mentioned in the Introduction, we do not feel there is a precise order in which the lessons in this book should be used. However, for particular lessons, we feel there are some prerequisite concepts and skills that will help you and the students focus on the goals or objectives of that lesson without having to simultaneously fill in gaps for students who are conceptually behind the majority of their classmates. We believe the following vignettes and notes can help you in one or both of two ways:

1. To provide insight into how your students are thinking about two fundamental ideas (patterns and functions) and how proficient they are with related procedures (using T-charts and graphing on the coordinate plane) that are needed for many of the lessons in this book

2. To provide examples of how such ideas and procedures might be introduced to your students, if needed

These vignettes do not include the same level of detail as the lessons that follow, but we hope they can help you assess some of your students' understandings and/or introduce them to fundamental ideas and procedures related to the development of algebraic thinking.

CHAPTER 1

Patterns and T-Charts

Introductory Experiences

Over the years we have refined the ways we help our middle school students develop proficiency in finding rules for patterns. We have found that the approach that works best for us incorporates a wide variety of content and pedagogical focuses, including the following.

Content Focuses

- Exposing students to a variety of patterns over time

- Using relevant/real-world patterns early and often

- Working with students to recognize and describe, extend, and generalize each pattern whenever possible

- Starting with patterns created using concrete objects and encouraging use of drawings, words, and symbols as individual students are ready

- Beginning with simple, unambiguous patterns but progressing rapidly to more complicated ones

- Spiraling use of vocabulary such as *stage, constant, variable, iterative rule,* and *explicit rule*—students refine definitions over time

- Encouraging multiple interpretations of each pattern whenever appropriate

- Incorporating the use of a T-chart/table for each pattern

- Validating correct iterative rules while encouraging searches for appropriate explicit rules

- Asking students to use their rule(s) to predict what each pattern will look like or what its value will be for *several stages*

- Asking students to use their rule(s) to predict what each pattern will look like or what its value will be for *some large stage number*

- Asking students to use their rule(s) to predict what each pattern will look like or what its value will be for *any stage number*

- Asking students to find the appropriate stage number for a description or value of a particular stage of a pattern

- Moving as quickly as possible to working almost exclusively with patterns embedded in problem situations

Pedagogical Focuses

- Exploring one pattern at a time, followed by students' written reflections

- Working in a whole-class setting with built-in "think time" for the first few patterns—allowing students to work alone, then share their ideas with the class

- Working with individual students who need extra practice as the need arises

- Working in small groups and sharing ideas with the rest of the class as soon as appropriate in a particular class

- Having students write their reflections about a pattern early and often

The following vignette is from a lesson we used with a class of sixth graders, some of whom had very little experience working with patterns. We presented a simple pattern every few days early in the new school year. On each day following the exploration of a particular pattern, the students wrote brief reflections about the pattern they encountered the day before.

Exploration: The Rocket Pattern

Each student had a pencil and paper and was given a small bag of pattern blocks. I asked the students how many of them had worked with finding rules for patterns in their math classes in earlier grades, and nearly all raised their hands. I explained that the class would examine several patterns in the next few days and would be (1) sharing ways of thinking about various patterns, (2) practicing using a T-chart, and (3) hopefully, adding techniques for finding rules for patterns to each student's mathematical toolbox. I then used overhead pattern blocks to build the first three stages of the Rocket Pattern and projected them on the screen at the front of the room (see Figure 1–1).

I asked that each student look carefully at the first three stages of the pattern as they appeared on the screen and then build what he or she thought a Stage 4 rocket would look like.

Barry immediately raised his hand and asked, "What's a Stage Four rocket?"

There are usually sixth graders in any class who are not familiar with or do not remember the terms *stage* and *stage number*. Since it is essential that each student understand terms like these to be successful in our study of patterns, it is important to go over those terms with each new pattern until all the students are comfortable with sensible working definitions.

I asked whether anyone would like to say what he or she thought I meant, and Jack volunteered, "A Stage One, a Stage Two, and a Stage Three rocket are on the screen. They are the first three steps, or parts, in a pattern. If you look at how the pattern is going, you can tell what the next step in the pattern—a Stage Four rocket—will look like, and that's what you build with your pattern blocks."

Barry indicated that he understood Jack's explanation and each student successfully produced a Stage 4 rocket, as shown in Kenya's drawing in Figure 1–2.

I then asked that each student build, draw, or describe in words a Stage 5 rocket. Most of the students chose to build or draw a Stage 5 rocket. All except one of these students correctly depicted the figure. Sean had placed four blue rhombi under his three-piece model of the rocket. When I leaned over his shoulder and asked Sean to explain his thinking, he quickly exclaimed, "Oh, I meant to put five blue pieces there!" as he added a fifth rhombus to his model.

A few students chose to describe the Stage 5 rocket in words. Cemmie wrote, *A Stage 5 Rocket is just like all the others except it has 5 puffs of smoke.*

When asked to explain her thinking, Cemmie replied, "A Stage One rocket [pointing to the appropriate image on the screen] has a rocket made from three pieces plus the one puff of smoke. A Stage Two rocket has a rocket and two puffs of smoke [again pointing to the screen], and so on, so a Stage Five rocket has five puffs of smoke." When asked whether they agreed with Cemmie's line of reasoning, all the students nodded.

"So who can describe a Stage Ten rocket?" I asked. Several hands went up. I paused to give other students more time to think and about three-fourths of the students soon had their hands in the air.

I called on Suzi, who said, "It would be a rocket with ten puffs of smoke."

I asked whether everyone agreed and Camille spoke up. "Well," she said, "I would say it is a rocket made from a square, a triangle, and a trapezoid, and ten rhombuses for the puffs of smoke." Everyone agreed that

FIGURE 1–1

The rocket pattern

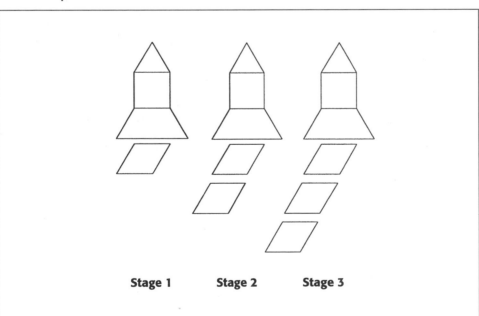

Stage 1   Stage 2   Stage 3

FIGURE 1–2

Kenya's drawing of a Stage 4 rocket

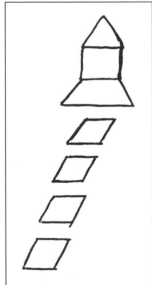

Camille's description was correct and also made it possible for someone who could not see a model or drawing to visualize the figure more clearly in his or her head.

I asked why some people had not raised their hands earlier, and Robbie volunteered that he got the same answer as Suzi and Camille but was not quite sure enough to raise his hand. I asked what he might do to be sure he was right. He replied, "Build or draw each one up to Stage Ten."

When asked, "Can you think of another way?" Robbie had no answer, so I asked him to choose another student to offer a suggestion. He called on Chelsie.

"Draw a T-chart," she offered. When Robble indicated that he had never seen a T-chart, I asked Chelsie to draw a T-chart for the Rocket Pattern on the board and explain it to the class. Figure 1–3 shows Chelsie's chart and explanation.

I still find that many students come to middle school claiming never to have heard of or seen a T-chart. Unfortunately, it is not simply that the term *T-chart* is unfamiliar: these students either have never been asked to record and examine data in a table, or they don't remember having done so. Either way, I make sure that early in the school year each of my classes is introduced to or reminded of using tables to record and interpret data. Through the years I have become convinced that using tables is the single best path to developing understanding of variables, a vital concept in the development of algebraic thinking. I want every student to develop facility with this powerful problem-solving tool during the middle school years.

To check his understanding, I asked Robbie to tell, in his own words, what Chelsie had said. He explained, "A T-chart is a way to write down and keep up with what is happening in a pattern. It can help you realize what is happening or, like for me, help you to know you are thinking right.

FIGURE 1–3   Chelsie's chart and explanation

Stage	Total # of Pieces
1	4
2	5
3	6
4	7
5	8
6	9
7	10
8	11
9	12
10	13

Chelsie's Comments

A T-chart has at least two parts, one column for the stage numbers and one for the numbers that match up with each of the stage numbers. For the Rocket Pattern—and a lot of other patterns—the second column is the total number of pieces or parts you get for that stage. You can count them from drawings, but soon you notice that the total number of pieces gets bigger by one each time, so you just fill in the rest of the chart.

For the Rocket Pattern you start with four pieces and add one more for each stage, so a Stage Ten Rocket has a total of thirteen pieces."

Emily raised her hand. "It makes sense to me that the total number of pieces increases by one for each stage because we added one puff of smoke each time. But if I think about it without looking at the chart, I get confused. We started with four pieces, so why isn't the total for a Stage Ten rocket fourteen pieces—four to start with and then ten puffs?"

Scot tried to explain. He pointed out, "Actually, Emily, you had only three pieces to start with—the triangle, the square, and the trapezoid (or the rocket). And then you added one rhombus (or the puff of smoke) to get a whole Stage One rocket."

Emily still looked confused, so I used her question as an opportunity to show the class how to expand the use (and often the value) of a T-chart. I pointed out that many people find it helpful to add a column to their T-chart, and I projected the image shown in Figure 1–4 onto the screen.

Next I asked Suzi to reread her description of a Stage 10 rocket. When she finished reading, I asked the class, "So what did Suzi see as the parts of each stage?"

Jared answered, "She said each stage has a rocket and some puffs of smoke."

I wrote the words *Rocket Pieces* and *Puffs* in the center column, then asked, "And what do you do to get the total number of pieces needed for any stage?"

"Add," the students said in unison, so I put a plus sign in the center column between the two phrases, as shown in Figure 1–5.

Next I asked whether anyone could look at the Stage 1 rocket, break it into the parts listed in the center column, and tell what numbers to write for Stage 1. Robin quickly waved her hand in the air and waited patiently while I gave the other students some time to try to find the an-

---

FIGURE 1–4   Blank T-chart for the rocket pattern

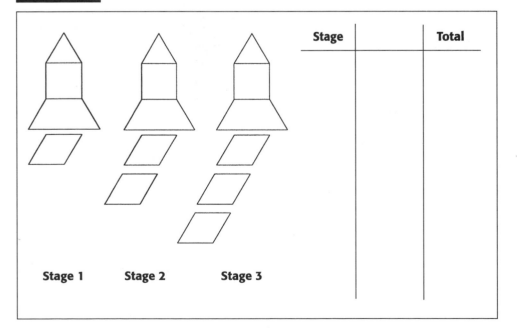

Stage		Total

Stage 1   Stage 2   Stage 3

FIGURE 1-5   Adding to the T-chart for the rocket pattern

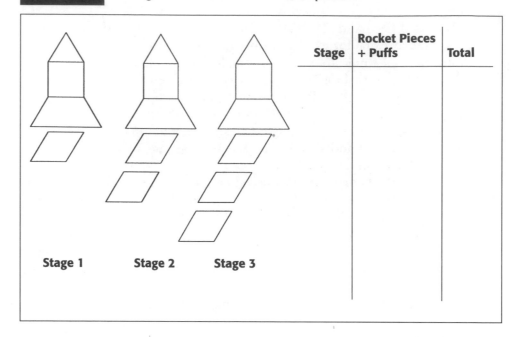

swer for themselves. I then asked Robin to come to the overhead, explain her thinking, and write the appropriate numbers in the chart. She said the following while she filled in the chart, as shown here. "For the Stage One rocket there are three pattern blocks, or pieces, in the rocket itself. Also, there is one pattern block for the puff of smoke, so there is a total of four pieces."

Stage	Rocket Pieces + Puffs	Total
1	3 + 1	4

Teddy raised his hand to comment, "I think we need to call the last column 'Total Number of Pieces' because all the pieces are not the same size or shape and that might confuse someone." Several students nodded and Teddy rewrote the caption as he filled in the numbers for Stage 2 in the T-chart, saying, "For Stage Two, the rocket has the same three pieces, but there are two puffs of smoke, so the total is five pieces."

Stage	Rocket Pieces + Puffs	Total # of Pieces
1	3 + 1	4
2	3 + 2	5

Emily agreed to do Stage 3. She smiled as she wrote the numbers and explained, "For Stage Three, you add three pieces for the rocket and three puffs of smoke, making a total of six pieces."

Stage	Rocket Pieces + Puffs	Total # of Pieces
1	3 + 1	4
2	3 + 2	5
3	3 + 3	6

Next I asked the students to look carefully at the center column of our T-chart, try to find any overall pattern there, and raise their hands when they found such a pattern. Soon nearly every hand was raised. I then asked whether anyone could express the pattern he or she found in words. Daniel responded, "For every stage, there are three pieces in the rocket and one more puff than in the last stage." I asked for a show of hands by students who agreed and every student so indicated. I was surprised that no one first isolated the pattern of threes or the increasing pattern 1, 2, 3 . . . , but was thankful they seemed to grasp the overall pattern at once.

I asked whether anyone saw the pattern in a different way, but no one volunteered. I was hoping someone would offer the explicit pattern "For each stage there are three pieces in the rocket plus a number of smoke puffs that is the same as the stage number," but I decided not to push for this observation on the first day of our pattern explorations. Most middle school students come to us thinking iteratively—basing their understanding of a pattern on the change from one stage to the next. I think it is important to validate this way of thinking and not to rush students to find explicit patterns and rules, so I decided to revisit this pattern after a few more experiences and see whether I could push the students further at that time.

During this part of the exploration, I asked two more questions to introduce the ideas of constant and variable. First, I asked, "Who can tell us which part of the Rocket Pattern stays the same?"

Several students quickly answered, "The threes," or "The three pieces of the rocket," or simply, "The rocket." I affirmed their answers and explained that mathematicians refer to a part of a pattern that remains the same for every stage as a *constant*. In this way, I introduce essential vocabulary as it applies in a relevant context (in this case, the Rocket Pattern). I have found that this increases the students' initial understanding of vocabulary and makes it more likely that they will recall the meaning of such terms later. Marilyn announced that *constant* was a "sensible name" since her mother often used the word when Marilyn did something again and again, like "tease my brother *constantly*." I suspect that this comment will probably serve as a mnemonic device that will help some of the students remember the term better than the three pieces of the rocket in this pattern!

The second, related question I asked was, "Who can tell us which part of the pattern changes from stage to stage?" All agreed it was the number of puffs of smoke that changed, so I explained that mathematicians call any part of a pattern that changes *variable*. At this point, I did not expect the students to remember precise definitions but hoped instead that they would begin to develop an intuitive understanding of these important ideas.

Next I asked that each student try to think of a rule for the total number of pattern block pieces for any stage in the Rocket Pattern and write it down. I explained that someone should be able to read the rule and then find the total pieces needed for any stage of the Rocket Pattern. When everyone had something written down, I asked the students to share their rules. I also told them they would be able to write a revised version of their rule if they wished after hearing all the ideas. Jeremy's rule was "To get the total for any stage, add one to the total for the stage before it."

I asked whether this rule would work and most of the students nodded. I asked for a volunteer to use the rule for Stage 11. Teddy volunteered. "For a Stage Eleven rocket there would be fourteen pieces because there were thirteen pieces in Stage Ten and thirteen plus one equals fourteen." His classmates agreed.

I asked whether anyone else had written the same rule as Jeremy and over half the students raised their hands. Because this was our first exploration, I asked that each student read his or her rule aloud if it was different in any way—even if it was just one word—from Jeremy's rule. Many, like Sarah, indicated that they wanted to modify their rules slightly after hearing Jeremy's. She said, "I wrote, *Total equals add one*, but I need to add 'to the stage before' for my rule to be clear." I agreed with Sarah's conclusion.

Next I asked whether anyone had a different rule. Camille volunteered, "Total pieces equals three, plus one more than the rhombuses in the stage before." When asked to do so, Cemmie used Camille's rule for Stage 11 by adding three plus *eleven*, the number of rhombuses or puffs from Stage 10, plus one. Most of the remaining students basically expressed their rule like Cemmie.

I then asked whether the two rules were the same. Josh volunteered, "They are not exactly the same, but they both work. And for both rules, you have to know something about the stage before it to get the answer."

I explained to the class that Josh's comment had two important mathematical ideas we should discuss. First, as Josh pointed out, while the rules were not worded exactly the same, they both worked for the Rocket Pattern. I told the class that when this is true, the rules are called *equivalent*. I explained that there are often several equivalent rules for a pattern—that might look or sound very different—all of which give the same results and all of which are correct. Again, I wanted to introduce the students to an idea that would be very important in our exploration of patterns.

Second, I explained that the rules were alike in another important way: both rules depended on knowing the results of the previous stage. I told the students that such rules are called *iterative* rules. I elaborated that such rules can be used to describe many real-world situations and are used in computer spreadsheets. I think it is important that students realize the value of iterative rules as well as their limitations.

When I asked whether anyone had another rule to share, Thomas raised his hand. "My rule is 'three plus the number of puffs, which is the same as the stage number,' or three plus *s*."

There were, as I anticipated, more than a few frowns around the room. I asked Thomas to explain his thinking and use his rule for Stage 11. Thomas put the transparency the students had constructed earlier back on the overhead (shown below).

Stage	Rocket Pieces + Puffs	Total # of Pieces
1	3 + 1	4
2	3 + 2	5
3	3 + 3	6

He said, "For every stage, you have the three pieces in the rocket [pointing to the 3s in the column under "Rocket Pieces"]. And for every stage you have some puffs of smoke [pointing to the column of numbers under "Puffs"]. But I noticed that the number of puffs is always the same as the stage number; like for Stage One, there is one puff, for Stage Two, there are two puffs, and so on. So, for any stage, you can always add the three pieces of the rocket and the number of puffs, which you know matches the stage number. For Stage Eleven, you would add three plus eleven equals fourteen."

Several of the other students immediately seemed to understand Thomas's reasoning and its implications. "With Thomas's rule," Chelsie blurted, "I can do *any* stage quickly. That's cool."

"I don't get it," Barry said. "Can you show me the rule again? And what is the *s*?"

I interrupted to comment on Barry's questions. "In our class," I explained, "it is one of every student's jobs to ask questions when you don't understand. We want a classroom where we all work together to share ideas and understand as many mathematical ideas as possible. This is not possible without your asking questions. We won't all think the same way, and we won't all understand ideas at the same time or in the same way, but sharing ideas and asking questions will help us all to grow and to enjoy doing mathematics." During the first part of the school year I use every opportunity I can find to help foster the learning environment I hope to establish in that class. Meanwhile, I added, "Thomas, can you explain your rule again?"

This time, Thomas went to the overhead projector. He added a row in the T-chart for Stage 20 as he spoke.

Stage	Rocket Pieces + Puffs	Total # of Pieces
1	3 + 1	4
2	3 + 2	5
3	3 + 3	6
20	**3 + 20**	**23**

"My rule is 'Total equals three plus *s*.' For Stage Twenty, you would add three, the number of pieces in the rocket, plus twenty, the number of puffs of smoke. You know there are twenty puffs because the number of puffs is always the same as the stage number [pointing back and forth to the columns under "Stage" and "Puffs"]. Three for the rocket plus twenty puffs equals twenty-three total pieces. The *s* just stands for 'stage number.' I learned you can do that last year."

Barry nodded slowly. "I think I understand what you are saying. I might be able to use your rule, but I would never have thought of it."

I assured Barry that, soon, every student in the class would be discovering rules like Thomas's. I asked everyone to try using Thomas's rule for Stage 100. I suggested that each student try to picture the rocket in his or her head and look back at the table on the screen before he or she started using the rule. I then asked Barry to try to explain what he did. He went to the overhead and said, "For Stage One Hundred [writing *100*], there would be three pieces in the rocket [writing the *3*] plus [writing the + sign], mmmm, one hundred for the puffs of smoke [writing *100*], for a total of one hundred three pieces [writing the sum]."

Stage	Rocket Pieces + Puffs	Total # of Pieces
1	3 + 1	4
2	3 + 2	5
3	3 + 3	6
20	3 + 20	23
100	**3 + 100**	**103**

"Did everyone get that answer?" I asked. Suzi and three other students indicated that they did not write anything, but followed Barry's explanation and now thought they understood. Based on that input, I had the students try using $T = 3 + s$ for Stage 50, without writing in the T-chart if they could. All reported success.

"Thomas's rule," I explained, "is called an *explicit* rule, because you do not have to know the answer to the previous step in order to use the rule and get an answer for any stage. The s in the rule is called a *variable*, because it stands for a value in the pattern that changes from stage to stage. In this rule, s stands for the stage number, or the number of puffs, and s equals twenty for Stage Twenty while s equals one hundred for Stage One Hundred. Does that make sense to you?"

The students nodded and I did not question them further, although I knew it was most likely that some had only a glimmer of what I had just said. After all, this was our very first exploration! Understanding of variables does not come instantly for most students, but, over time, with many varied experiences, every student can develop meaning for this and other important mathematical concepts that comprise algebraic thinking.

I concluded by saying, "I want you to think about the Rocket Pattern and what you learned today overnight. Tomorrow I am going to ask you to write a short paragraph about our exploration. Are there any questions?"

Sarah asked, "Will we have to write about *everything* we did?"

I laughed and assured Sarah and the rest of the class that they would simply explain the Rocket Pattern and a rule for finding the total number of pieces needed to build any stage.

As expected, it took quite a while for the class to complete this first pattern exploration. For most students in the class, only the first layer of understanding about finding rules for patterns was developed. Also, important concepts such as variable were only introduced or were addressed briefly, while others did not emerge at all. However, I am confident that working slowly through the first few explorations and discussing concepts and vocabulary as they arise naturally during those explorations is best. This approach results in a stronger foundation and more long-term success than trying to cover a larger number of examples quickly or simply presenting concepts in an order that seems logical to me. I know the content and pedagogical objectives I hope to accomplish by the end of a number of explorations and have confidence, based on past experience, that these objectives will be met for almost all the students by the end of several explorations. Thus, I ended the class feeling optimistic and looking forward to reading the students' reflections about their experience with the Rocket Pattern.

I started class the next day by placing the transparency shown in Figure 1–6 on the overhead projector.

I also explained, "You can write out the method you used yesterday to describe the Rocket Pattern and how it grows, a different method, or more

Yesterday we explored the Rocket Pattern shown below. Explain in writing a rule for what the pattern looks like, how it grows, and how many total pieces are needed to build it for any stage.

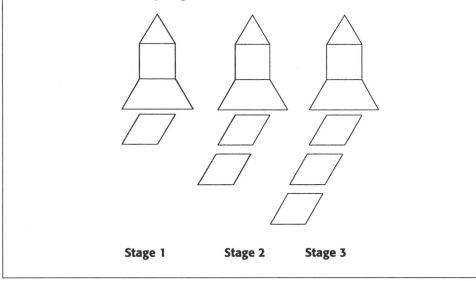

Stage 1   **Stage 2**   **Stage 3**

than one method. I want to know your ideas and how you think about this pattern."

The students took a few minutes to complete their reflections and then turned in their papers. We spent the rest of class on another topic and I read their papers that night in preparation for our second patterns exploration the following day.

Emily's paper was typical of most of the students' reflections (see Figure 1–7).

Emily's writing showed that she could describe the pattern adequately and provide an appropriate iterative rule. Like most of the students in this class, her reflection was not very detailed. I have found that most students need to hear several examples from their classmates that are more expansive and clearer than their own before they begin to include important details in their own reflections.

The writing of some students showed more understanding than that of their classmates. Kenya, for example, wrote the reflection in Figure 1–8 on page 14. A few students' reflections indicated some incomplete or inaccurate understandings (see Barry's writing in Figure 1–9 on page 14).

FIGURE 1–7   Emily's reflection

Each stage of the pattern includes a rocket with 3 pieces plus some puffs of smoke. Each stage has one more puff so there is one more total number of pieces.

FIGURE 1–8   Kenya's reflection

> To build the Rocket Pattern, you always use 3 pieces for the rocket itself. Then you have a number of puffs of smoke which gets bigger for each stage. There is 1 puff of smoke for the first stage, 2 for the second stage, 3 for the third stage, and so on. So you can think of the rule as adding one puff of smoke to the stage before it to build each new stage. But you can also think of the rule as always having 3 pieces (the constant) and adding one more puff of smoke for each new stage (the variable). This is easy if you remember that the number of puffs of smoke is always the same as the stage number.

FIGURE 1–9   Barry's reflection

> The rule for the Rocket Pattern is that you start with 4 pieces and add one more for each new step.

While Barry's iterative rule yields the correct total number of pieces for any stage, his writing shows no understanding of the constant and variable parts of the pattern. Of course, he might have just failed to write down this information—understanding it after all—but, with the most generous interpretation, his writing indicates that he did not think this information was important. His reflection indicates that Barry needed more experiences with finding rules for patterns.

Only Thomas included the explicit rule with a variable in his reflection.

The next day in class we had a brief discussion about the reflections. I reported that most members of the class wrote the rule as, "The total number of pieces for any stage equals the number of pieces in the previous stage plus one." I made a transparency of Kenya's reflection and had her read it to the class. The other students agreed that the details she included made her explanation about the pattern and the connection of the rule to the models or drawings clearer than simply stating the rule. They also agreed that Kenya's writing indicated understanding of the terms *constant* and *variable* as well. I acknowledged that I knew other students in the class understood these same ideas and connections, and encouraged all the students to include such information in their reflections in the future. I felt the class was ready for another exploration.

Follow-Up Explorations

Figures 1–10 and 1–11 show two additional patterns that I have used with middle school students on days soon after the student exploration of the Rocket Pattern. The iterative and explicit rules are given following an illustration of the first three stages of each pattern. Notice that each of these patterns is simple and unambiguous. I do not push the students to arrive at an explicit rule at this point.

The following elements of the exploration with the Rocket Pattern should be repeated with patterns like these:

- Describing, building a model for, and/or drawing Stages 4 and 5 of the pattern

- Predicting, then verifying, what Stage 10 of the pattern would look like

- Using a T-chart to record information, search for patterns, and find and check a rule for the pattern

- Finding an iterative and explicit (*if* it comes from the students) rule for the pattern

- Using the rule(s) to find any stage of the pattern

- Writing and sharing reflections the following day

Another pattern that is appropriate to use with students at this beginning level of experience, titled "Exploring Houses," including a Blackline

---

FIGURE 1–10 Hexagonal sun pattern

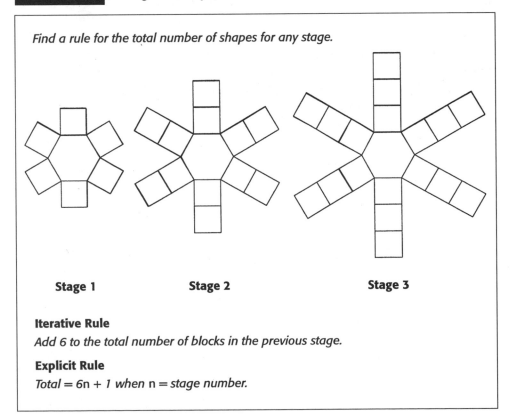

Find a rule for the total number of shapes for any stage.

Stage 1   Stage 2   Stage 3

Iterative Rule
Add 6 to the total number of blocks in the previous stage.

Explicit Rule
Total = 6n + 1 when n = stage number.

FIGURE 1–11   Toothpick perimeter

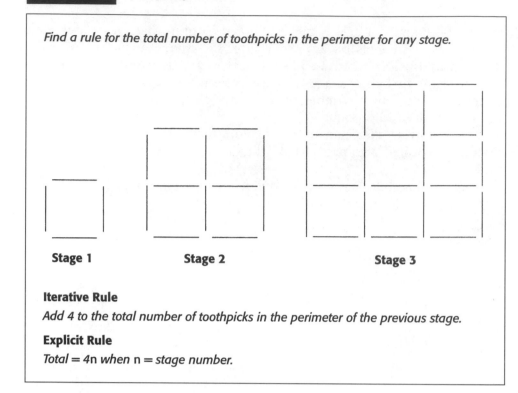

Find a rule for the total number of toothpicks in the perimeter for any stage.

Stage 1   Stage 2   Stage 3

Iterative Rule
Add 4 to the total number of toothpicks in the perimeter of the previous stage.

Explicit Rule
Total = 4n when n = *stage number.*

Master and discussion, can be found in *Navigating Through Algebra in Grades 6–8* (Friel et al. 2001, 9, 74).

Often a class will need only one follow-up pattern before I feel comfortable proceeding to patterns that lend themselves to more than one interpretation. Occasionally, a class or group of students will need to work with several additional simple patterns before encountering less straightforward patterns.

When most of the students in a class appear comfortable with extending patterns, using a T-chart, and finding iterative rules for patterns, it is appropriate to use the lesson *Surprising Squares*, which emphasizes finding explicit rules for patterns.

CHAPTER 2

Functions and Graphing
Introductory Experiences

The concept of *function* is one of the main building blocks of algebra. Understanding of this concept develops gradually through numerous experiences. We have found that the approach that works best for us incorporates a wide variety of content and pedagogical focuses, including the following.

Content Focuses

- Exposing students to patterns that are functions and patterns that are not functions early and often

- Emphasizing that functions represent the relationship between two variables

- Starting with functions that can be illustrated with concrete objects and/or real-life situations

- Validating iterative function rules offered by students, but demonstrating their limitations

- Asking students to derive explicit function rules when appropriate

- Encouraging multiple representations for each function whenever appropriate (models/drawings, T-chart/table, graph, function rules using words, function rules using symbols)

- Spiraling the use of vocabulary such as *function, function rule, domain, range, coordinates,* x-*coordinate,* y-*coordinate, ordered pair, axis, axes,* x-*axis,* y-*axis,* and *origin,* and helping students to refine definitions over time

- Asking students to use *x* values and function rules to find *y* values and ordered pairs

- Asking students to use *y* values and function rules to find *x* values and ordered pairs

- Asking students to use ordered pairs to find a function rule

- Eliciting informal definitions of *slope* and *intercept*

- Asking students to use function rules to predict what the corresponding graph will look like

- Exposing students to different kinds of functions (constant, linear, quadratic, and exponential) early and often

- Having students find function rules to approximate real-world situations

Pedagogical Focuses

- Working in a whole-class setting with built-in "think time" for the first few functions

- Working with individual students who need extra practice as the need arises

- Working in small groups and sharing ideas with the rest of the class as soon as appropriate

- Having students express their mathematical ideas and reasoning orally

- Having students write their reflections about a function or investigation of the relationship between two variables early and often

- Encouraging use of multiple representations and understanding the relationships among them early and often

Despite these extensive lists, we have found that one lesson (completed in two sixty-minute class periods), such as the one described in this chapter, can serve as an effective introduction to many of the big ideas related to functions and graphing on the coordinate grid. These ideas are developed more deeply over time through experiences like those described later in this book.

I used the following lesson with a class of seventh graders, who had experience working with patterns and finding both iterative and explicit rules for those patterns, including writing their rules using variables. Many of the patterns they had encountered could be represented by linear functions, but the students had not been exposed to any of the vocabulary or traditional conventions associated with functions. In addition, the students had very limited experience with negative numbers. They had done only a few introductory explorations, including graphing negative values on the number line. If you prefer to introduce graphing only in the first quadrant, you can omit the round of *Guess My Rule* described in the section titled "Exploration: Graphing on the Coordinate Plane" (see page 27) and the graphing of that function rule ($f = s - 7$). Of course, that portion of this lesson can be done later by your students.

Notice that throughout the lesson I tried to incorporate use of vocabulary that I want students to *begin* to understand and use. I certainly do not expect the students to fully grasp the mathematical meaning of these words or phrases during introductory experiences of this type. They are italicized simply to make it easier for the reader to identify vocabulary that I believe is appropriate to target for long-term mastery by middle school students.

Exploration: Guess My Rule

Each student had a pencil and paper. I told the students that we would start class by playing a game called *Guess My Rule*. I explained that we would play a few rounds and then examine the game in a way that would introduce some new and important mathematical ideas, terms, and procedures.

I explained how we would play the game:

- I would begin each round of the game by giving the students a starting value for imaginary coins in my pocket (for example, twenty cents).

- Using an unstated mathematical rule to change the starting value, I would then announce the final value for the coins (for example, thirty cents). I would continue to announce starting and final values, using the same rule, until a student indicated that he or she thought he or she knew my rule. I would then give a new starting value and that student would predict the final value, using the rule he or she guessed. I would announce whether the final value followed my rule.

- Two students must correctly predict the final value for two different starting values before anyone could try to verbalize my rule.

- The rule must be stated in a particular form (for example, "The final value of the coins equals the starting value plus ten.").

Students asked a few clarifying questions, such as, "What happens if the rule I give is wrong?" (nothing) and "What if I can't remember how to state the rule?" (another student can help you). Then we began the first round of the game. I drew the following expanded T-chart on the board, including the labels shown for the three columns:

Starting Value	Using the Rule	Final Value

"The starting value of my coins is six cents," I stated, writing *6* in the left-hand column. "And the final value after using my rule is twelve cents," I continued as I wrote *12* in the right-hand column.

Starting Value	Using the Rule	Final Value
6		12

There were several raised hands. I called on Chip. He stated, "I think I know the rule."

"OK, Chip, use the rule you think I have in mind to predict the final value of the coins if the starting value is five cents," I said, writing *5* in the column for starting values.

Starting Value	Using the Rule	Final Value
6		12
5		

"The final value for five is ten," Chip stated confidently.

"No," I answered. "The final value, if you start with five cents, using my rule, is eleven cents," I explained as I wrote *11* in the column for final values.

Starting Value	Using the Rule	Final Value
6		12
5		11

A few students frowned, but Sally immediately blurted, "I know the rule now. I am sure of it!"

"OK, Sally, use the rule to predict the final value of the coins if the starting value is ten cents," I said, writing *10* in the column for starting values.

Starting Value	Using the Rule	Final Value
6		12
5		11
10		

"I think the final value for ten cents is sixteen cents," Sally offered.

"That is correct," I affirmed, adding sixteen in the table. "If the starting value of the coins in my pocket is ten cents, and I use my rule, the final value is sixteen cents. Is there anyone else who has found a rule that fits all the pairs of numbers in the table and is ready to make a prediction?"

Several hands were raised and I called on Amrita. "Amrita, use the rule to predict the final value of the coins if the starting value is twenty cents," I said, writing *20* in the table.

Amrita promptly offered twenty-six as the final value, and I verified that her answer followed my rule. Now the table contained the information shown below.

Starting Value	Using the Rule	Final Value
6		12
5		11
10		16
20		26

"We now have two correct predictions," I reminded the class, "so anyone can volunteer to guess my rule if you think you know it. I want each of you to take a few moments to think before I call on anyone. Remember that my rule must work for every pair of numbers in the table. If you think you know the rule, check that rule by using it for each pair of values in the table, and anyone who does not yet have a rule in mind, look at the pairs to see whether you can find one." Thus, I offered each student a constructive way to utilize some "think time," an important ingredient to maximize the success of this activity.

Despite the fact that most hands were waving in the air, I waited a full minute before calling on Chip to state the rule. "Remember," I cautioned him, "you must start the rule using the words, 'The final value of the coins equals.' "

Chip took a breath and stated, "The final value of the coins equals the starting value plus six cents."

"Raise your hand if you agree that Chip has guessed my rule," I requested, and all the students raised their hands, though a few obviously thought a moment before doing so. "Yes," I stated, "for each starting value, I used the rule 'The final value of the coins equals the starting value plus six cents' to find the final value of the imaginary coins in my pocket. Let's look back at the T-chart to make sure that rule works for each pair of values."

With help from various students, I filled in the center column of the T-chart as shown:

Starting Value	Using the Rule Final value = starting value + 6	Final Value
6	6 + 6	12
5	5 + 6	11
10	10 + 6	16
20	20 + 6	26

"Now, can anyone write the rule using a variable?" I asked.

Misha volunteered, "If s stands for the starting value, the rule could be 'Final value equals s plus six.' " I added the expression $s + 6$ in the center column of the T-chart.

I called on Cory to use Misha's rule to find the final value for imaginary coins with a starting value of eighty-seven cents. He came to the board and gave the explanation shown in Figure 2–1. (The writing he did on the board is labeled "Notation," and his spoken words, "Comment.")

When the class indicated that Cory's explanation was clear, I asked, "So

FIGURE 2–1   Cory's explanation

Notation	Comment
Final value = $s + 6$	Misha's rule says that for any starting value of coins, you can find the final value by adding six to s, the starting value.
Final value = 87 + 6	Since the starting value is eighty-seven, you add the eighty-seven plus six more cents.
$FV = 93$	So the final value is ninety-three, or ninety-three cents.

can everyone use my rule to find the final value of my imaginary coins if the starting value is three hundred ninety-two cents?"

A chorus of "three hundred ninety-eight" rang out.

"And what if the final value of my coins is four hundred nineteen cents? What was the starting value?" I queried.

Most students answered, "four hundred and thirteen."

"Who can show us how to get that answer?" I asked. Ray came to the board and gave the explanation shown in Figure 2–2.

FIGURE 2–2 Ray's explanation

Notation	Comment
Final value = $s + 6$	Our rule says that for any starting value of coins, you can find the final value by adding six to s, the starting value.
Final value = 419 $419 - 6 = s$	Since the final value, four hundred nineteen, is given, you must work backwards or subtract to get the starting value.
$s = 413$	So the starting value is four hundred thirteen, or four hundred thirteen cents.

"Before we start the next round, does anyone have a comment or question that you think might help the class?" I asked.

Chip raised his hand and offered, "I guess everybody noticed: I learned the hard way that you need more than one pair of numbers to make sure your rule is correct. After the first example, I thought the rule was 'Final value equals starting value times two' because that was what I thought of to get the final value twelve cents when you started with six cents. My rule worked for those two amounts of money. But, if I had waited to find out that starting with five cents and using the rule gave you eleven cents, I would have known my rule was not the one you were using. So we need to check a guess before we try to predict."

"I saw some frowns when I told Chip ten was not the final value if I started with five cents. Were you thinking of the same rule as Chip?" I asked. When several students nodded, I added, "So do you think Chip's suggestion is a good one, to check a rule several times before trying to predict?" The class agreed that it was.

Andrew then commented, "I didn't get the rule as fast as Sally or Amrita. How did they know so quickly what it was?"

Amrita said, "Partly, I think I was lucky. After we found out Chip did not guess the correct rule, I tried to think of other ways to get from six to twelve. 'Adding six' just popped into my head and I checked it for the next several pairs."

Sally added, "I went backwards from twelve to six. Since the difference between them was six, I tried adding six to the starting value. When that worked twice, I felt like I had found the rule."

I noted that everyone should keep the suggestions offered by Chip, Amrita, and Sally in mind to see whether those strategies were useful in the next rounds of the game, then began Round 2 of *Guess My Rule*. I left the first T-chart on the board, drew a new one, and stated the following as I entered the values appropriately in the new T-chart: "The starting value of my coins is five cents, and the final value, after using my rule, is thirteen cents."

Starting Value	Using the Rule	Final Value
5		13

No one offered to make a prediction, so I asked for a new starting value. Scott suggested ten. Other students suggested one and twelve, with no one offering a prediction. Then Taylor asked for the final value if the starting value was zero. After I gave three as the final value using my rule, he studied the table as shown below and declared he was ready to make a prediction.

Starting Value	Using the Rule	Final Value
5		13
10		23
1		5
12		27
0		3

"OK, Taylor, use the rule to predict the final value of the coins if the starting value is nine cents," I said, writing 9 in the column for starting values.

Taylor took only a second to reply, "Using your rule, the final value for nine cents is twenty-one cents."

I announced that Taylor was correct and Maury quickly volunteered to make a prediction. When I announced four cents as the starting value, Maury confidently gave the corresponding final value as eleven cents, the correct amount using my rule.

At this point, I repeated the procedure we used in the first round of the game, including the following steps:

1. "Think time" for everyone before a rule is offered

2. Confirmation of the correct rule: Final value = 2 × starting value + 3

3. Writing the rule and substituting in that rule for each row in the center column of the T-chart, as shown here:

Starting Value	Using the Rule Final value = 2 × starting value + 3 Final value = (2 × s) + 3, 2 • s + 3, or 2s + 3	Final Value
5	2(5) + 3 = 13	13
10	2(10) + 3 = 23	23
1	2(1) + 3 = 5	5
12	2(12) + 3 = 27	27
0	2(0) + 3 = 3	3
9	2(9) + 3 = 21	21
4	2(4) + 3 = 11	11

4. Writing the rule using a variable: Final value = $(2 \times s) + 3$, $2 \bullet s + 3$, or $2s + 3$

The class first offered the rule as $(2 \times s) + 3$. Then I gave a short explanation about the other ways the rule could be written. I began by asking the class, "What food do you think I mean if I say, 'I'd like a burger for lunch'?"

Ray answered, "You want a hamburger," and the other students agreed.

I explained that when a person uses the word *burger*, everyone knows that the person must mean a hamburger. If a person wanted to talk about a turkey burger or a veggie burger, everyone would expect him or her to say the whole phrase. Using "burger" to mean "hamburger" is a generally accepted shortcut or convention in our language. I went on to explain that in mathematics there are also many shortcuts or conventions—practices that have become accepted, even preferred, in the world of mathematics. For example, to write "three times two," you may write 3×2 or $3 \bullet 2$. When writing "three times the variable s," you may write $3 \times s$, $3 \bullet s$, or even $3s$. Any time there is no sign between a number and a variable, mathematicians mean multiply the number by the value of the variable. It is just a shortcut that has become the preferred way to write such an expression. If you want to add to, subtract from, or divide by a variable, you must include a sign, but not with multiplication. Why multiplication? Who knows? Why $3s$ and not $s3$? Who knows? The point is that there are many such conventions in mathematics, most of which use fewer symbols than other, equivalent ways of writing or doing things. I concluded by telling the students that writing the rule as $2s + 3$ signaled that they were beginning to learn the conventions of mathematicians, although any of the equivalent ways were acceptable until they felt comfortable using this way. (Similarly, later in the year we talk about not always needing to write $+2$ for positive 2 while we must always write -2 for negative 2; not needing to write $\sqrt[2]{16}$ for $\sqrt{16}$ while we must write $\sqrt[4]{16}$ for the fourth root of 16, etc.)

5. Using the rule with a variable to find the final value for a given starting value (for example, *Find the final value for a starting value of 15 cents, using the rule 'Final value = 2s + 3')*

6. Finding the starting value for a given final value (for example, *If 37 is the final value, what was the starting value?*)

7. Students sharing explanations of the thinking they used to derive the rule

Taylor, for example, explained that he noticed the final value was always larger than the starting value, so he tried adding and then multiplying by the same amount for each starting value. When neither operation worked alone, he tried multiplying and adding together. He said comparing the pair 5 (starting value) and 13 (final value) to the pair 10 (starting value) and 23 (final value) helped him find the rule. He also pointed out that he used 0 as the starting value to verify the rule. "Since two times zero equals zero, the final value of three had to come from adding three cents," he explained. A few of the other students expressed how impressed they were with the "try zero as the starting value" strategy.

I left the T-chart on the board, and the students played one more round of *Guess My Rule*. The rule for that round was "Final value = 3 × starting value + 5" ($3s + 5$). **Note:** Avoid rules that will make the final value a negative number in these first few rounds. Such rules should be avoided because they don't fit within the context of imaginary coins in your pocket (You can't have a negative value for coins!). Also, by avoiding negative numbers, you can restrict the introduction to graphing on the coordinate plane (see the next section of this lesson) to include only points in Quadrant I if you wish.

When the class had successfully completed Round 3, I felt the students were ready to be introduced to the idea of function. This introduction was, of necessity, primarily my imparting information to the students (since they could hardly divine the mathematical names for the terms involved). However, I tried to lead the discussion in a way that involved the students as much as possible instead of simply presenting an informative lecture. This way the students could derive their own informal definitions for the appropriate terms—definitions that had meaning for them, definitions that could be refined over time, and definitions that would, hopefully, enable the students to feel ownership of their learning.

I began by asking the students to look at the three T-charts on the board and to identify any characteristics that all three T-charts had in common.

"They all have three columns," Maury announced.

"That's true, Maury," I conceded, "but, instead of focusing on the appearance of the charts, I want you to concentrate on the content—the information that is found in the columns. Can you look again at the T-charts and tell me one way in which their content is the same?"

Maury stared at the board for a few moments and then tentatively offered, "Well, all three have a list of starting values."

"Yes," I answered, and wrote, *List (group or set) of starting values* on the board. Soon the class had compiled the following list of common elements in the T-charts:

- List (group or set) of starting values

- List (group or set) of final values

- Rule that is used to find the final value for each starting value

- Pairs of numbers in the first and third columns of each row that all follow the same rule

If the class had not offered all of these elements, I would have asked questions to elicit those responses. (For example, to elicit the last item in the list, I would have asked, "What can you say about these pairs of numbers [pointing left and right at the values in each row of the charts]?")

I then explained, "In this list you have included most of the important parts—or, as mathematicians refer to them, *elements* or *components*—of a very important concept in mathematics called *function*. To have a function, you must start with a group or set of numbers called the *domain*. In the rounds we played of *Guess My Rule*, the starting values or domain was the group or set of all the whole numbers. I could use any whole number as a starting value. Does that make sense?" The students nodded and I wrote *domain* above the left-hand column of each T-chart.

"Next, to have a function, you must have a rule to follow. Each of our rules [pointing to the heading for the center column of each T-chart] is a *function rule*. A function rule is a mathematical rule that can be used with each number in the domain to find a particular final value. Who can tell me the function rule for Round One of our game?"

Mattie raised her hand and answered, "The function rule was 'The final value equals the starting value plus six.'"

"Yes," I replied, and asked other students to give the function rules for Rounds 2 and 3 of the game. I wrote *function rule* above the center column of each T-chart.

"Finally, every function has a group or set of final values, one for each of the values in the domain. This group or set of numbers is called the *range* of the function. Who can tell me where members of the range appear in our T-charts?

Andrew spoke up. "That's easy. The numbers in the range for each function are in the column we called 'Final Value,' the last column in each T-chart."

I nodded and wrote *range* above the right-hand column of each T-chart. I then continued, "The last item in your list, 'Pairs of numbers in the first and third columns of each row that all follow the same rule [pointing to the writing on the board], is also very important. When working with functions, we can take each pair of numbers linked by the function rule and write them as what is called an *ordered pair*. Look back at the T-chart for Round One. The ordered pairs we found for our first function were (six, twelve), (five, eleven), (ten, sixteen), and (twenty, twenty-six). What do you notice about how ordered pairs are written?" While explaining, I wrote on the board: *(6, 12)*, *(5, 11)*, *(10, 16)*, and *(20, 16)*.

Javier offered, "Each pair has parentheses around it."

"Yes," I repeated, "each ordered pair is surrounded by parentheses. Anything else?"

"The starting value is listed first in each pair," Misha noted.

"Yes, the starting value (the element from the domain) is always listed first in an ordered pair," I affirmed, continuing to purposefully use the appropriate vocabulary, "and the final value, an element from the range, must be listed second in each ordered pair. Can you see why that is important?"

After a moment, Sally spoke up. "Yes, it makes sense. Our first ordered pair is 'six, twelve'; you start with six, use the rule, and get twelve. If you wrote the ordered pair 'twelve, six,' it doesn't make sense with the function rule: you can't start with twelve, use the rule 'Add six,' and get six."

"I guess that's why they call it an *ordered* pair, huh?" Gina commented. "The numbers have to be in a certain *order*—the starting value first, then the final value (after using the rule) second."

"Do the ordered pairs have to be listed in the order we have them?" Angelo asked.

"What do *you* think?" I asked.

"I don't know," Angelo answered.

"Well, let's try rearranging the ordered pairs," I suggested. I wrote *(5, 11)*, *(20, 26)*, *(6, 12)*, and *(10, 16)* on the board. "Does this new order suggest anything different about the function to you?"

Angelo shook his head "no" and the rest of the students agreed when I posed the same question to them. "You're right," I said. "The order in which you list ordered pairs makes no difference. Also, could I add more ordered pairs to the list?"

"Of course," Sally answered. "Since we could have any whole number as a starting value, we could find as many ordered pairs as we want."

"There are some other special symbols and ways of writing expressions related to functions that we will discuss soon, but I think you have plenty of new words and ideas to think about for now. Would you agree?" The students nodded enthusiastically.

"So, do you have any final questions for today?"

"I have one," Misha said. "How are functions and function rules different from the patterns and rules we have worked with in the past? They seem the same to me."

"I am glad you asked that question, Misha. Many of the patterns you have explored *are* functions, but some are not. For example, the H Pattern and all of the personalized patterns that you created represent functions [see *Personalized Patterns* lesson, Chapter 4], but a pattern like 1, 2, 2, 3, 3, 3, 4, 4, 4, 4 . . . does not fit the requirements for a function. We'll be examining a lot of patterns this year to determine whether or not they are functions."

Since there were no more questions, I asked, "Who can summarize what you have learned about functions today?"

Erin volunteered. "To have a function, you must have a domain, a function rule, and a range. You can take any number from the domain, use the function rule, and you will get a member of the range. You can also write each member of the domain you have used with the member of the range you get by using the function rule. This makes a list of ordered pairs."

"I'd like to ask just one clarifying question," I added. "For any member of the domain, how many ordered pairs will there be for a particular function and why?"

After a moment, Javier spoke up. "Each member of the domain is paired with just one member of the range because the function rule gives only one final value for each starting value. That also means that no two pairs will have the same first member, right?"

After making sure the other students understood Javier's answer, I dismissed class for the day.

Exploration: Graphing on the Coordinate Plane

The next day the students entered the classroom eager to play more rounds of *Guess My Rule*. I assured them that we would play the game throughout the rest of the year but added that we would play just one round today because we were going to learn to do a new kind of graphing. The students seemed excited to start, so I outlined a new situation they should imagine. The starting value would be the temperature in degrees Celsius on an imaginary day. The final value would be the temperature on the same day after a change in the weather. Otherwise, the game would be played as before.

When everyone was ready to start, I drew an expanded T-chart on the board, including the labels for the three columns, as shown:

Starting Temperature	Using the Rule	Final Temperature

"The starting temperature is fourteen degrees," I stated, writing *14* in the left-hand column. "And the final temperature after using my rule is seven degrees," I continued as I wrote 7 in the right-hand column.

Starting Temperature	Using the Rule	Final Temperature
14		7

Apparently learning from their experiences the day before, the students waited for more values before offering a prediction for the final temperature. I announced the next pair of values, 10 degrees as the starting temperature and 3 degrees as the final temperature, writing them in the next row of the T-chart.

"I'm ready to predict," Cory declared.

I entered *8* as the starting temperature and asked Cory his prediction for the final temperature. He predicted 1 degree and I wrote it in the final column as I announced that he was correct. The chart then appeared as shown:

Starting Temperature	Using the Rule	Final Temperature
14		7
10		3
8		1

"This is an easy one," Janet announced. "I'm ready to predict."

"OK. The starting temperature is four," I told her and waited for her prediction. Janet paused for a few seconds and then said, "Maybe it isn't so easy after all. I think the answer is less than zero and we haven't had any numbers like that before in this game."

"Well, Janet," I offered, "remember that the situation for this round of *Guess My Rule* is different from the one we played with yesterday. It wouldn't have been realistic to have a number less than zero for the value of coins in my pocket. Could the temperature on an imaginary day be less than zero on a Celsius thermometer?"

"Sure," she said, "so I'll predict negative three degrees as the final temperature if you started at four degrees."

"Janet is correct," I announced. "Is anyone ready to guess my rule?"

Ray studied the chart for a moment, then raised his hand. "I think the rule is 'Final temperature equals starting temperature minus seven degrees.'"

"You got it," I told Ray, and the class proceeded to carry out the same follow-up steps we did in the other rounds. The final T-chart looked like this:

Starting Temperature	Using the Rule Final temperature = starting temperature – 7 Final temperature = s – 7	Final Temperature
14	14 – **7** = 7	7
10	10 – **7** = 3	3
8	8 – **7** = 1	1
4	4 – **7** = –3	–3

A few students had trouble using the rule for a starting temperature of 4 degrees, but Janet came to the board and explained the procedure (shown in Figure 2–3), incorporating the use of a number line.

If Janet had not incorporated use of the number line in her explanation, I would have asked for a volunteer to show precisely what she did. Not only did it remind students about negative integers, but it also involved using a number line that included such numbers and I knew this was a timely reminder for the upcoming part of our lesson.

As a quick review, I asked the students to identify the domain and range of the function, write the function rule using variables ($f = s - 7$), and list the ordered pairs from the T-chart. They successfully did this.

When there were no further questions, I announced that the class would now learn how to make a new kind of graph, one that is very useful in creating visual representations of functions. I briefly projected a transparency of a coordinate grid on the front wall showing all four quadrants. I said, "This is a *coordinate grid*, a grid that is formed by two perpendicular number lines that intersect at a point, called the *origin*. We will make a *coordinate graph* using this grid. What do I mean by 'perpendicular number lines'?"

FIGURE 2–3 Janet's explanation

Notation	Comment
Final temperature = s – 7	Our rule says that for any starting temperature, you can find the final temperature by subtracting seven from s, the starting temperature.
8 – 7 = 1 –5 0 1 5 8	For any starting temperature, you can think of subtracting seven as moving seven to the left on the number line. For example, if the starting temperature is eight degrees, you move seven to the left, ending at one. Eight minus seven equals one.
4 – 7 = –3 –5 –3 0 4 5	So if the starting temperature is four degrees, you still move seven to the left on the number line to subtract seven. This time you end at negative three degrees. Brrrrrr!

Luke replied, "There is a ninety degree angle at the intersection—a perfect corner."

I nodded and continued, "You can draw each of the number lines to show as many or as few numbers as you wish. For example, on this grid [indicating the projected image], you see negative twenty through twenty on the horizontal number line and negative twenty through twenty on the vertical number line. You see arrows at the ends of each number line, indicating that the grid shows only part of the coordinate plane. As you know, a plane goes on and on indefinitely in two directions. Of course, you use only part of that plane for any graph. You can also use any *scale* you wish on the number lines. For example, you could have one centimeter between each pair of integers or one inch—any distance you choose as long as you use the same distance between each pair of numbers that differ by the same amount. You must choose the part of the plane and a scale that fit the values you are going to graph, just as you have done when making other kinds of graphs, remember? Are you with me so far?"

The students nodded, so I continued. "One of the neat things about a coordinate graph is that each point shows information about two variables (values that change), and the overall graph gives a visual representation of how changes in those variables are related or not related to each other.

"First, let's look back at our rounds of *Guess My Rule* from yesterday and see how to make a coordinate graph to represent each round." As I made this statement, I passed each student a sheet of paper with three grids. (See the *Grids for Coordinate Graphing* activity sheet in the Blackline Master section.)

I then pointed to the T-chart and list of ordered pairs for Round 1 of *Guess My Rule* that were still on the board from the day before, as shown here:

domain **Starting Value**	*function rule* **Using the Rule** **Final value = starting value + 6** **Final value = s + 6**	*range* **Final Value**
6	6 + **6**	12
5	5 + **6**	11
10	10 + **6**	16
20	20 + **6**	26

Ordered Pairs: (6, 12), (5, 11), (10, 16), (20, 26)

"I mentioned that each point in a coordinate graph shows information about two variables. What two sets of variables did we list in this T-chart?"

Gina promptly answered, "We had starting values and final values."

"Correct," I said. "And which set of values varies or changes?"

"Both sets vary," Andrew declared.

"Yes," I said. "So we have *two* sets of values that change in our chart, the starting values and the final values. You already chose a symbol or variable to represent any member of one group. What was the set of values and what was the variable?"

"We represented the starting values using s in our rule 'Final value equals s plus six,' " Angelo stated. "We used each member of the domain for s in the center column."

"Yes. So who can suggest a variable to represent the final values, or the range for this function?" I asked.

"Why not use *f*?" Erin suggested.

"Fine," I answered, and then continued, "Can anyone rewrite the function rule using both variables?"

No one volunteered for a while, so I reworded the question. "Who can use *f* as well as *s* in the function rule so that it still means the same as the version that uses words?"

"I get it," Javier chimed in. "We could say our rule, *f* equals *s* plus six [$f = s + 6$], because the final value of the coins changed each time the starting value changed. They both *varied*."

"You're almost ready to begin graphing," I said. "Look at the board once more and tell me where I can find pairs of numbers linked by the function rule *f* equals *s* plus six."

"Pairs of numbers like that show up in our ordered pairs!" Maury noted with evident pride. "The first number in each pair is a starting value and if you add six to it, like our rule says, you get the final value that is the second number in that ordered pair."

"On to graphing then," I declared. "First let's look at the *horizontal* number line on the first grid. It is called an *axis* when you are making a co-ordinate graph. Which number line would that be?" I asked.

"The one that goes across, like the horizon," Gina quickly contributed.

"Yes." I answered. "The *horizontal axis* is often used to show the starting values or the stage numbers."

"So we'll use it for the starting values of the coins," Taylor finished for me.

I nodded and asked what scale we should use.

After a pause, I called on Chip and he declared, "There are thirty squares along each side of the grid. Looking down the left-hand column in the T-chart, the smallest starting value is five, and the largest starting value is twenty, so I guess we can just start at zero and number the horizontal axis in order, zero through thirty, from left to right. And we can use the same scale along the left side of the grid, since the largest final value in the right-hand column of the T-chart is twenty-six," he added, anticipating my next question.

The rest of the class agreed with Chip that the *vertical axis* should be used for the final values and that it should be numbered 0 through 30 as well. I reminded the students that each axis should have a label as well as numbers and they agreed that the horizontal axis would be labeled *Starting Values* or *s* and the vertical axis, *Final Values* or *f*.

As the students labeled their axes, I circulated around the room. I also asked each student to swap papers with another student to verify that the axes (Taylor pointed out that the plural for *axis* was like that for *parenthesis*—just change the *-is* to *-es*) were labeled correctly.

The students were finally ready to graph! I asked them to look at the list of ordered pairs on the board. I reminded them once more that each ordered pair had two parts, a starting value and a corresponding final value, according to the rule $f = s + 6$. I also explained that each of the numbers in an ordered pair is called a *coordinate* and together they indicate an exact location on the coordinate plane. They were clearly eager to hear how this process worked. "There are just two steps to follow to graph an ordered pair:

1. Start at the origin. Move along the horizontal axis until you find the location of the first coordinate. Place your pencil point there.

2. Now use the vertical axis as your guide. Move your pencil point vertically (straight up or down along an imaginary number line) until you find the location of the second coordinate. Mark, or *plot*, the point at that location."

Most of the students were eager to graph a point, so I told them they could try plotting our first ordered pair, (6, 12), or they could wait and go through the steps as I did them on a transparency. After a few moments, I placed a transparent grid, labeled to match those of the students, on the overhead projector and read the two steps aloud again as I demonstrated how to use those steps to *plot the point* (6, 12). Again I asked each student to swap with another student to verify that the work was done correctly. It is critical that students avoid doing a procedure they will need often, like this one, incorrectly in the beginning. Otherwise, the erring student can possibly imprint that incorrect sequence of steps into his or her thinking and have a difficult time undoing it. Therefore, I think it is well worth the time to check every individual's work for the first few attempts.

After all the students had graphed the first coordinate pair correctly, I asked them to plot the remaining three points, (5, 11), (10, 16), and (20, 26), while I circulated to check their work. When all the students indicated that they had completed graphing all four points, I had Mattie, Erin, and Javier each come to the overhead projector and plot one of the other points, explaining the procedure as they did so. I asked each student to check his or her own graph by comparing it to the one projected on the wall. All the students correctly plotted the four points; Mattie's work is shown in Figure 2–4.

As they completed their graphs, several students remarked that their points made a "line of dots." I explained that this always happened when the values for a function change in a certain way and asked them to think about what might cause that visual image to occur. I assured them that what they had noticed related to an important mathematical idea that we would explore and discuss often in the coming months. (See the *Bulging Backpacks*, *The Window Problem*, and *Stretching Slinkies* lessons in this book.)

"So who can explain to me where the ordered pair (ten, sixteen) appears on your graph and how it gives information about Round One of the *Guess My Rule* game?" I asked.

Rebecca answered this way: "The point (ten, sixteen) is ten spaces to the right and sixteen spaces up from the origin of the graph. That is because it shows a starting value of ten and a final value of sixteen going by the rule we used in the first round of our *Guess My Rule* game."

"Here's a challenge for you," I said to the class. "Think about what Rebecca said. Look at the information on the board and your graph for Round One of our game yesterday. Then plot the point that shows what happens using our rule if I begin with fifteen cents in my pocket." All except a few students began working immediately. After a few moments, I announced, "If you are having trouble getting started, you can ask a classmate a question to help you get started." I noticed only a couple of students asking questions.

"So who can tell us what you did and plot the point on our overhead graph?" I asked.

Chuck came to the overhead and reported. "If you start with fifteen cents, our Round One function rule, *f* equals six plus *s*, says to add six to the starting value. That gives you twenty-one cents for the final value, so the

FIGURE 2–4 Mattie's graph for Round 1

Functions and Graphing

33

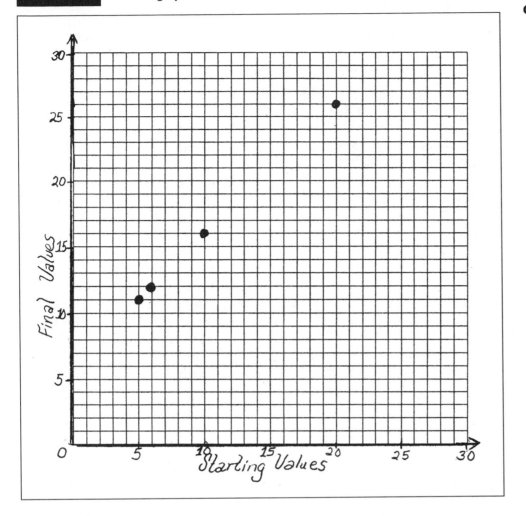

ordered pair (fifteen, twenty-one) makes sense on the graph. To plot the point at (fifteen, twenty-one), I moved fifteen spaces along the bottom axis for starting values and then up twenty-one spaces according to the vertical axis since it was for final values. So there's my point [as he plotted the point correctly on the transparency]. I knew I was right when the point ended up on the same line with the others on this graph."

Chuck's observation about a line of points was an important one, but I decided to postpone any discussion of its implications during this beginning experience. Instead, I announced, "OK. I think we are ready to make the graph for our second round of yesterday's game. Look at the second grid on your paper and the information about Round Two of *Guess My Rule* on the board. What should we do first?"

The class repeated the steps we had just used and plotted the ordered pairs for Round 2 of the *Guess My Rule* game, including the following:

■ Scaling and labeling the axes

■ Plotting the first point together (this time a student led the class)

■ Plotting the remaining ordered pairs

■ Checking the graphs for accuracy

- Discussing the meaning of the points in relation to the function rule and the context of the imaginary coins in my pocket

- Plotting a point for a starting value that did not occur during the original round of play

When the class had finished graphing the ordered pairs for Round 2, I announced that I would like us to skip to the round of *Guess My Rule* with which we had started class today. As we began to discuss drawing and labeling the axes, Angelo exclaimed, "Uh oh, I think we're in trouble. How can we graph a point like (four, negative three)?"

I asked whether anyone had a suggestion to offer and several hands went up. Amrita expressed her idea this way: "When Janet had to find the final temperature for a starting temperature of four degrees, she used a number line that went below zero. It had negative numbers like minus one, minus two, minus three, and so on. I think we just need to make the axis for final values keep going down below the axis for starting values."

Despite the brief peek I had given the students earlier that day of a coordinate grid showing four quadrants, I was impressed that Amrita made this suggestion on her own. Often I need to ask students leading questions before they can come up with a way to extend their grid beyond Quadrant I. Amrita's insight reminded me that we as teachers should always give students the opportunity to discover solutions for themselves before we offer answers or even ask leading questions.

I asked Amrita to come to the overhead and show us what she meant, using the transparency that showed the same grids as those on the students' papers. "For the graphs we have done up until this one, we needed only numbers zero and higher, so we made the bottom left corner (zero, zero)—the origin. Now we need to have more of the number line—with some negative numbers—so we can just make the origin in the middle of the grid like on the transparency we saw earlier today. Put (zero, zero) here [drawing two perpendicular lines and pointing to their intersection] and you have places for the negative numbers we need below the axis for one of the final values." She proceeded to draw and label the axes as shown in Figure 2–5.

The other students were also impressed by Amrita's suggestion and embraced it immediately. They had no trouble graphing the first three ordered pairs—(12, 5), (10, 3), and (8, 1)—but several were hesitant about how to locate (4, –3). I encouraged those having difficulty to confer with another student and followed up with a demonstration by Amanda at the overhead.

After all the graphs were deemed correct, I presented the class with one additional scenario. "Suppose the starting temperature is negative five. Use the same function rule to find the final temperature and plot the ordered pair on your graph." Determining the ordered pair was more challenging for this class than plotting the appropriate point. Taylor had to draw a number line on the board, similar to the one Janet had used earlier, and visually demonstrate subtracting 7 from –5. All the students indicated that they understood this model; once again a drawing made a concept clearer to students than any words or algorithm could possibly have done! Taylor's drawing is shown in Figure 2–6.

In order to plot the point, the students first needed to locate –5 on the horizontal axis. This time most of the students added the appropriate labels on the horizontal axis without hesitation. They also extended the vertical

FIGURE 2-5 Amrita's coordinate grid

Functions and Graphing   **35**

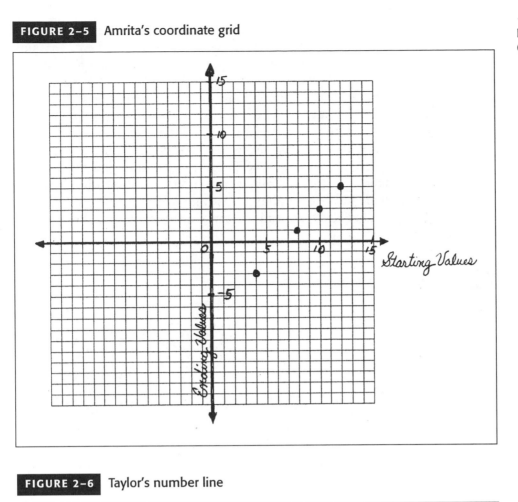

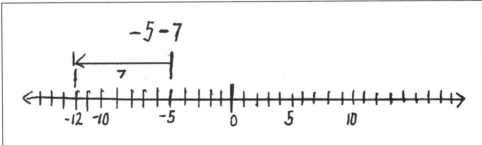

FIGURE 2-6 Taylor's number line

number line downward to at least –12 and were not the least nonplussed to plot a point (–5, –12) in Quadrant III. Sometimes we teachers make too big a fuss over natural extensions of situations!

As class ended, I felt confident that the students had started to build a foundation of understanding about functions and graphing on the coordinate plane. I looked forward to the experiences I had planned for them—experiences that would continue to increase their understanding of these important components of algebraic thinking.

The next day in class I asked the students to write brief reflections about the lessons of the previous two days. I wrote the following instructions on the board:

We have been exploring functions and graphing on the coordinate plane. Write a paragraph that explains what you now know about these mathematical ideas.

The students' written reflections included a range of responses, as indicated by how much those reflections revealed about their mathematical understandings. Lack of detail and clarity is typical of many students' first few written reflections (see Rebecca's response in Figure 2–7, for example). While it is clear that Rebecca understood how to play the *Guess My Rule* game and used that context to help her "define" *function* and *graph*, her reflection indicates only emerging understanding of these ideas.

Andrew demonstrated facility using the vocabulary associated with functions and appeared to have a conceptual understanding of this important idea (see Figure 2–8). However, he included no indication that he grasped the fundamentals of graphing. His final sentence suggests that he recognized only a superficial connection between functions and their graphs on the coordinate plane.

FIGURE 2-7   Rebecca's reflection

> To me, a function is like a game. You look at two numbers at a time and try to find the rule that makes them go together. Example: If you look at (1 and 4) (2 and 5) and (3 and 6) you can tell the first number + 3 = the second number, so that is your function. You can show the rule on a graph too because you always go to the right some amount and then go up three more than that.

FIGURE 2-8   Andrew's reflection

> A function is a mathematical idea. You start with some numbers called the domain. Then there is a rule, like $F = 2\underline{s} + 3$, called the function rule.
>
> When you take any number from the domain and use it for $\underline{s}$ in the rule (like $F = 2(\underline{5}) + 3 = 13$), you get a partner for that number and you can write an ordered pair (5, 13). All the second numbers together are called the range. You can graph the ordered pairs.

Javier's writing reflects basic understanding of the concepts of both function and graphing on a coordinate plane, including the connections between a function rule and its graph (see Figure 2–9). Moreover, the fact that he explained his thinking in a new context indicated his ability to generalize this learning.

I was pleased that the students' writing did not reveal any obvious misconceptions. Also, I know from experience that many students will benefit greatly from hearing a few of the written reflections of their classmates, like Javier, who more clearly expressed their thinking. Based on their performance and comments in class, I felt the students had begun to lay a foundation of understanding about functions and graphing on the coordinate plane.

FIGURE 2–9 Javier's reflection

> A function is a way to look at a situation. If I eat 5 donuts today and then eat 2 more each day after that, the function would be $f(n) = 5 + 2n$ (function rule). The number of days is the domain like 1, 2, 3, and so on. The total of donuts I will eat is the range like 5, 7, 9, and so on. These numbers show up on a graph in a line of points (1 day, 5 donuts) [point (1,5)], (2 days, 7 donuts), and so on.

Follow-Up Explorations

Students can benefit from playing additional rounds of the *Guess My Rule* game, followed by graphing the ordered pairs produced in each round of the game.

For each such exploration, the following elements should be considered and employed when appropriate:

- Discussing the meaning of the points in relation to the function rule (and the given context, when appropriate)
- Plotting a point for a starting value that did not occur during the original round of play
- Asking students to use x values and a function rule to find y values and ordered pairs
- Asking students to use y values and a function rule to find x values and ordered pairs
- Eliciting informal definitions of *slope* and *intercept*

- Asking students to use function rules to predict what the corresponding graphs will look like

- Exposing students to nonlinear functions (constant, quadratic, and exponential)

- Having students express their mathematical ideas and reasoning orally

- Having students write reflections about a mathematical concept involved in the game

Lessons like *Personalized Patterns* can be carried out with an emphasis on the idea of function and the addition of graphing the ordered pairs for each pattern. If your students do that lesson as presented in this book before they do these explorations, it is appropriate to revisit *Personalized Patterns* to incorporate finding ordered pairs and graphing each pattern. The *Surprising Squares* lesson can be extended in this same way.

Go Figure and *The Window Problem* can offer the students opportunities to explore nonlinear functions, and *Stretching Slinkies* introduces finding function rules to approximate real-world situations.

PART TWO

The Lessons

As stated in the Introduction, the lessons in Part Two offer a wide variety of experiences. Each of these lessons involves significant mathematics and emphasizes many components of algebraic thinking.

The problems presented in the lessons often can be solved using several different strategies and often have multiple solutions. In all the lessons students are encouraged to use various representations—models, drawings, tables, graphs, words, and symbols. After many experiences, students are able to move comfortably among the different representations. It is the mental processes used to connect these representations that enable students to analyze and understand rates of change, uses of variables, and the concept of function—in short, to develop algebraic thinking.

CHAPTER 3

Surprising Squares

OVERVIEW

This lesson provides experiences with recognizing patterns, extending the patterns, and finding general rules for them. Given the first three stages of patterns that are arrangements of squares, students first attempt to produce the next two stages for the pattern. They next try to describe the pattern that leads them from one stage to the next. Usually they find an iterative pattern and rule (one that expresses how each stage in the pattern evolves from the stage just before it). Once students are comfortable with a pattern, they reexamine it to try to find a visual way to break down the pattern—a way that can be used to describe the beginning stages they have constructed, the tenth stage of the pattern, and the one hundredth stage of the pattern. Finally, they find an explicit rule to predict the total number of squares needed for any stage of the pattern.

This approach is designed to coincide with the way the thinking of most middle school students progresses in working with the concepts of patterns and rule making. In dealing with patterns, students almost invariably succeed first by providing the next stages for a pattern, usually based on an iterative pattern they notice. When asked to give a rule for the pattern, they usually start with something like "Just keep adding three" or "Add three to get the next answer." This seems to be the natural first step in making rules for patterns. It is important to us that we allow student thinking in this area to evolve comfortably at first. If we move too quickly, many students seem to get the impression that "magic" is involved in deriving function rules and some students get lost along the way. So, at this point, we would merely restate their suggestions in standard iterative form with the rule "For any stage, add three to the previous stage."

Once students are comfortable with the iterative pattern and rule, we ask them to describe the tenth stage of the pattern and then the one hundredth stage. These questions impel the students to find a rule to predict the total number of squares needed for any stage. At this point in the lesson students almost always see the limits of an iterative rule. We encourage them to reexamine the pattern in order to find a visual way to break down the pattern that can be used to describe each of the stages they have constructed, and new stages as well. Students explain their thinking, providing their classmates with opportunities to develop new strategies for finding patterns and their own rules.

As the lesson proceeds, we emphasize finding rules based on the stage number of the pattern and discuss the power of explicit, as contrasted with iterative, rules. Additionally, this lesson is intended to establish that various strategies may be used to find the rule for a pattern, that a general rule must work for every stage of the pattern, and that several seemingly different rules may be correct if they are equivalent.

Middle school students need to have many experiences with finding and making rules for patterns before they enroll in a formal algebra course. Proficiency with patterns will help these students build a foundation for understanding functions and their rules. In turn, these understandings will help students succeed in Algebra I, other future mathematics courses, and many problem-solving situations.

BACKGROUND

Prior to this lesson, this class of seventh-grade students had limited experience investigating patterns. In previous mathematics classes, they had produced the next stages for visual and numerical patterns but had gotten very little experience with finding a general rule for such patterns. They had completed a few explorations immediately prior to this one (see Chapter 1) in which the terms *stage of the pattern, constant, variable, iterative rule,* and *explicit rule* were introduced. In general, their computational skills were not particularly strong and their confidence levels were low.

PREREQUISITE CONCEPTS OR SKILLS

- Extending visual and numerical patterns
- Finding iterative and explicit rules (*if* they are offered by students without prompting) for simple, unambiguous patterns (optional)

VOCABULARY

constant, equivalent rules, explicit rule, iterative rule, order of operations, stage number, T-chart, variable

TIME

The lesson was completed in a sixty-minute class and student reflections were written the following day. If your classes are only forty-five minutes long, we suggest doing only the first pattern and follow-up discussion and/or student writing on the first day, with the other patterns and written student reflections on the second day.

MATERIALS

- Colored squares (tiles or paper), up to 15 per student
- Transparent overhead squares, 15 each of two colors

At the beginning of class, each student was given square tiles of several colors. I placed transparent colored squares on the overhead projector to form the first three stages of a squares warm-up pattern, as shown below:

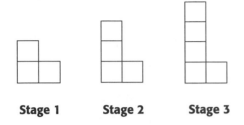

Stage 1   **Stage 2**   **Stage 3**

I chose to start the lesson with this warm-up problem for two reasons. First, I wanted to use the vocabulary and establish the general procedures that I wished the students to follow with the subsequent patterns in the lesson. I felt this modeling was especially important given the limited experience of these students with the concepts I had targeted for the lesson. Second, I hoped that working through an initial problem together would boost the confidence of the students in their ability to successfully carry out the objectives of the lesson.

I told the students, "The figures projected on the screen represent the first three stages of a pattern. As you can see, they are labeled Stage One, Stage Two, and Stage Three. Use your colored squares to construct what you believe Stage Four and Stage Five of the pattern look like."

I provided the students with colored squares because I believe that using materials that are both tactile and visual provides students with concrete examples for concepts like constant and variable. These examples can then serve as the basis for developing understanding of those concepts.

I circulated around the room to check the accuracy of the students' figures. I was pleased to find that every student in the class constructed Stages 4 and 5 as I had hoped they would (see below).

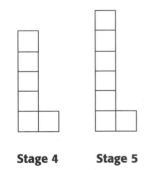

Stage 4   **Stage 5**

Sometimes, of course, a student interprets a pattern differently than the teacher or text intended. When this happens, I always ask the student to explain her or his thinking because I would never want to assume that there is only one correct interpretation for a pattern, especially when only a few terms or stages are given (e.g., the sequence 1, 2, 4, . . . could be interpreted as successive powers of two and extended 1, 2, 4, 8, 16, . . . or it could be interpreted as increasing the difference between successive terms and extended 1, 2, 4, 7, 11, . . .). Certainly, good mathematical discussion can grow from examining such a situation. For this lesson, however, I tried to choose configurations of squares with growth patterns that were not ambiguous because I wanted to avoid distractions from the emphases of the lesson. I also chose only patterns that modeled linear functions, again to avoid distractions from this early exploration about finding explicit rules.

As soon as I verified that every student had constructed the expected configurations for Stages 4 and 5, I asked the students to look carefully at all five stages. I asked them to express their thinking for producing the fourth and fifth stages. Clara offered that each stage had one more square added to the stack on the left side than in the previous stage. Everyone agreed.

"So what is a rule for this pattern?" I asked.

As expected, several students raised their hands and each essentially stated the same iterative rule: for each stage, you have one more square than in the previous stage. An overwhelming proportion of middle school students come to us thinking iteratively. I think it is important to recognize the accuracy and validity of this kind of thinking. Iteration is embedded in a lot of important mathematics, and finding iterative rules for patterns can often help students find explicit rules for those same patterns. (For example, when a student notices that each stage in a pattern increases by three, the explicit rule may contain three times a variable, as in $y = 3x + 1$ for the sequence 4, 7, 10, 13 . . . .) More important, we teachers need to validate students' thinking whenever we can in order to encourage them and to signal that we value that thinking.

Simultaneously, I want students to continue to expand their thinking. In this lesson, my objective was to help students learn to derive explicit rules for patterns as well as iterative ones. Thus, after acknowledging the accuracy and validity of the students' iterative rule for the warm-up pattern, we moved on.

I asked the students to break each stage of the pattern down into several parts in a way that made sense to them and that could be used to describe how the pattern grew from stage to stage. "Use squares of different colors to illustrate your thinking more clearly." As a starting point, I asked the students to focus on Stage 3 of the warm-up pattern. I asked them to imagine how they might use different colored squares to show the composition of that stage visually. I knew from experience that this is difficult for students to verbalize at first.

No one volunteered, but Allen at least had eye contact with me, so I said, "Allen, would you be willing to try?"

Allen stated, "I see four up-and-down squares and one that sticks out to the right."

"Can you show us with colored squares what you mean?" I asked.

Allen dutifully came up to the overhead and arranged an array congruent to the one already there, using four red squares for the vertical column and one yellow square.

I then asked, "Can you build Stages One and Two using the same way to visually show how you see the pattern put together?" He nodded and constructed the arrays shown in Figure 3–1.

"Can anyone say in words the way you believe Allen is viewing each stage?"

FIGURE 3–1 Allen's interpretation of squares warm-up pattern

FIGURE 3–1 Allen's interpretation of squares warm-up pattern

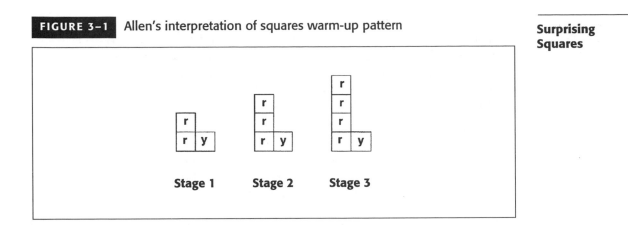

Will volunteered, "I think Allen made a stack of red squares and one yellow square out to the side for each stage." Allen nodded.

"So Allen sees each stage as a vertical (up-and-down) column of red squares and one yellow square at the bottom of the column on the right side." I repeated Allen's description of the pattern for clarity and to incorporate the use of appropriate vocabulary (*column* and *vertical*). I left Allen's models on the projector and asked, "Now, does anyone see another way to think of each stage of the pattern?"

There was a long pause. Again, because I know it often takes students some time to go through this process at first, I waited. Eventually, Sally asked, "Could you see each figure as two on the bottom and then some sticking up?"

"Come show us what you mean at the overhead, Sally."

Sally built the three stages, using two yellow squares along the bottom row and a column of one, two, and three red squares, respectively, above the yellow square on the left side, as shown in Figure 3–2.

"Can someone describe in words how Sally separated each figure into two parts?" I asked.

"She has a row of two yellow squares along the bottom and a stack of red squares above it on the left side for each stage," Fernando offered.

After Sally confirmed Fernando's description, I restated, "So Sally sees each stage as a row of two yellow squares along the bottom and a column of red squares above the yellow square on the left side." Again I included in the description some vocabulary that I wanted the students to begin to use.

"Now let's look at each of these ways of viewing the pattern and try to make a rule for the total number of squares. Let's look at Sally's version

FIGURE 3–2 Sally's interpretation of squares warm-up pattern

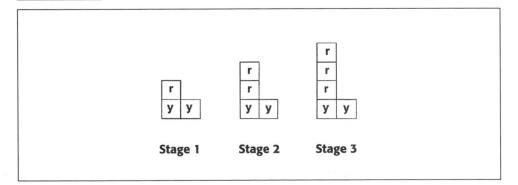

first," I said, covering Allen's figures with a sheet of paper. "Does anyone have a rule to suggest?" When no one volunteered a rule, I asked, "What do you notice about the number of yellow squares in each stage?" to get the process started. I have found that it is not unusual for students to need prompts during an early exploration of this type.

"There are always two," Gina offered.

"Yes," I affirmed, "looking at Sally's models, the two yellow squares are the *constant* part of each stage of the pattern. There are always exactly two yellow squares for each stage. And what about the number of red squares?"

"Well," Fernando said, "there is one more red square for each stage."

"Tell me more, Fernando," I urged.

"There is one red square for Stage One, two red squares for Stage Two, and three red squares for Stage Three."

"Exactly," I said. "Both of Fernando's statements are correct. But one of them helps us make the kind of rule we are looking for today—an *explicit* rule, a rule that uses the stage number in some way and can also be used to find the total number of squares for any stage. Which of Fernando's statements relates the number of red squares to the stage number?"

Clara raised her hand. "I think one of Fernando's statements says that the number of red squares is the same as the stage number. Stage One has one red square, Stage Two has two red squares, and so on."

"So who can make a rule in words to give the total number of squares in any stage, using Sally's model?" No one volunteered. "Well, what did Gina notice about the number of yellow squares?"

A chorus replied, "There are always two."

"Yes, we can use that as part of the rule." So I wrote on the overhead film, *Total number of squares for any stage = 2 (yellow squares)*. . . .

"The two yellow squares are in every figure, so they are the *constant* part of the rule," I said, again using the vocabulary I hoped they would absorb. "And what about the red squares?"

Fernando said, "There are always as many red squares as the stage number."

"Yes." I skipped a space after "2 (yellow squares)" on the transparency and wrote *stage number (red squares)*. Then I stated, "The number of red squares *changes*, or *varies*, from stage to stage. That is the *variable* part of the pattern, but the number of red squares remains the same as the stage number. So what do I do with these two parts of the rule?"

"Add them!" Sally contributed.

"Yes," I said, inserting a plus sign into the rule so that it now read "Total number of squares for any stage = 2 (yellow squares) + stage number (red squares)." Then I asked, "Now, who can give us an example of how this rule works?"

Charlie raised his hand. "Like for Stage Three, the number of squares is two yellow ones, plus three reds (the stage number of reds), or five total squares."

"I don't get it," Tony said.

"OK, Tony, let's try using the rule for Stage Two," I offered. "Tell me the rule again."

Tony reluctantly read, "Total number of squares for any stage equals two (yellow squares) plus stage number (red squares)."

"What does the rule tell you to do first?" I asked.

"I don't know," Tony replied.

"Who can help Tony get started?" I asked. Several hands went up. Tony pointed to Greg.

Greg said, "The rule says, 'Total equals two plus something,' so first you put down a two and a plus sign."

"OK," Tony answered, and wrote 2 + ... "But what do you add?" he asked.

Greg continued. "Look at Stage Two. It has two red squares, so you add two. Two plus two equals four squares for Stage Two."

"But the rule says, 'Two plus stage number,' " Tony protested.

"Yeah, you're right. But look: the number of red squares and the stage number are always the same," Greg explained. He pointed to each stage on the overhead. "That's why the rule works for any stage. You always have the two yellow squares and then add on the red ones."

"Does that make sense to you, Tony?" I asked.

When he nodded "yes," I asked him to use the rule to tell me the total number of squares needed for Stage 4. He said slowly, "Two plus stage number, so two plus four equals six squares."

"Yes," I said, "and can you show us Stage Four, according to our rule, on the overhead?"

Tony came up and placed two yellow and four red squares on the bed of the overhead projector (see below) next to the Stage 3 model and wrote *Stage 4*.

Tony's comments may have revealed that he was struggling with a very common conceptual hurdle, grasping the concept of a variable. Like many students, Tony seemed to have trouble recognizing that the stage number for the figures can represent a value that changes. He indicated that he understood there was a quantity (the number of red squares) that was different from one stage to the next, but he did not yet grasp how using the term *stage number* in a rule could represent change. Once he connected that the number of red squares and the stage number changed in the same way, I felt he was making progress toward understanding the critical algebraic ideas of change and variables.

"So, Tony," I began, "can you do Stage Five?" He nodded and quickly used two yellow squares and five red ones to construct Stage 5 as Sally's interpretation would dictate.

"Describe that stage in words for me, please, Tony."

He answered, "There are two yellow squares on the bottom and five red ones in a column above them on the left side."

"Can you describe Stage One Hundred, Tony?" I asked.

He confidently stated, "It would have two yellow squares on the bottom and one hundred red ones in the column on the left." Tony returned to his seat.

In addition to building Tony's confidence and allowing him to regain any self-esteem he had lost, I wanted to make another point. "Would Tony or any of you been able to describe Stage One Hundred quickly if we had stopped after noticing that each stage has one more red square than the previous stage?" As the students shook their heads "no," I added, "Tony has just demonstrated the need for a rule that relates to the stage number, an *explicit rule*, and the power such a rule gives us. Thanks, Tony."

Then I asked, "Does this rule make sense to everyone?" When all the students nodded, I asked, "Can someone explain again how this rule matches with the way Sally built her models for this pattern on the overhead?"

Danita summarized, "Sally showed each stage with two yellow squares and some red squares. The number of red squares always matched up with the stage number, so we can use the rule 'Total number of squares equals two plus stage number.'"

"Let's do one more example before we look back at Allen's way of breaking down the pattern," I suggested. "Will everyone please use Sally's rule to find the total number of squares needed for Stage Seventy-Three of this pattern?"

All except a couple of students wrote something quickly and raised their hands. Gina explained, "Since the total number of squares equals two plus the stage number, I did two plus seventy-three, for a total of seventy-five squares."

Seeing a couple of frowns, I said, "Gina, can you come to the board and show us your steps? Remember to explain each step as you go."

Gina came to the board and gave the explanation shown in Figure 3–3. (The writing she did on the board is labeled "Notation" and her spoken words are labeled "Comment.")

"I see how you used the rule," Albert said, "but I still don't see where the 'stage number' part comes from."

Gina pointed back to the models on the overhead. "See, for Stage Two, there are two red squares, for Stage Three, there are three, so for Stage Seventy-Three, there would be seventy-three. We noticed the pattern and it went along with the stage number. That means we can add the two yellow squares and know that the red ones will be the same as the stage number."

"I got it. I got it," Albert declared.

"So, Albert," I began, "are you ready for a tough question?" Even though Albert looked dubious, I went on. "How many total squares would be in Stage Four Hundred Eighty-One of this pattern?"

FIGURE 3–3   Gina's explanation

Notation	Comment
Total = **2** + stage number	Our rule says that for any stage, you can find the total number of squares by adding the two yellow ones and the stage number.
Total for Stage 73 = 2 + 73	Since we are working on Stage Seventy-Three, we add the two yellows and seventy-three reds. There would be seventy-three reds because that is the stage number.
Total for Stage 73 = 75	So there are seventy-five squares in all in Stage Seventy-Three.

Albert thought a second, wrote on his paper, and then announced, "I think you would have two yellows and four hundred eighty-one reds, or four hundred eighty-three squares."

"Exactly," I said.

I chose to have the class examine Sally's way of viewing the pattern before looking at Allen's version because I knew the link between the stage number and the rule would be easier for the students to find with Sally's models. Because we had spent so much time with "Sally's rule," I momentarily considered skipping detailed examination of Allen's way of seeing the pattern, but I returned to it for two important reasons. First, one of the ideas I wanted to emphasize in this lesson is that many patterns, even simple ones, can be visualized in different ways that may all be correct. Similarly, seemingly different (although equivalent) rules for the same pattern can be derived, again all of which may be correct. Too many of us were taught that mathematics is a discipline in which nearly every problem has one, and only one, correct answer, and one and only one method for obtaining that answer. This perception not only stifles creative thinking but also tends to focus the efforts of students on "learning the one right way" as defined by the teacher or textbook author. It is my strong belief that this mindset is counterproductive if the goal is to help students become thinkers and creative problem solvers. Thus, I demonstrate to students that I value different ways of seeing and solving problems whenever I can. Of course, this also coincides nicely with the needs of middle schoolers for self-expression and their desire to do things their own way!

I also wanted to return to Allen's way of viewing this pattern because it would illustrate for the students a less direct, but often needed, way of connecting the stage number of a pattern with a general rule. Therefore, I removed Sally's models from the overhead projector and uncovered Allen's models. "Allen used a different way of visualizing each stage of the pattern," I noted. "What is the *constant* part in each stage as Allen viewed it?"

Ming said, "I think the constant is the one yellow square at each stage."

"Yes," I answered. "So what do you think Allen's rule might be?"

Will stated, " 'Total number of squares equals one (yellow square) . . . plus . . .' something."

"OK. Now, what does anyone notice about the number of red squares in each stage?"

As before, Fernando volunteered. "There is one more red square for each stage than for the stage before it."

"Yes; can you use your observation to make an iterative rule?"

Fernando completed the thought: "For any stage, the total number of squares will be one more than the total for the stage before it."

"And we know that kind of rule is often useful. But what have we found the drawback or limitation of an iterative rule to be?"

"You can only find the answer if you know the answer for the step before the one you want to know," Cecie answered.

"That's right. Remember, everyone, today we are looking for *explicit* rules, rules that do not depend on knowing the answer for the previous stage, rules that can be used to find the answer for *any* stage of a pattern. So look back at the red squares in Allen's models. What do you notice?"

"I notice that the number of red squares is *not* the same as the stage number," Charlie observed.

"Correct, Charlie," I noted, "and who can explain why Charlie's observation is important?"

"Because," Danita offered, "if the stage number matches part of each figure you can usually find a rule pretty easy."

"Yeah," Clara added, "like with Sally's rule."

"Can anyone make another observation about the number of red squares for each stage number?" I asked.

After the students were quiet for almost a minute, I decided to help them organize the information they had provided in a different way that would model an approach I knew they would find useful with the other patterns in this lesson and in many future situations. (**Note:** This information could also be entered in a three-column T-chart. I chose to do it using the way described here in order to demonstrate an alternate method that is more beneficial for some students.)

"Well, let's see what we know so far," I said, starting to construct a table on the overhead. I wrote the headings *Stage 1, Stage 2, Stage 3, Stage 4,* and *Stage 5* in the first column. Next I asked, "And what do we know about the number of yellow squares?"

Danita answered, "There is always one yellow square in each stage."

I wrote *1 yellow* in each row of the second column. "And what will we do with the number of red squares for each stage?" I asked.

"Add it to the yellow one," Ming offered.

"Yes," I agreed, adding the symbol and words in each column so that the table looked as shown:

Stage 1	1 yellow + ____ reds
Stage 2	1 yellow + ____ reds
Stage 3	1 yellow + ____ reds
Stage 4	1 yellow + ____ reds
Stage 5	1 yellow + ____ reds

"Fill in the other information you know and look for a pattern that *relates to the stage number*," I instructed. Students began to copy the table and fill in the number of red squares for each stage number.

I led the students through building the table at this point in the lesson for two reasons. First, I have found it useful to model for students possible methods for organizing information they know, to help them look for patterns in that information, and then to help them relate such patterns to stage numbers. Also, I knew that the difference between using the phrase *the stage number* and using the phrase *one more than the stage number* or *one less than the stage number* in a rule is a big one for many middle school students. I hoped, if possible, to use this table to make that step easier for some of the students.

Soon the students had completed the table:

Stage 1	1 yellow + <u>2</u> reds
Stage 2	1 yellow + <u>3</u> reds
Stage 3	1 yellow + <u>4</u> reds
Stage 4	1 yellow + <u>5</u> reds
Stage 5	1 yellow + <u>6</u> reds

"Who has found a pattern that relates the number of red squares for any stage to the stage number?" I asked.

Several hands went up. "The number of red squares is one more than the stage number," offered Danita.

"Exactly," I said. "So what is the rule for the total number of squares for any stage?"

Again several hands went up. Michael said, "The total number of squares equals one plus one more than the stage number."

"Yes. Did anyone word it in a different way?" I asked.

"I did," Julie offered. "Total number of squares equals one plus the stage number plus one."

I pointed out that Julie's version was exactly the same as Michael's: adding "one more than the stage number" signals a person to do exactly the same calculations as adding "the stage number plus one." Michael and Julie simply wrote the same rule using slightly different words.

Sally spoke up. "Actually, Allen's rule is the same as the rule I got before, isn't it? I mean 'two plus the stage number' is the same as 'one plus the stage number plus one,' right?"

I acknowledged that the two rules were *equivalent*; that is, they would produce the same results for each stage. I emphasized that the two rules (Sally's and Allen's) were expressed differently because the two students had viewed the pattern in different ways: each rule was derived directly from a visual way of breaking down (or putting together) each stage of the pattern. I am repeatedly reminded that the reason for working with concrete models is to build a tangible, visible pattern that can help lead students to "see" and understand the abstract concepts toward which we are aiming.

I also pointed out that students should listen carefully when their classmates explain their ways of thinking; they might discover new strategies for finding patterns and their rules.

Before moving to the next pattern, I asked the students to find the total number of squares in Stage 10 of the pattern using Allen's rule. After everyone had written down an answer, Greg gave the explanation shown in Figure 3–4.

Everyone agreed that Greg had correctly used Allen's rule for Stage 10. Again I pointed out that twelve was the same answer that was obtained using Sally's rule because the rules are equivalent. I also repeated that for any pattern, all correct rules will yield the same results for any and every stage.

FIGURE 3–4 Greg's explanation

Notation	Comment
Total = 1 + 1 more than the stage number	Allen's rule says that for any stage you can find the total number of squares by adding the one yellow one and one more than the stage number for the red squares.
Total for Stage 10 = 1 + 10 + 1	For Stage Ten, we add one yellow and ten reds. You add ten reds because that is the stage number. Then you add one more red.
Total for Stage 10 = 12	So there are twelve squares in all in Stage Ten

Finally we could move to another pattern! Although almost half the class period had been spent working through the warm-up problem, I was pleased that students seemed to be focusing on and discussing exactly the ideas I had targeted for the lesson. I have found that working slowly and thoroughly with students through the first few examples related to any new concept or skill usually results in a stronger foundation than trying to cover a larger number of examples more quickly. Again, with this lesson, that strategy paid off.

Next I presented the students with the following pattern:

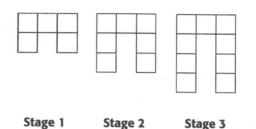

Stage 1   **Stage 2**   **Stage 3**

I asked the students to do the following:

- Draw what you think the fourth and fifth stages look like.

- In a sentence or two, describe what the tenth stage would look like.

- In a sentence, write a rule that describes how to build any stage of the pattern.

I circulated as the students worked. Everyone was able to draw the expected versions of the fourth and fifth stages, as shown here.

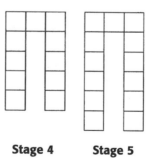

Stage 4   **Stage 5**

As students described the tenth stage of the pattern, there were three different interpretations of the pattern among the class members. Most of the students saw the pattern as Michael did (see Figure 3–5).

The majority of the class, like Michael, described Stage 10 as having the top three squares (the constant part), with ten squares in each leg. Michael pointed out that ten was the same as the stage number. He chose Will from among the students who saw the pattern in this way to give the rule for any stage of the pattern. Will said, " 'The total number of squares equals three plus the stage number plus the stage number,' or 'three plus two times the stage number.' "

I asked the students to use this rule to find the total number of squares needed to build Stage 100, and everyone except Carla got 203. Carla got

Stage 10
It would have the three constant ones on the top
with ten squares going down matching.
On both sides. The equation is 3+10+10

Any Stage
Keep the very top squares (3)
then find the # of chips in each
leg and multiply by 2

23 Total chips

Total = 3+N×2 =

500 because she added 3 + 2 and then multiplied by 100. Beyond helping Carla, analyzing her error gave me the chance to review the order of operations for the class. Will explained his calculations, shown in Figure 3–6.

"It makes sense when you explain it that way," Carla said. "But the way you wrote your rule, it looks like I should add the three and two first. Three plus two equals five and then five times one hundred equals five hundred."

Will paused, then answered, "Well, you could write the rule 'Total equals two times the stage number plus three.' Would that help?"

"Yeah," Carla said, "but is that the same rule?"

I asked who could answer Carla's question and explain why. Fernando volunteered. "Remember the order of operations, Carla? You always multiply before you add. But I think the rule would make more sense if we used parentheses, like this." He wrote the following on the board: $Total = 3 + (N \times 2)$.

Carla nodded, but Clara raised her hand and asked, "What does the N in that rule mean?"

FIGURE 3-6   Will's explanation

Notation	Comment
Total = 3 + 2 × the stage number	Our rule says that for any stage you can find the total number of squares by adding the three across the top plus two times the number of squares in each column. The number of squares in each column is always the same as the stage number.
Total for Stage 100 = 3 + 2 × 100	For Stage One Hundred, we first multiply two times one hundred for the squares in the two columns. Then we add the three across the top.
Total for Stage 100 = 203	So there are two hundred three total squares for Stage One Hundred.

I asked Fernando to explain. He said, "A couple of times we have talked about how you can use a letter to stand for the variable part of the rule, so I just used *N* to stand for the stage number."

I added, "Clara, the rule still means 'Add the constant three squares to twice the stage number.' The *N* is called a *variable* because it stands for a changing amount."

Clara asked whether she had to use *N* in her rule. I told her she should write the rule using words until she was comfortable replacing some of the words with a variable, and I cautioned Fernando that you should always explain what a variable stands for. I added that all the students would eventually need to use variables in rules but there was no rush to do so. Clara seemed satisfied.

Ming and a few other students saw the middle square in the top row as the constant in this pattern (see Figure 3–7).

FIGURE 3–7 Ming's description of Stage 10 and rule

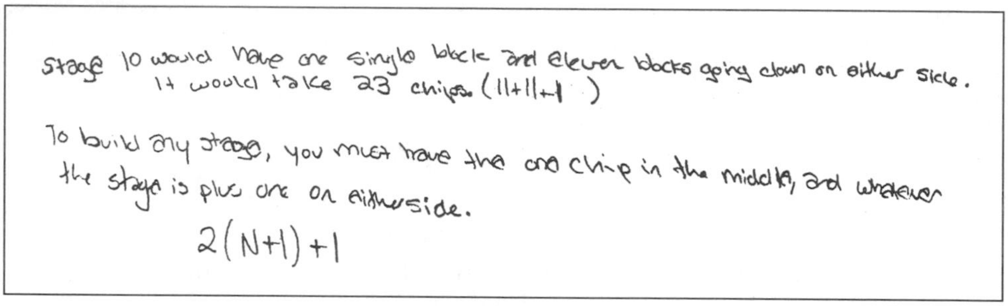
Stage 10 would have one single block and eleven blocks going down on either side. It would take 23 chips. (11+11+1)

To build any stage, you must have the one chip in the middle, and whatever the stage is plus one on eitherside.

2(N+1)+1

These students viewed Stage 10 as having eleven squares in each leg. Ming pointed out that the number of squares in each column was one more than the stage number.

Michael explained the general rule: "To build any stage, you have one square in the middle and a number of squares that is one more than the stage number going down on each side of that square." When asked whether he could write the rule using the variable *N* to stand for the stage number, Michael wrote $Total = 1 + 2 \times N + 1$.

Ming raised her hand and suggested, "Michael, you need to put parentheses around the '*N* plus one' part of your rule." Michael nodded and rewrote his rule: $Total = 1 + 2 \times (N + 1)$.

"Why do we need the parentheses?" Seth asked.

"Because," Ming explained, "you multiply by two *after* you add one to the stage number. Without the parentheses a person would have to multiply two times *N* and then add one. That would not be right because each stage has two parts that have one more than the stage number of squares."

Seth still looked puzzled, so we asked Ming to use the rule with and without the parentheses, following the rules for the order of operations, for Stage 10. She wrote the following:

No ( )s	With ( )s
Total = 1 + 2 × ***N*** + 1	Total = 1 + 2 × (***N*** + 1)
Total = 1 + 2 × **10** + 1	Total = 1 + 2 × (**10** + 1)
Total = 1 + 20 + 1	Total = 1 + 2 × 11
Total = 21 + 1	Total = 1 + 22
Total = 22	Total = 23

Ming explained each step and how it followed the rules for the order of operations. Seth then demonstrated his understanding by using the correctly written rule to find the total number of squares needed for Stage 100 of the pattern.

Will asked whether the multiplication sign was necessary in front of the parentheses. I answered that it was not necessary but students could continue to include the symbol until they were comfortable with omitting it.

Danita was the only student in the class to view the pattern in a third way (see Figure 3–8).

For Stage 10, she saw the top three squares as the constant and the two columns as containing eleven squares each. Thus, as she explained it, she counted each corner twice and therefore needed to subtract two from her sum to get the correct total number of squares. She was completely comfortable with this view, and several other students remarked that they would have never thought to look at it that way.

FIGURE 3–8   Danita's description of Stage 10 and rule

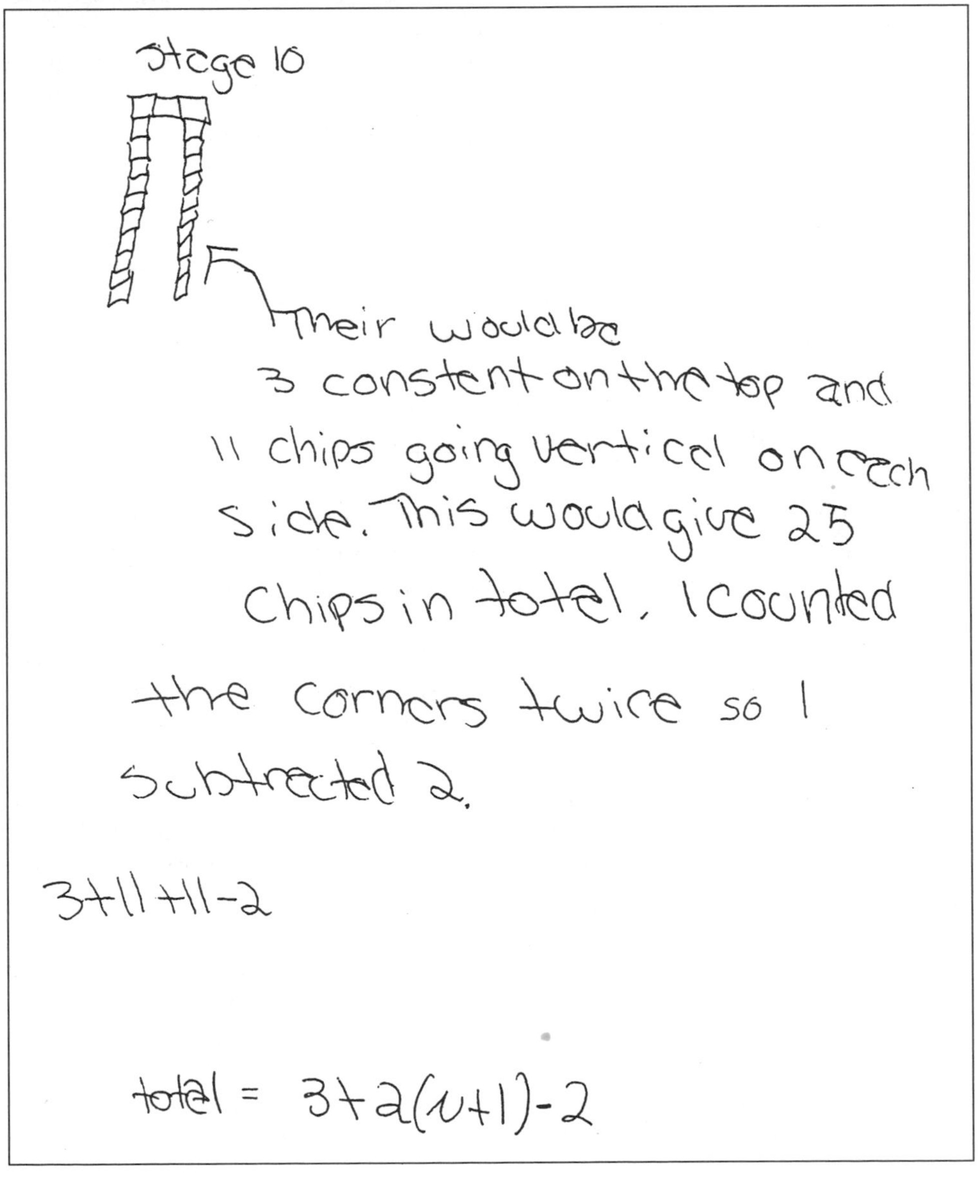

Stage 10

Their would be 3 constent on the top and 11 chips going vertical on each side. This would give 25 Chips in total. I counted the corners twice so I subtracted 2.

$3 + 11 + 11 - 2$

total $= 3 + 2(N + 1) - 2$

Julie asked Danita what made her think to use overlapping squares as part of the pattern. "To tell the truth, I didn't know I had done that at first," Danita admitted. I encouraged her to explain the steps she went through. "When I first tried Stage Five with my rule, I added three for the top part and two sixes for the columns, so I got a total of fifteen squares. This didn't match with the number of squares I counted in the model, so I thought my rule was wrong. I had to play with several stages before I realized that I had counted the squares on the top corners twice, so all I had to do was subtract that extra two each time to get the correct total. I tried this same thing with several stages and it always worked. I guess when something doesn't quite work you just have to think about it a little more, because it all came out OK in the end."

I was pleased that Danita had shared her experience. I pointed out that most students (and adults as well) sometimes have to try a "rough draft" of a rule and then revise it if it doesn't quite work. I pointed out that this method is quite valuable in solving problems.

Danita's interpretation also reminded me of another common occurrence when students are trying to find rules for visual patterns. When students see a pattern in a particular way, they will often go to great lengths to find a rule that matches that visual interpretation. In this case, Danita saw an intact group of three squares at the top of the array for each stage, and also two intact columns on the sides. It was this way of seeing the pattern that caused her to double-count the corner squares. However, when faced with a mismatch between her rule and the way she viewed the arrays, Danita chose to shoehorn the rule to fit her image rather than to rethink her interpretation. This tendency by Danita and many other students to stick with what makes sense to them corroborates what research tells us about the way we learn: people build knowledge based on what they already understand, not on what is unknown to them. This is why I avoid the "one right way to do it" approach to the teaching of mathematics: the learning process for each student is as unique as the knowledge and experiences she or he brings to class. It is my obligation to try to link new ideas to those the students already understand.

Next I asked each student to write a rule to describe how to build any stage of the pattern in the way that Danita viewed it. After giving the students a minute or so to work, I asked Julie to share her rule. "I think the rule is 'Total number of squares equals add three to two times one more than the stage number, and then subtract two.' " She wrote *3 + 2 × (1 more than stage number) − 2* on the board.

I asked whether anyone could write the rule using *N* to stand for the stage number. Several students raised their hands. After seeing that several students had correct responses, I asked Julie to put her answer on the board. She wrote *Total = 3 + 2 × (N + 1) − 2*.

I believe the relative ease with which these students incorporated the expression *N* +1 into their rules was a direct payoff for the slow, thorough discussion the class had earlier in determining how to incorporate a variable expression for "one more than the stage number" into a function rule. The early stages of introducing new ideas and concepts sometimes seem almost agonizingly deliberate and drawn out, but I have found that time spent to establish a solid foundation of understanding—even of some important details—is time well spent.

I asked Julie to explain her rule and how to use it for Stage 10. She presented the example shown in Figure 3–9.

I asked Seth whether he thought Julie needed to include the parentheses in

FIGURE 3-9 Julie's explanation

**Surprising
Squares**

57

Notation	Comment
Total = 3 + 2 × (**N** + 1) − 2	The rule says that for any stage you can find the total number of squares by adding the three across the top plus two times the number of squares in each column. The number of squares in each column is always one more than the stage number, *N*. Then you have to subtract the two squares you counted twice.
Total = 3 + 2 × (**10** + 1) − 2 3 + 2 × 11 − 2 3 + 22 − 2 25 − 2 23	So for Stage Ten, you add one to ten to get the number of squares in each column, multiply two by eleven for two columns (twenty-two), add the three across the top (twenty-five), and subtract the two you counted twice. You get the twenty-three squares needed.

her rule. He replied, "Yes, I think it's just like before. Without the parentheses a person would get the wrong answer. It's the order of operations thing."

I asked Seth to explain his phrase "the order of operations thing" a little more clearly. He said, "Without the parentheses, a person would just multiply two times the stage number, but Julie wanted them to do two times one more than the stage number, so you have to put the parentheses there to let other people know that." While Seth's answer was not exactly what I was looking for, he clearly understood why parentheses were needed in this particular case.

I chose to add only the comment, "That's right, Seth. The parentheses indicate that the one should be added *before* multiplying. Without them, the order of operations would say multiply first, then add." I felt that Seth was most likely still shaky with the order of operations and use of parentheses, but he seemed to understand the need for parentheses in the context of the particular cases we were discussing.

It is invaluable for students to learn mathematical procedures within a meaningful context, in part so that later they can use that experience as a reference. I have found that saying to a student who can't remember a mathematical rule or procedure, "Remember when we . . ." often eliminates the need for further explanation. Students connect something they did in the past with a new situation *because it had meaning for them in the previous context*. I hoped this would be the case with Seth.

We had time for only one more pattern during the class period. Again, I presented the students with a pattern of squares and asked them to do the same steps.

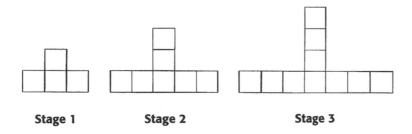

Stage 1   Stage 2   Stage 3

■ Draw what you think the fourth and fifth stages look like.

■ In a sentence or two, describe what the tenth stage would look like.

■ In a sentence, write a rule that describes how to build any stage of the pattern.

Again, I circulated as the students worked, and once more everyone was able to draw the expected versions of the fourth and fifth stages, as shown here.

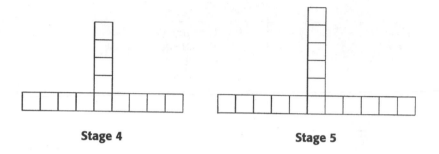

Stage 4   Stage 5

With this pattern, there were only two different interpretations by the students. Actually, everyone except Greg saw the pattern as Albert did (see Figure 3–10).

The students viewed the center square on the bottom row as a constant, with three identical sections, one vertical and two horizontal, each containing the same number of squares as the stage number, attached to that center

FIGURE 3–10 Albert's description of Stage 10 and rule

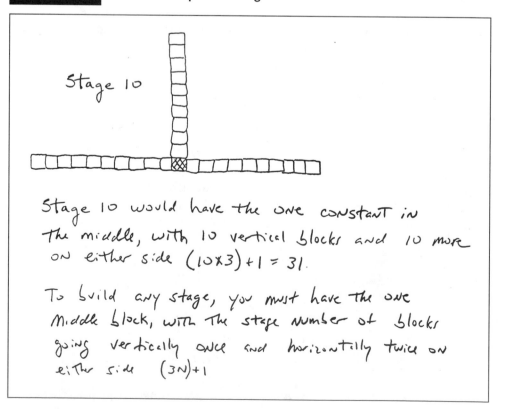

Stage 10

Stage 10 would have the one constant in the middle, with 10 vertical blocks and 10 more on either side $(10 \times 3) + 1 = 31$.

To build any stage, you must have the one middle block, with the stage number of blocks going vertically once and horizontally twice on either side $(3N) + 1$

square. Thus, Stage 10 contained 1 (the constant) + 3 × 10 (the congruent sections), or 31 squares. The general rule, as Albert expressed it, was "To build any stage, you must have the one middle block with the stage number of blocks going vertically once and horizontally twice on either side."

When asked to express the rule using a variable, Julie volunteered $3n + 1$ and the rest of the class agreed. Each student then used the rule to find the total number of squares for Stage 100—301.

Greg interpreted the pattern in a slightly different way (see Figure 3–11). He used the squares of Stage 1 as the constant. Therefore, he viewed Stage 10 as containing the four squares from Stage 1 and three other pieces, each containing nine squares. He calculated the number of squares needed for Stage 10 by doing 9 × 3 + 4, for a total of 31. He described how to build any stage of the pattern by writing *Stage 1 chips (4) are the constants and you add one less than the stage number on each side.*

I have found that a student will often use Stage 1 as a whole, like Greg did, or the basic outline of the pattern's shape, as the constant portion of the pattern and rule. While this way of interpreting the pattern usually makes the rule messier than necessary, when a pattern or rule is consistent with the way the student visualizes the pattern, the whole process is easier for that student. I have also observed that students seldom stick with this strategy, or way of seeing patterns, very long, instead learning to search for

FIGURE 3–11 Greg's description of Stage 10 and rule

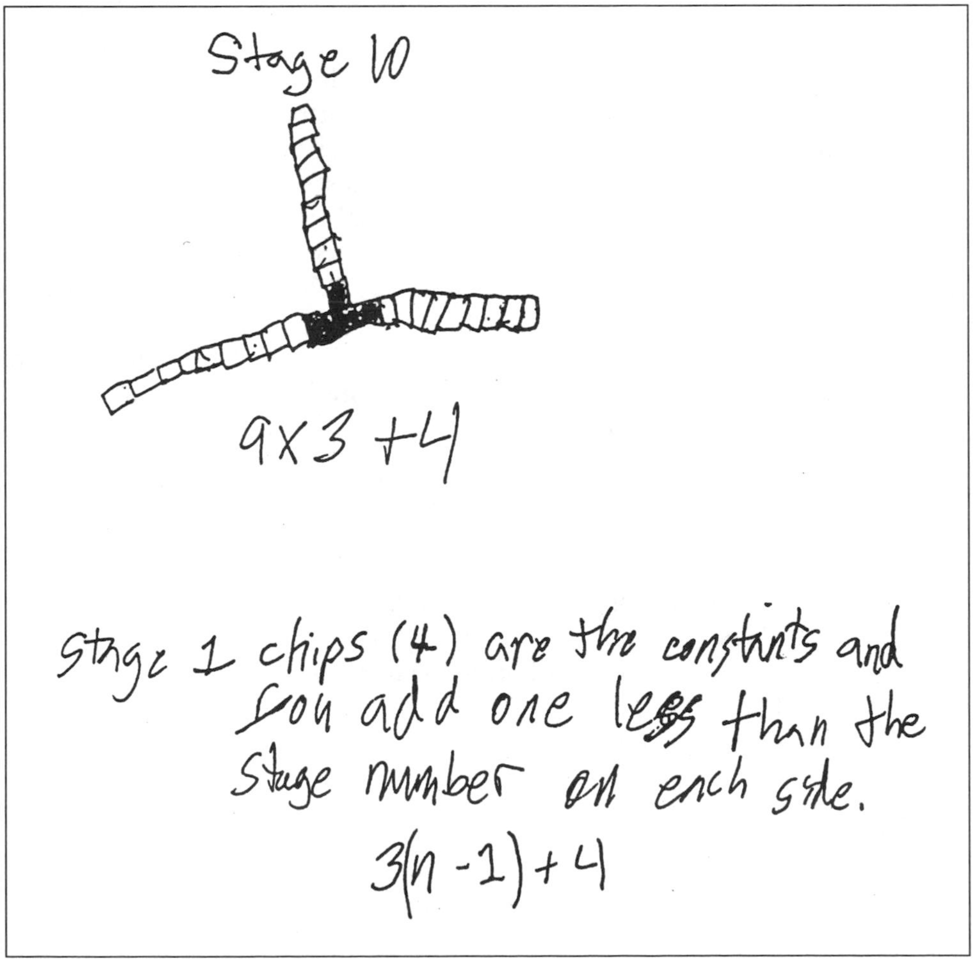

the simplest constant. So I opt not to emphasize finding the simplest form of a constant or even of a rule when another way makes more sense to an individual. Again, I believe making sense of mathematics is far more important than being efficient, certainly when confronting new concepts.

When asked to write Greg's rule using a variable, a few students had some difficulty. Cecie spoke up. "I can get the constant part, four, and I know I need to multiply three by one less than the stage number, but I don't know how to write that part."

I asked who could help Cecie and she chose Sally from the students who raised their hands. "Remember when we wrote the rule for one more than the stage number?" Sally asked.

Cecie nodded but did not speak. "Well, do you remember, with the other pattern, what we wrote for one more than the stage number?" Sally asked. When Cecie shook her head from side to side, Sally added, "We wrote *n* plus one because we wanted to make each stage, *n*, one bigger, so we *added* one to *n—n* plus one. To show one more than something, we *added*."

Cecie slowly nodded. "This time," Sally continued, "we want to write one *less* than the stage number, so . . . ." And she paused. Again, Cecie didn't say anything. "When you want to take one away from something, Cecie, what do you do?"

"Subtract?" Cecie asked quietly.

Sally said. "You got it! So you write *n* minus one, since Greg's rule needs to have that part in it."

I gave the students who were having trouble writing the rule using a variable a little more time and then asked for a volunteer to share what he or she thought with the class. Charlie said, "I think the rule for any stage is 'three, open parenthesis, *n* minus one, close parenthesis, plus four.' " We asked him to show the rule on the overhead and he wrote $3(n - 1) + 4$.

Cecie exclaimed, "I got it! I mean, I wrote four plus three times *n* minus one, but that's the same thing, right?" I assured her that it was, looking over her shoulder to make sure she had used parentheses.

I look for opportunities to let a student help one or more classmates when they are struggling. Of course, I try to listen to what the student helper is saying when I can, but even when I can't hear what is being said, I find several advantages to this technique. First, accepting help from another student usually seems to feel more comfortable for the struggling student than when an adult steps in. Also, the helping student often seems to word things in ways that are more understandable to the student who is having trouble. And, finally, I believe the student doing the helping often clarifies his or her own mathematical thinking by verbalizing it. The only caveat I offer is that I caution my students to avoid *telling* the struggling student the answer. I suggest that a student ask questions to help the other student find the answer for him or herself. Early in the year students need to be reminded to use this questioning-rather-than-telling approach, but soon they really seem to get satisfaction and pride from the successes of their efforts. I am confident that more learning goes on in a mathematics classroom where such collaborative learning is an integral part of instruction.

As with the previous rules, I asked the students to use Greg's rule to find the number of squares needed to build Stage 100 of the pattern. I asked Seth to do the steps at the overhead and he did so with no trouble.

"Is everyone comfortable now using a rule for this pattern to find the total number of squares used to build any stage of the pattern?" I asked. After all the students gave the "thumbs up" signal, I added, "So can you think about the pattern and the rule to tell me for which stage of this pattern would you use twenty-five squares?"

Some hands were quickly raised. After giving the rest of the students some extra time to think, I called on Julie to explain her answer and her thinking. She said, "I think Stage Eight of this pattern would use twenty-five squares. To get this answer, I worked backwards. The one square in the middle of the bottom row is not part of a group, so I took it away. The other twenty-four squares are divided into three equal sections, so I divided twenty-four by three and I got eight. Since the stage number is always the same as the number of squares in each of the three equal groups, I knew the answer must be Stage Eight."

Although everyone indicated that they understood Julie's reasoning, I had her build a model using the colored squares on the overhead and talk through her solution again. The class then worked in pairs to find the stage number that would use 151 squares (Stage 50). This gave any of the students who were not quite ready to use this process of "undoing" independently an opportunity to do collaborative thinking.

Although I knew some of the students were probably saturated with new ideas at this point in the lesson and thus not ready to fully grasp the process of "undoing," I wanted to introduce the process at this early stage in the students' experiences with algebraic thinking. A lot of algebra (e.g., factoring), as well as problem solving in general, requires an understanding of undoing a process to get to an earlier stage or to the starting point. I have found that the sooner students are asked to "undo" as a natural extension of "doing" algebraic thinking, the more success they have. After all, students, for example, "undo" adding to subtract in the primary grades. It is not a difficult task for most students to apply this same kind of thinking in new situations. It is primarily a matter of the teacher providing appropriate opportunities and asking the right questions for students to build on their previous mathematical experiences and to expand their understanding and skill in working through a process either forwards or backwards.

Seeing that there were only a couple of minutes left in the class period, I reviewed the major objectives of the lesson by asking a few informal questions.

"So, quickly, who can tell what a constant is?" I asked.

"The constant is the part of a pattern that stays the same, like the yellow squares on the overhead," Gina volunteered, "when it stays the same for every stage."

"And it can be a number in the rule, like the two in 'stage number plus two,' " Charlie added.

"What is a variable?" I asked.

"The part of the pattern that changes for each stage," Fernando contributed, "like when there was one red square in Stage One, two in Stage Two, and all."

"How might you use a variable in a rule?" I asked.

"You can say 'the stage number,' " Clara answered.

"Or use a letter to stand for the part that changes," Michael added.

"Can there be more than one version of the rule for a pattern?" I ventured.

"Yes!" a chorus of voices practically shouted.

"And should every *correct* rule for a pattern give the same answer for each stage?"

Again a chorus of "Yes!"

"What a great class," I exclaimed as the students gathered their books to go the next class.

Similar Problem | The Stairs Pattern

The Stairs Pattern is appropriate for a lesson similar to *Surprising Squares*.

Find a rule for the total number of dots for any stage.

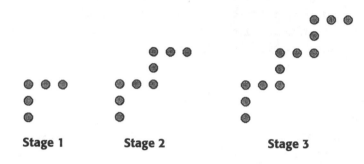

Stage 1   Stage 2   Stage 3

Iterative Rule: Add 4 to the total number of dots in the previous stage.

Explicit Rule: Total number of dots = $4n + 1$, or $5n - (n - 1)$, or $3n + n + 1$ when n = stage number.

Several colors of manipulatives (colored disks would be nice for this pattern) should be used by students to show the visual interpretation that underlies their explicit rules. In this way, all students have the opportunity to expand their ways of visualizing patterns.

For example, for the rule $4n + 1$, a student might illustrate his or her interpretation of Stage 2 in the following way:

Total = 4n + 1

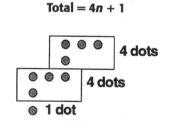

In Stage 2 of the Stairs Pattern there are two groups of four dots (the variable part) and one constant dot.

Extension Problem | The Blockhouse Pattern

The Blockhouse Pattern may be built using one-inch cubes.

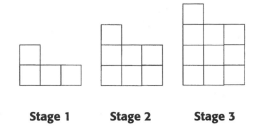

Stage 1   **Stage 2**   **Stage 3**

Comments

The following elements of the *Surprising Squares* lesson should be repeated with both the Stairs Pattern and the Blockhouse Pattern:

- Describing, building a model for, and/or drawing Stages 4 and 5 of the Blockhouse Pattern

- Predicting, then verifying, what Stage 10 of the Blockhouse Pattern would look like

- Using a T-chart to record information, search for patterns, and find and check a rule for the Blockhouse Pattern

- Finding iterative and explicit rules for the Blockhouse Pattern

- Using the explicit rule to find any stage of the Blockhouse Pattern

- Working backward from a given total number of pieces to find the appropriate stage number of the Blockhouse Pattern

  Example: What stage of the Blockhouse Pattern contains 55 cubes?
  $$55 = 3 \times n + 1$$
  $$54 = 3 \times n$$
  $$54/3 = n$$
  $$18 = n$$
  Stage 18 of the Blockhouse Pattern contains 55 cubes

- Noting that there is more than one way to visually interpret the pattern and that each way may be reflected in a different-looking (but equivalent) form of the rule (Note that each of the first three rules listed here corresponds with the three expanded T-charts shown on pages 64 and 65.)

  1. $n + n + n + 1$: three columns of squares, each containing a number of squares that is the same as the stage number (stage number + stage number + stage number, or $n + n + n$), plus one cube on top of the left-hand column

  2. $3 \times n + 1$: a group of cubes that is three cubes wide and as many cubes tall as the stage number ($3 \times$ the stage number, or $3 \times n$), plus one cube on top

  3. $(n + 1) + n + n$: a column on the left that contains one more square than the stage number ($n + 1$) and two additional columns, each of which contains n squares ($n + n$)

  4. $3 \times (n + 1) - 2$ (rarely): a group of cubes that is three cubes wide and as many cubes tall as the stage number plus one [$3 \times$ (the stage number + 1) or $3 \times (n + 1)$] minus two missing cubes in the top row

- Writing and sharing reflections

Ideas/concepts that may be new for some students that often emerge during exploration of this pattern include the following:

- Writing the expressions in the center column of the T-chart in expanded form. At first, students often create the following expanded T-chart for the Blockhouse Pattern:

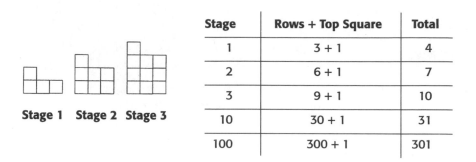

Stage	Rows + Top Square	Total
1	3 + 1	4
2	6 + 1	7
3	9 + 1	10
10	30 + 1	31
100	300 + 1	301

Stage 1   Stage 2   Stage 3

Writing the expressions in the center column of the T-chart in an expanded form helps students find the rule(s) more easily. If needed, it should be pointed out that each of the following expanded forms reflects how the pattern is changing in a way that relates to the stage number.

1.

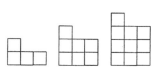

Stage 1   Stage 2   Stage 3

Stage	Columns + Top Square	Total
1	(1 + 1 + 1) + 1	4
2	(2 + 2 + 2) + 1	7
3	(3 + 3 + 3) + 1	10
10	(10 + 10 + 10) + 1	31
100	(100 + 100 + 100) + 1	301
n	(n + n + n) + 1	

or, 2.

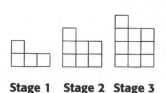

Stage 1   Stage 2   Stage 3

Stage	Rows + Top Square	Total
1	(1 × 3) + 1	4
2	(2 × 3) + 1	7
3	(3 × 3) + 1	10
10	(10 × 3) + 1	31
100	(100 × 3) + 1	301
n	(n × 3) + 1 *or* ($3 × n$) + 1	

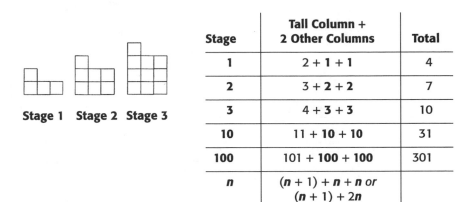

Stage	Tall Column + 2 Other Columns	Total
1	2 + 1 + 1	4
2	3 + 2 + 2	7
3	4 + 3 + 3	10
10	11 + 10 + 10	31
100	101 + 100 + 100	301
n	$(n + 1) + n + n$ or $(n + 1) + 2n$	

- Noting that the consistent increases of three in the total number of pieces from stage to stage is a part of both the iterative rule (Total = total from previous stage + 3) and the explicit (Total = $3 \times n + 1$) rule for the pattern and making sense of that observation

- Verifying that equivalent forms of a rule produce the same results

  Example: For Stage 20 of the Blockhouse Pattern,
  $n + n + n + 1 = 20 + 20 + 20 + 1 = 61$ total squares
  $3 \times n + 1 = 3 \times 20 + 1 = 61$ total squares
  $(n + 1) + n + n = 21 + 20 + 20 = 61$ total squares
  $3 \times (n + 1) - 2 = 3 \times (20 + 1) - 2 = 3 \times 21 - 2 = 61$ total squares [*if* this form of the rule is offered by a student]

- Noting that $n \times 3 + 1$ and $3 \times n + 1$ may be written $3n + 1$ [also that $3 \times (n + 1) - 2$ may be written $3(n + 1) - 2$ *if* this form of the rule is suggested]

Another lesson appropriate for use after *Surprising Squares* can be found in *Navigating Through Algebra in Grades 6–8* (Friel et al. 2001, 63–64, 86). It is titled "Tiling Tubs" and emphasizes equivalent variable expressions for a given situation.

Comparing Equivalent Rules

Technology Connections

If graphing calculators are available, the equivalent forms of the explicit rule for each pattern explored in the *Surprising Squares* lesson can be entered in the *y* = menu and the tables can be viewed. These tables, shown on the following page, can be compared to verify that equivalent forms of a rule produce the same results for any stage and to show values for large stage numbers.

If you feel it is appropriate for your students at the time of this lesson, the calculators can also display scatter plots that can verify in a visual way that equivalent forms of a rule produce the same results. Directions for creating such scatter plots using TI-73 calculators can be found in the "Technology Connections" section of the *Personalized Patterns* lesson.

Alternatively, students can create a spreadsheet on a computer to display the various forms of the rule for a pattern that were found in their class and the values each rule generates.

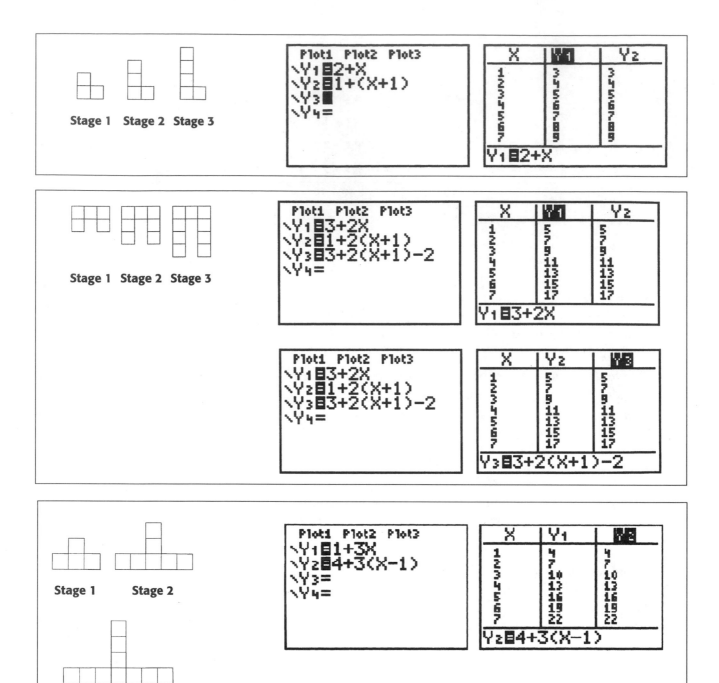

Starting with Spreadsheets

The first three stages of the last pattern used in *Surprising Squares* are shown below.

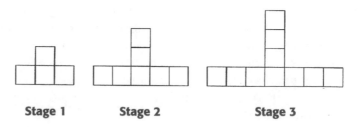

Stage 1   Stage 2   Stage 3

Iterative Rule: For any stage of the pattern, the total number of squares equals three more than the total of the previous stage.

Explicit Rule: For any stage n, the total number of squares $= 3n + 1$.

A spreadsheet can be created by students to display the values produced by these rules. The spreadsheet can be used to verify that the rules produce the same values as those calculated by the students for any stage, to emphasize the constant and variable parts of the explicit rule, and/or to show values easily for large stage numbers.

Before students enter data into a spreadsheet, first have them agree on the column titles for the spreadsheet so that it will be easy for you or any student to refer to a particular column or cell when discussing the completed spreadsheet. For patterns like those in *Surprising Squares*, the following titles work well in initial spreadsheets: *Stage Number* in the first column, *Result Using Iterative Rule* in the second column, *Value of Constant in Explicit Rule* in the third, *Value of Variable Part in Explicit Rule* in the fourth, followed by *Result Using Explicit Rule* in the fifth. (These titles can be shortened as soon as your students are ready to do so.) Note that it is helpful for students to separate explicit rules into two parts, the constant part and the variable part. The last column displays the sum of those two parts, showing the value generated by the entire explicit rule, as illustrated below. This format helps solidify the meaning of *constant* for students as they see the same value in the appropriate column (Column C in this example) for every stage. Similarly, students will notice that the values in the column for the variable part (Column D in this example) change for every stage.

Next students should enter the column titles and type in the data gathered by the students for stages one through five, as illustrated below.

	A	B	C	D	E
1	Stage Number	Result Using Iterative Formula	Value of Constant in Explicit Rule	Value of Variable Part in Explicit Rule	Result Using Explicit Rule
2	1	4	1	3	4
3	2	7	1	6	7
4	3	10	1	9	10
5	4	13	1	12	13
6	5	16	1	15	16

Students should then enter formulas to generate values for subsequent stages in the next row. For this example, students can enter the rules in Row 7, as shown below.

	A	B	C	D	E
1	Stage Number	Result Using Iterative Formula	Value of Constant in Explicit Rule	Value of Variable Part in Explicit Rule	Result Using Explicit Rule
2	1	4	1	3	4
3	2	7	1	6	7
4	3	10	1	9	10
5	4	13	1	12	13
6	5	16	1	15	16
7	=SUM(A6,1)	=SUM(B6,3)	1	=PRODUCT(A7,3)	=SUM(C7:D7)

You may have to vary formulas slightly to fit those required by your software.

Once the formulas have been entered, students can produce values for as many stages as desired by using the following steps:

1. Hold down the mouse button to select the row of cells containing formulas.

2. Continue to hold down and drag to select as many rows as desired.

3. Choose *Fill Down* from the *Edit* menu.

With formulas displayed, the spreadsheet for this example will appear as shown below for the first ten stages:

	A	B	C	D	E
1	Stage Number	Result Using Iterative Formula	Value of Constant in Explicit Rule	Value of Variable Part in Explicit Rule	Result Using Explicit Rule
2	1	4	1	3	4
3	2	7	1	6	7
4	3	10	1	9	10
5	4	13	1	12	13
6	5	16	1	15	16
7	=SUM(A6,1)	=SUM(B6,3)	1	=PRODUCT(A7,3)	=SUM(C7:D7)
8	=SUM(A7,1)	=SUM(B7,3)	1	=PRODUCT(A8,3)	=SUM(C8:D8)
9	=SUM(A8,1)	=SUM(B8,3)	1	=PRODUCT(A9,3)	=SUM(C9:D9)
10	=SUM(A9,1)	=SUM(B9,3)	1	=PRODUCT(A10,3)	=SUM(C10:D10)
11	=SUM(A10,1)	=SUM(B10,3)	1	=PRODUCT(A11,3)	=SUM(C11:D11)

With values displayed, the spreadsheet for this example will appear as shown below for the first ten stages:

	A	B	C	D	E
1	Stage Number	Result Using Iterative Formula	Value of Constant in Explicit Rule	Value of Variable Part in Explicit Rule	Result Using Explicit Rule
2	1	4	1	3	4
3	2	7	1	6	7
4	3	10	1	9	10
5	4	13	1	12	13
6	5	16	1	15	16
7	6	19	1	18	19
8	7	22	1	21	22
9	8	25	1	24	25
10	9	28	1	27	28
11	10	31	1	30	31

Once appropriate explicit rules have been discovered and entered into the spreadsheet, students can find the exact results for any stage quickly without filling all the rows for stages up to the one they wish to display, as illustrated below.

	A	B	C	D	E
1	Stage Number	Result Using Iterative Formula	Value of Constant in Explicit Rule	Value of Variable Part in Explicit Rule	Result Using Explicit Rule
2	1	4	1	3	4
3	2	7	1	6	7
4	3	10	1	9	10
5	4	13	1	12	13
6	5	16	1	15	16
7	6	19	1	18	19
8	7	22	1	21	22
9	8	25	1	24	25
10	9	28	1	27	28
11	10	31	1	30	31
12	20	?	1	60	61
13	50	?	1	150	151
14	100	?	1	300	301
15	1234	?	1	3702	3703

Thus, the use of spreadsheets also rewards students for deriving correct explicit rules, which can focus their efforts on searching for efficient mathematical rules and motivate them to persevere.

Creating and analyzing a spreadsheet of the rules and values for patterns can help many middle school students gain understanding about iterative and explicit function rules. By relating the information in specific cells, columns, or rows to the same information in, for example, models of the pattern's stages or rules for the pattern written in words, students can establish connections between multiple representations. Understanding these connections is an important part of algebraic thinking.

CHAPTER 4

Personalized Patterns

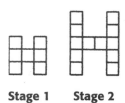

H Pattern

Stage 1   **Stage 2**

L Pattern

Possible Stage 1

OVERVIEW

This lesson provides experiences with finding general rules for given patterns and creating patterns that follow general rules. First, students explore the H Pattern. Given the first two stages of the H pattern (see left), students are asked to produce the next stages of the visual pattern and find a rule to predict the total number of squares needed for any stage. Then each student creates a geometric pattern to represent one of the initials in his or her name (e.g., for the letter L, also shown) and models or draws several stages of that pattern. Students work with each other's models or drawings to identify the pattern, discover an iterative rule that fits the pattern, and, hopefully, find an explicit rule that will generate any stage of the pattern. Students explain their thinking, providing their classmates with opportunities to develop new strategies for finding patterns and their rules. This lesson is intended to establish that various strategies may be used to find rules for patterns and that several different forms of a rule may be correct if they are equivalent.

Students use a different kind of thinking when they create original patterns following a rule than when they simply create new stages or even find a rule. Such thinking helps build an intuitive understanding about how formal function rules are derived. Too often students enter Algebra I devoid of familiarity with contextual function rules. Even fewer students have had opportunities to create their own patterns that model the composition of a function. The lack of this kind of experience adds to the intimidation some students feel when faced with formal function rules and notation.

This lesson should help students develop understanding of functions and the composition of simple rules for linear functions. These understandings will help students succeed in Algebra I, other future mathematics courses, and many problem-solving situations.

BACKGROUND

Being proficient at finding patterns and function rules for patterns requires many experiences for most students. Prior to this lesson, this class of sixth-grade students worked in groups, in pairs, and alone with a variety of patterns to complete each of the following tasks:

- Produce the next stages for a given geometric or numerical pattern.

- Express an iterative rule for a pattern (e.g., "To get a new term in this pattern, add 5 to the previous term.").

- Express an explicit rule for a pattern (e.g., "For any stage in the pattern, the rule is 'The total = 2 more than the stage number.' ").

They used manipulatives, drawings, and tables to help them, and they shared their thinking, methods, and results with the rest of the class.

PREREQUISITE CONCEPTS OR SKILLS

- Recognizing, describing, and extending visual and numerical patterns

- Finding iterative and explicit rules for patterns

VOCABULARY

constant, equivalent rules, explicit rule, iterative rule, stage number, T-chart, variable

TIME

The lesson was completed in two sixty-minute classes plus the time spent by students between the classes creating their own personalized patterns. If your classes are only forty-five minutes long, we suggest going as far as possible during the first day (the students probably will not get to the questions described on page 78). On the second day, again go as far as possible, but be sure to discuss the directions for creating their own personalized patterns with the students. Perhaps there will even be time for students to start on them in class. At least one more class period will be needed for students to check and share each other's personal patterns.

MATERIALS

- *Personalized Patterns: Part One* and *Part Two* activity sheets, 1 of each per student (see Blackline Masters)

- Colored tiles, chips, or other manipulatives for each student

Investigating the H Pattern

The Lesson

Students were presented with the following problem:

Exploring the H Pattern

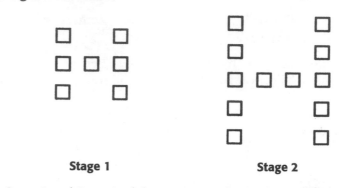

Stage 1   **Stage 2**

Given Stage 1 and Stage 2 of the H Pattern, do the following:

- Draw Stages 3 and 4 of the H Pattern.
- Find a pattern to predict the number of squares needed for higher stages of the H Pattern.
- Give a rule that will work for any stage of the H Pattern.

The *Personalized Patterns: Part One* activity sheet (see Blackline Masters) varies slightly from the one used with this class in order for the form to be most useful for the reader.

This problem was chosen partially because it is often viewed and solved in more than one way. With such a problem, almost every student in the class has the opportunity to add to his or her "mathematical toolbox" by listening to other students' strategies and conclusions. Because they had done several activities prior to this one that were similar to this first part of the lesson, my students worked alone on this part of the lesson. However, they were free to consult with each other whenever they were stuck or wanted verification of their thinking. One-inch square tiles were available for the students to use, but most were able to go directly to drawing the stages of the pattern on their papers.

Many students solved the problem with little difficulty. One solution, provided by Andrew, is typical of those provided by students who fairly quickly arrived at both an iterative and an explicit rule. Andrew expressed the iterative rule as "Add five to the previous stage." When asked to explain this rule, Andrew related it to the visual representation. He said, "Each stage you go up, you add one horizontally and two on each vertical bar (plus five)." I feel it is important to validate iterative rules but also to make students aware of their limitations (inability to predict the answer for a stage without knowing the value for the previous stage). When Andrew was asked how many tiles would be needed for the hundredth stage, he clearly saw the need for an explicit rule. He said, "I don't want to do each one up to ninety-nine to find the answer for the hundredth stage, so I need to find another rule." He provided an explicit rule almost immediately: "For Stage n of the H Pattern, $5n + 2 =$ the number of squares." (See Figure 4–1.)

Andrew explained the thinking behind his rule this way: "For each stage, I need five groups of squares and two extras [pointing to the two squares circled on his diagram]. The number of squares in each group equals the stage number." Next I asked Andrew to explain how his rule worked for the hundredth stage and he stated with confidence, "Do five times one hundred for the five parts [pointing to each group in his Stage n drawing] and add the two extras you always have." I then asked Andrew to

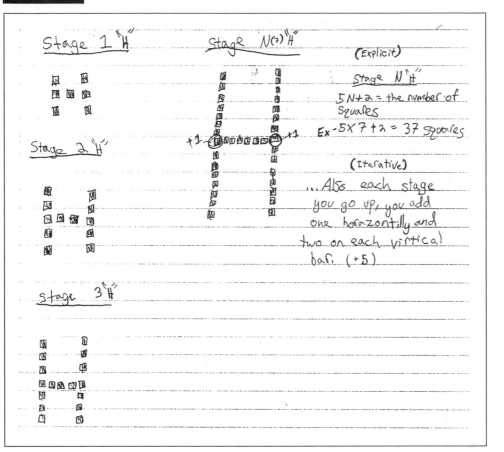

explain how he came up with the two extra squares. He thought for a minute and then said, "I always try to find something related to the stage number. For the H Pattern it is easy to see the five groups of squares that are the same size as the stage number just from the shape of the H. Then there are always two squares left over. I tried it on several stages and it always worked."

I felt it was valuable for the other students to hear Andrew's explanation, especially the part about trying to relate something about the pattern to the stage number, since a lot of middle school kids don't come up with that idea on their own.

Some students, like Carlos, provided drawings that more clearly reflected their thinking (see Figure 4–2).

As Carlos showed in his drawing, he broke down the H Pattern in each stage into five congruent parts, two in each column and one in the row across the middle of the figure. Like Andrew, he observed that each of these parts always contained a number of squares equal to the stage number, and that there were always two squares that were not used in any of the five parts. These observations led him directly to the explicit rule "To find H for Stage n, the formula is $5n + 2$."

As Carlos explained his solution, many students nodded, but a few needed to see more examples or to work with the manipulatives or drawings themselves before they could follow his reasoning. As one student expressed it, "Those groups labeled n don't mean anything to me. I need to count the squares." It seemed to help these students when Carlos explained that he

FIGURE 4–2 Carlos's solution

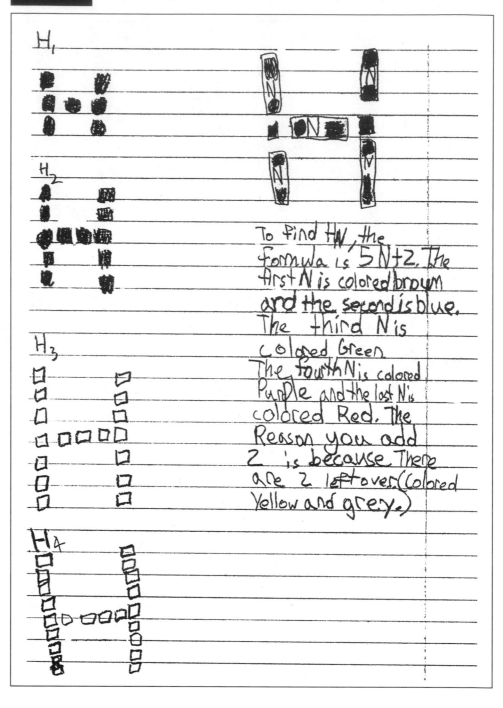

To find HN, the formula is 5N+2. The first N is colored brown and the second is blue. The third N is colored Green The fourth N is colored Purple and the last N is colored Red. The Reason you add 2 is because There are 2 leftover (colored Yellow and grey.)

too had to count the squares at first until he noticed that each of the five groups always contained the same number of squares as the stage number. I feel that hearing that classmates don't immediately see the solution motivates kids who are struggling to keep trying.

Other students provided different solutions. Pete, for example, also saw the H Pattern as composed of five congruent parts and a constant number, but his interpretation of the breakdown was different (see Figure 4–3).

Pete saw each of the stages (he called them levels) as being made up of a constant of seven squares plus five congruent parts, each containing one less square than the stage number. Thus, his explicit rule was $7 + 5(L - 1)$. When asked to explain his rule, Pete pointed out that he chose 7 as the con-

FIGURE 4–3 Pete's solution

Personalized
Patterns

75

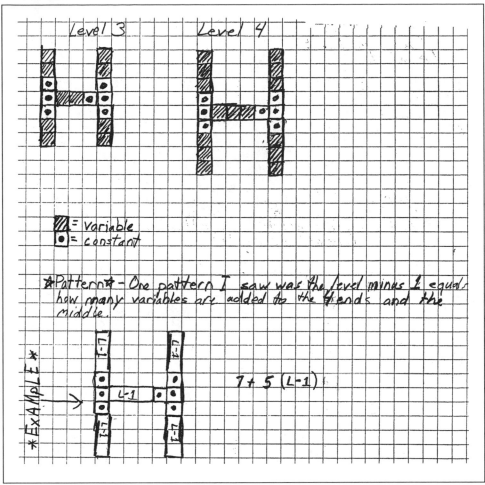

stant "because those squares made a shape like an H." He explained that "using up" seven squares left five equal groups. He admitted that these groups caused him some trouble when trying to express his rule because "the number of squares in each group did not match the level of the figure. I noticed that each group had a number of squares that was one less than the level number. Since I wanted to use the level number in my rule, I had to call that number L minus one." Other students liked his reasoning about the H shape and it was valuable for them to hear how he arrived at $(L - 1)$ as part of his rule.

Some students needed help to complete their solutions. For example, Amy could explain her thinking (see Figure 4–4 on the following page) but did not provide a rule using variables.

I asked Amy to choose any stage, talk through what she was thinking, and write the numbers and operations as she talked (see Figure 4–5 on the following page). (The writing she did is labeled "Notation" and her spoken word are labeled "Comment.")

I then asked her to repeat the process for a different stage and she used the same steps for Stage 4, ending with $\underline{4} + 2(2 \times \underline{4} + 1)$. She noticed on her own that the two sequences were the same except that 4 replaced 3, so I asked her to generalize by saying, "So now try to write the rule for any stage number." She wrote, *Total chips = number of chips in the middle (which = the stage number) + 2 × the stage number + 1 for each vertical portion.*" Look-

FIGURE 4–4 Amy's solution

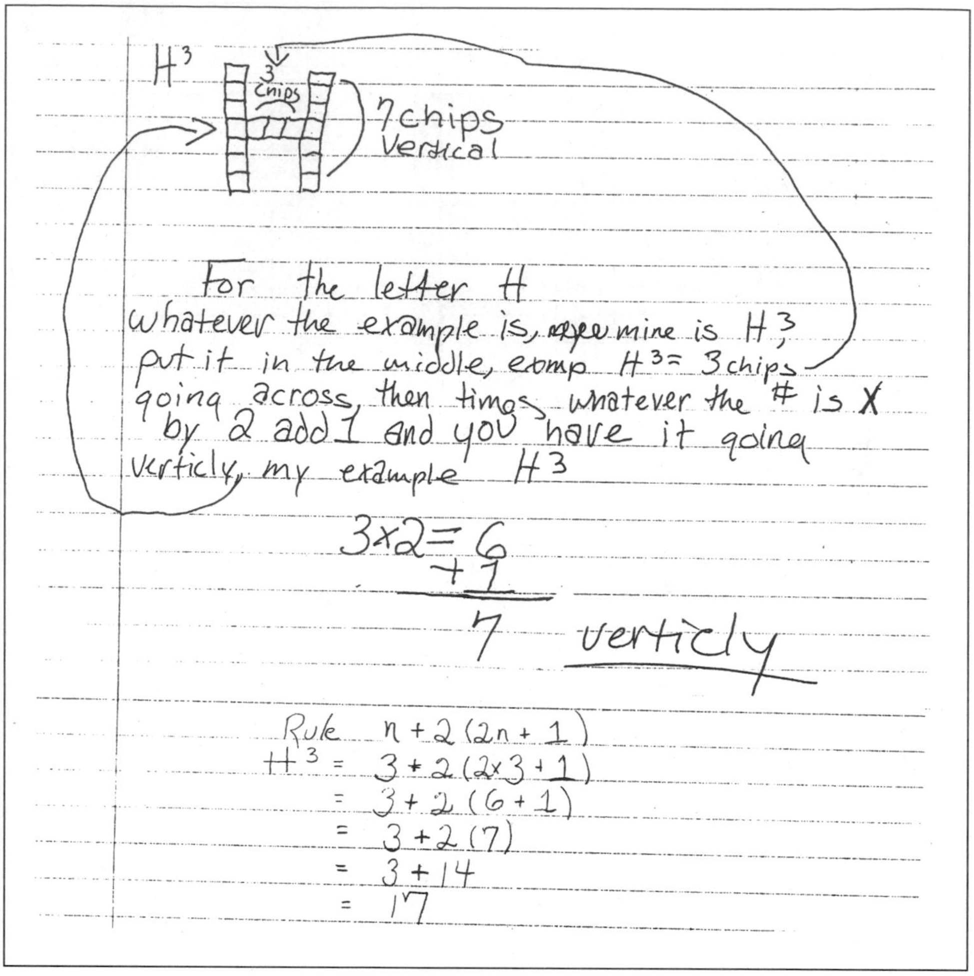

$$H^3$$

7chips Vertical

For the letter H whatever the example is, mine is H3, put it in the middle, H3= 3chips going across, then times whatever the # is X by 2 add 1 and you have it going verticly, my example H3

$$3 \times 2 = 6$$
$$+ 1$$
$$7 \quad verticly$$

Rule $n + 2(2n + 1)$
$H^3 = 3 + 2(2 \times 3 + 1)$
$= 3 + 2(6 + 1)$
$= 3 + 2(7)$
$= 3 + 14$
$= 17$

FIGURE 4–5 Amy's explanation

Notation	Comment
3	For Stage **Three**, I put **three** (that number) of chips across the middle.
$2 \times 3 + 1$	Then for **each** vertical part I added **three** twice and one more chip in the middle, so . . .
$+ 2(2 \times 3 + 1)$ [she added parentheses]	. . . I did that twice . . .
$3 + 2(2 \times 3 + 1)$	. . . and added it all together.

ing at her own words and previous expressions, she was able to write the rule $n + 2(2n + 1)$.

When a student has identified an underlying pattern but is having trouble expressing it as a rule, I have found that it is helpful to ask the student to go through such a sequence of explaining and examining her or his own way of seeing that pattern for several stages. Often the student can then write the rule in words and/or symbols.

Other versions of the rule are also possible, of course, and have been discovered in other middle school classes. It is crucial that students understand that all correct rules are equivalent. I asked the students in this class whether these rules were all correct. When they replied "yes," I asked them, "Tell me how you could be sure they are equivalent."

Most students agreed they would compare the table of values generated for each such expression (either by hand or by using a graphing calculator or a spreadsheet). As Michelle expressed it, "When the totals for each stage are the same using two or more rules, they must be basically the same, just written a little different."

I have observed that when results are the same for every value of n that is examined, most students become confident that the rules are equivalent. However, there are some middle school students who need to evaluate each expression for one or more values of n before they are convinced. For example, Austin said, "I'm not sure." So I asked the class, "Can you convince Austin that these rules are equivalent?" Amy suggested that a different student be designated to evaluate each suggested form of the rule at the board or overhead by substituting a particular value for each n in the rule. She chose $n = 10$, and students wrote the following:

	Andrew's Rule $5n + 2$	Pete's Rule $7 + 5(L - 1)$	Amy's Rule $n + 2(2n + 1)$
Value of expression when $n = 10$	$5(10) + 2$	$7 + 5(10 - 1)$	$10 + 2(2(10) + 1)$
	$50 + 2$	$7 + 5(9)$	$10 + 2(20 + 1)$
	52	$7 + 45$	$10 + 2(21)$
		52	$10 + 42$
			52

Since all three rules yielded fifty-two total squares for this stage and the same totals for any stage a student might try, Austin (and probably others) was convinced that the rules must be equivalent. This understanding is critical to the success of this lesson.

For some groups of students in middle school, using symbolic manipulation to simplify the various forms of the rule is appropriate. The students in this class had a little experience with the distributive property, so I asked them to look at two of the rules in their general form. I asked, "Can you show that these two rules are the same without substituting numbers for n?" No one could, so I said, "Time out: Does anyone remember the distributive property?"

Isabel said, "It's about adding and multiplying."

Pete added, "Oh, yeah, two times three-plus-five is the same as two-times-three plus two-times-five."

I asked Pete to write what he had said on the board and he wrote $2(3 + 5) = 2 \times 3 + 2 \times 5$. Then I asked, "So how does that help us?" and Pete applied the distributive property on the board as other students dictated to him to show that both $5(n - 1) + 7$ and $n + 2(2n + 1)$ are equivalent to $5n + 2$.

$5(n-1)+7$	$n+2(2n+1)$
$5n - 5 \times 1 + 7$	$n + 2 \times 2n + 2 \times 1)$
$5n - 5 + 7$	$n + 4n + 2$
$5n + 2$	$5n + 2$

This symbolic manipulation should not be used until you are confident that your students have reached the appropriate level of abstract thinking to make this process meaningful.

As part of the wrap-up for this part of the lesson, the students were asked questions, including the following, to assess their understanding of how a function rule works:

- How many squares would be in the 100th stage of the H Pattern?

- If 187 squares were used to build a stage of the H Pattern, which stage would it be?

All students answered the first question correctly. Most were able to figure out the answer to the second question, but a few required hearing the reasoning of another student. Isabel explained as she demonstrated with square tiles: "I worked with the rule $5n + 2$. I'll use Stage Three to show you." She built Stage 3 of the H Pattern out of square tiles. "First, I subtracted the two squares [as she removed them] because they are not part of any group (seventeen minus two equals fifteen). Then I divided by five to find the size of each of the five equal parts (fifteen divided by five equals three)." She pointed to each of the five groups of three squares. "This gave me the stage number because the size of each of these equal groups is always the same as the stage number for the H Pattern."

Then I asked Devon, who had been struggling with the question, to do a similar demonstration for Stage 4. He did this without any difficulty.

Students then repeated the process for 187 tiles:

$187 - 2 = 185$

$185 \div 5 = 37$

Finally, those who had trouble with the original question were given a different total number of squares and asked to find the stage number and explain their reasoning. They did this task successfully. This is another vital part of the lesson. I asked students to return to the tactile models and drawings in order to help those students who could not yet grasp the abstract version of the pattern. Students having trouble could see the two squares as the part of the expression that did not change, the part that remained the same for all stages. Then they could focus on the changing part of the model/drawing/ expression, which always increased by five. With this concrete handle, the remaining students were able to understand and apply the explicit rule.

Creating Personalized Patterns

Next students were introduced to the concepts of *constant* (a part of a pattern that stays the same for every stage) and *variable* (any part of a pattern that changes with each stage of a pattern in some predictable way). Working in pairs, the students applied these definitions to the H Pattern. I used the H Pattern to introduce these terms because it was a familiar context and thereby made the acquisition of these mathematical terms simple and sensible for them.

The students determined that the constant part (2) for the rule $5n + 2$ is the two shaded squares shown at right, and the variable portions are the five congruent, unshaded parts, each composed of a number of squares equal to the stage number.

Thus for Stage 3, there are two shaded *constant* squares and there are five *variable* parts, each containing three squares. Put together, these parts are consistent with the rule "Total number of squares for any stage equals two plus five times the stage number," written $2 + 5n$ or $5n + 2$. Of course, various forms of the rule provided other examples of these terms as well—in a now-familiar context. As Devon said, "What's hard about this?"

My next goal was to have students create patterns for their own initials. They were given several days to use any extra moments in class or outside of class to complete this activity. In this part of the lesson students were constructing rather than analyzing patterns that followed rules. Thus, I used this part of the lesson to build understanding about how function rules are derived. This learning objective and subsequent conceptual understanding are very different from what happens when students are "undoing" function rules they have been given. I believe it is a very valuable addition to the approach used by many of the function-based curricula now being used to help our students develop the ways of thinking they will need in introductory algebra and the mathematics courses beyond.

The assignment is shown in Figure 4–6. As with the H Pattern, I asked each student to create several stages for a pattern, identify the constant and variable portions, and provide an explicit rule for the pattern. Their prior experiences provided a foundation for generating an original pattern that followed a rule.

When the students had all completed a rough draft of their original personalized patterns, I asked them to share their patterns with a partner and make any revisions they felt were needed. When all pairs indicated that they were ready, each pair then exchanged their patterns with another pair to try them out—to examine the patterns and answer the three questions indicated in the assignment in Figure 4–6. They then gave the patterns and their answers back to the students who had created them to have their work

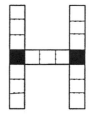

**Stage 3
of the H Pattern**

FIGURE 4–6   Creating your own personalized pattern

Create a personalized pattern for one of your own initials, similar to the H Pattern. Show Stages 1 and 2. Other students will be asked the following questions about your pattern:

    What do Stages 3, 4, and *n* look like?

    Which parts of the pattern are constant and which are variable?

    What is a rule for any stage of the pattern?

Create a separate key that provides answers for the three questions about your pattern.

checked. After a few rounds of these exchanges, I took up all the papers, looked over them, and posted all the original personalized patterns on the class bulletin board so students could view them and try any they had not previously attempted in class. I was pleased to find that many of the students in the class voluntarily worked with additional patterns on their own.

Besides accomplishing the objectives mentioned earlier, these student-generated problems provided more experience with finding rules for patterns, and I used them as an informal assessment of the students' levels of understanding with problems of this type.

Many of the students, like Aiden, were able to complete this activity with little trouble (see Figure 4–7). When I asked, "How did you build your pattern?" he showed understanding of both variable and constant.

He explained, "*N* can be any number. The *N* can change and will be used three times for each stage [pointing to the three sections in his Stage *N* drawing labeled *N*]. The constant part, three [pointing to the shaded portion of his Stage *N* drawing], is always the same."

Most of the students expressed both confidence and interest in completing the task and were eager to share their creations. However, I noticed that their patterns often had only one solution that was easy to derive. With Aiden's F Pattern, for example, it would be unusual for a student to extend

FIGURE 4–7 Aiden's F Pattern

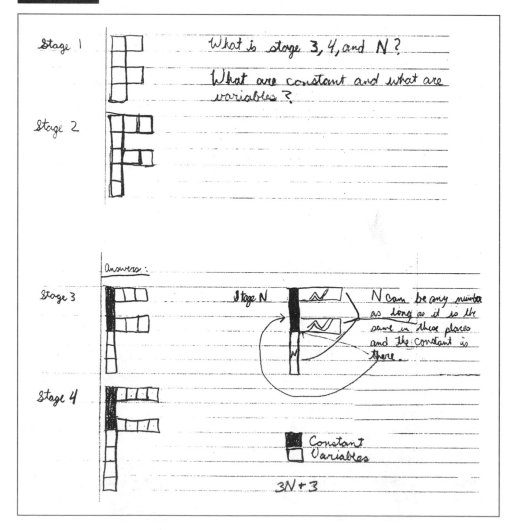

it in any way other than adding one square to each of the three main parts of the F figure for each new stage.

Some students created patterns that seemed to offer more opportunities for multiple solutions. Caitlin's C Pattern, for example, lends itself to several different interpretations, although all the correct interpretations, of course, produce equivalent rules (see Figure 4–8).

Using the part of the pattern Caitlin chose as the constant for her solution, she expressed the rule as $3n + 7$. She saw 7 as the constant because, like Pete in the first part of the lesson, "the constant part was shaped like my letter (C) and the three variable parts had the same number of squares as the stage number." Other students found the rules $3(n + 1) + 4$ and $2(n + 3) + (n + 1)$ for Caitlin's pattern.

When asked to explain her thinking for the rule "Total = $3(n + 1) + 4$" for the C Pattern, Lia drew the solution shown in Figure 4–9 and provided the following explanation: "I see each stage with the same four squares (the ones I have shaded), the constant part of the pattern. Each stage also has three other parts that are exactly alike. Each of these parts has one more square than the stage number, or (n plus one) squares. So the total number of squares for any stage is four plus three times (n plus one), or three times (n plus one) plus four."

Several students asked Lia to "remind us how the (n plus one) part works." She explained her thinking as shown in Figure 4–10.

FIGURE 4–8 Caitlin's C Pattern

FIGURE 4-9 Lia's solution for the C Pattern

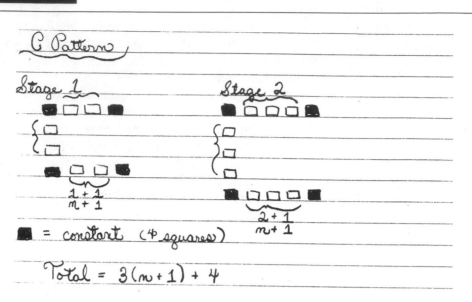

FIGURE 4-10 Lia's explanation

Drawing	Comment	Notation
	My rule is "Total squares equals three times (n plus one) squares plus four."	$T = 3(n + 1) + 4$
■ □ □ □ □ ■ □ □ □ □ ■ □ □ □ □ ■	Looking at Stage Three, first I put down the four squares that are the constant part of the pattern.	$T = 3(n + 1) + \mathbf{4}$
■ □ □ □ □ ■ □ □ For Stage 3, □ n = 3 □ n + 1 = 4 squares □ ■ □ □ □ □ ■	Then I put (n plus one) squares in each part of the C. Since it is Stage Three, I used four squares times (three plus one) for each set.	$T = 3(\mathbf{n + 1}) + 4$ $T = 3(\mathbf{3 + 1}) + 4$ $T = 3(4) + 4$
	So the total number of squares for Stage Three is twelve plus four, or sixteen squares.	$T = 12 + 4$ $T = 16$ squares

Questions and explanations such as this one helped some students expand their thinking to include expressions like $(n + 1)$ and $(n + 3)$ when building the variable portion of rules. As Carlos put it, "Now I can make more than one rule for my pattern since I am not stuck with plain n as the variable part."

I have found this understanding to be challenging for many students; they need several encounters with this type of situation to become proficient at interpreting and generating such expressions. But I also believe facility of this sort is important for success in algebra, so I provide opportunities for such encounters to foster the development of algebraic thinking.

Karelia's experience was unique. She created a pattern that could easily have several solutions. However, she guided the thinking of students investigating her pattern when she indicated the constant for her Z Pattern with a different color in her statement of the problem. Thus, students looking for a pattern from her drawings all concluded that one square is added to each of the three main unshaded parts of the Z figure (two horizontal and one diagonal) for each new stage (see Figure 4–11).

FIGURE 4–11 Karelia's Z pattern

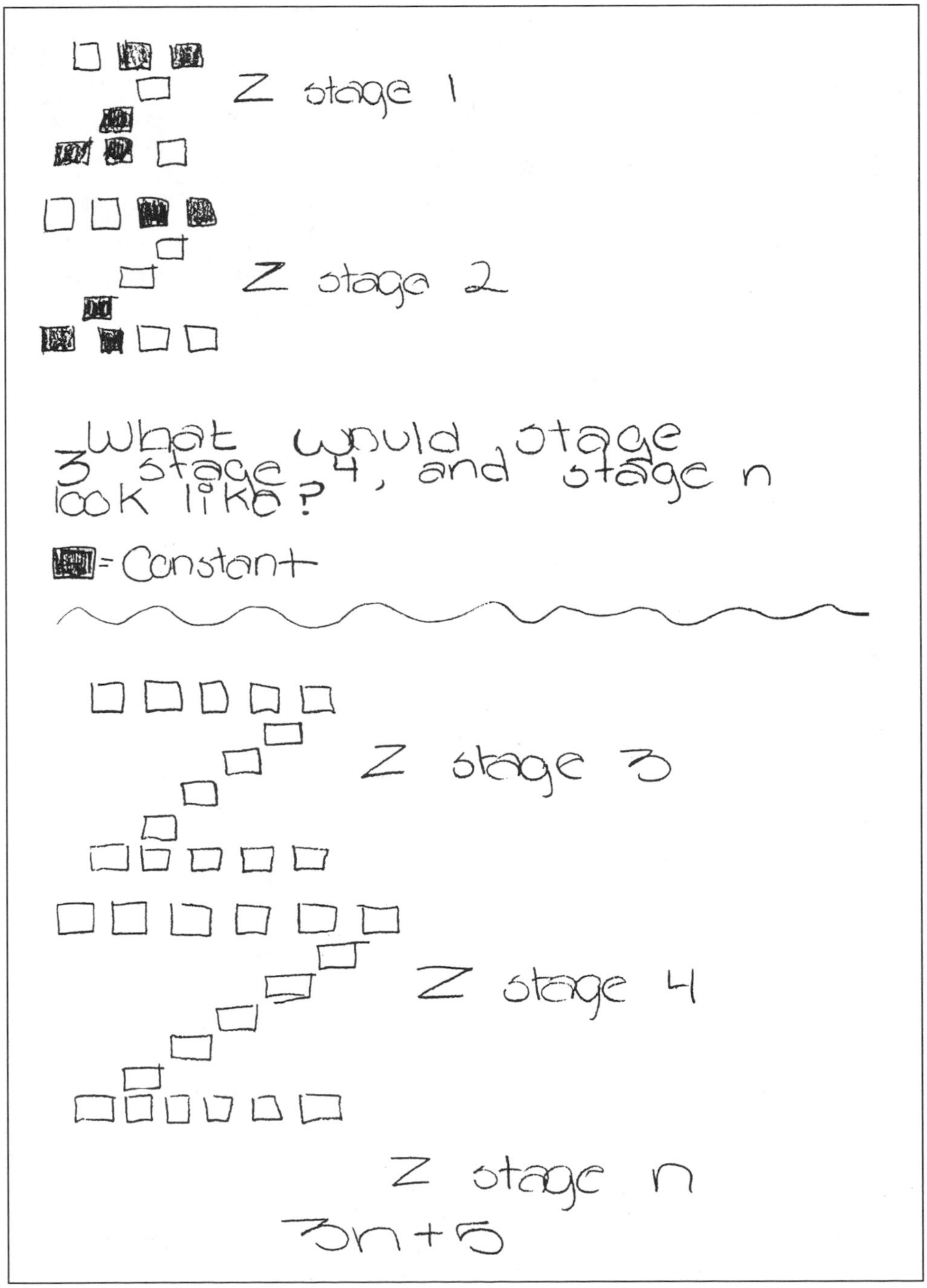

Karelia had used another way to state her rule and was anxious for the other students to find it, so I asked her, "Is there anything you could do to help students to think about your pattern in a different way?" After asking several students to explain their thinking about her pattern, Karelia realized that shading the constant guided the students' thinking so strongly that they practically had no alternative in how they viewed her pattern. So she redrew Stages 1 and 2 without the shading and was delighted to find that students found another form of the rule, $2n + (n + 1) + 4$ (see Figure 4–12).

Lex explained this solution in the following way: "For each stage of the Z Pattern I see four squares at the 'corners' of the Z shape. These are the constant part of the pattern. There are three other parts in each stage. Along the top and bottom row of squares there are n squares—one square in each row in Stage One, two squares in each row in Stage Two, and so on. Then, along the slanted part of the Z, there are $(n + 1)$ squares—two squares in Stage One, three squares in Stage Two, and so on. That means there are two groups of n squares, one group of (n plus one) squares, and one group of four squares for each stage. This rule for the pattern is 'Total squares equals two n plus (n plus one) plus four' for any stage."

It was nice that Lex's solution gave students another opportunity to see how an expression like $(n + 1)$ can be part of an explicit rule. Seeing an alternate interpretation also reinforced for the class that many patterns can be viewed in more than one way. These different views may lead to patterns that initially appear to be different, but are actually found to be equivalent after closer scrutiny.

I point out to the students that the shape of some letters inherently makes it easier to create a pattern that can be interpreted in several different

FIGURE 4–12 Lex's solution to the Z pattern

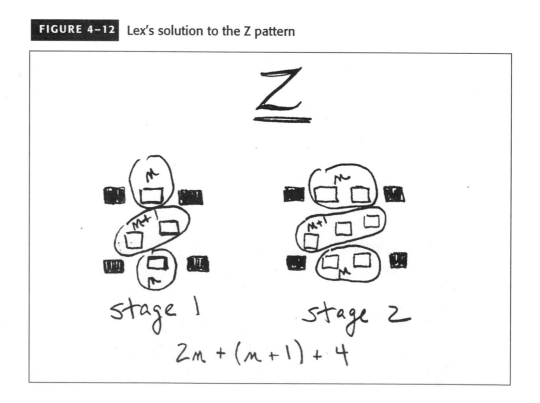

ways. I know that, with a little experience, students will probably realize this themselves, but I wanted to be careful not to imply that one student did a better job than another simply because his or her pattern lent itself to more solutions. On the other hand, I point out those patterns that do lend themselves to multiple interpretations and encourage students to try to see patterns in more than one way. Such emphasis increases both student involvement (more students share their thinking) and the impact of a lesson. I also send the message that multiple techniques and solutions are valued in the class.

The creation and interpretation of personalized patterns by these students indicated that almost all these sixth graders were proficient with this type of pattern problem, both analyzing and creating patterns that follow explicit rules. In this way, they were developing important algebraic thinking skills that would help them bridge the gap between concrete examples and more abstract function rules.

The Box Pattern | **Similar Problem**

The Box Pattern problem is appropriate for a lesson similar to the H Pattern lesson.

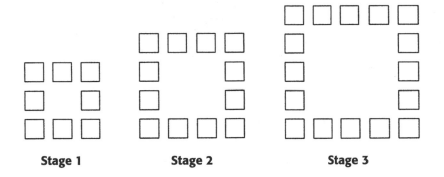

Stage 1   Stage 2   Stage 3

Given Stages 1, 2, and 3 of the Box Pattern, do the following:

- Draw Stages 4 and 5 of the Box Pattern.
- Find a pattern to predict the number of squares needed for higher stages of the Box Pattern.
- Give a rule that will work for any stage of the Box Pattern.

The Box Pattern lends itself to many interpretations. It is important to record student responses using notation that reflects the way the student interpreted the pattern. Students may offer the following interpretations, among others, for the Box Pattern:

Rule for Each Stage	Rule for Stage 4	Rule for Stage n
1. 4(length of side without corners) + 4(corners)	$4(4) + 4$	$4n + 4$
2. 2(length of side with corners) + 2(length of side without either corner)	$2(4 + 2) + 2(4)$	$2(n + 2) + 2n$
3. 4(length of side without a corner + 1 corner)	$4(4 + 1)$	$4(n + 1)$
4. (length of side)^2 – (two less than length of side)^2	$(4 + 2)^2 - 4^2$	$(n + 2)^2 - n^2$

This notation makes it easier for students to use a variable, such as n, to represent the stage number in their explicit rules, as long as they have the understanding that they need to generate such rules.

More patterns appropriate for use in lessons similar to *Personalized Patterns* can be found in *Navigating Through Algebra in Grades 6–8* (Friel et al. 2001, 10–12) in the section "Growing Patterns." The lesson "Building with Toothpicks" (Friel et al. 2001, 13–17) in the same publication also targets many of the same concepts as *Personalized Patterns*.

Extension Problem | Around the Blocks

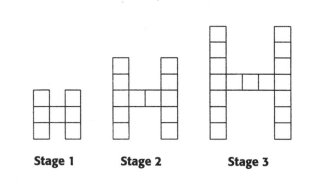

Stage 1   **Stage 2**   **Stage 3**

Shown above are the first three stages of the H Pattern constructed from squares. Notice that the sides of adjacent squares are touching. Do the following:

- Find the perimeter of each stage. Remember to count only the outside edges of each figure.

  Example: For Stage 1, the perimeter is 16.

- Draw Stages 4 and 5 of the H Pattern and find each perimeter.
- Find a pattern to predict the perimeter for higher stages of the H Pattern.
- Give a rule that will work to find the perimeter of the figure for any stage of the H Pattern.

Iterative Rule: For any stage, add 10 to the perimeter of the previous stage.

Explicit Rule: Total perimeter = $10n + 6$ for any Stage n. (Various forms of the rule should be compared to show that they are equivalent.)

Also, having the students graph their personalized patterns by hand, with a graphing calculator, or using both methods is an excellent extension of the *Personalized Patterns* lesson.

Technology Connections

Graph the H Pattern Using the TI-73

If graphing calculators are available, students can use scatter plots to display appropriate graphs for their personalized patterns. This activity would be a wonderful way to introduce the graphing of functions on the coordinate plane.

Clear any data in the lists L_1 and L_2 using the following keystrokes:

To clear data in ALL lists:

1. Press **2nd MEM.**

2. Choose **#6 ClrAllLists.**

3. Press **ENTER.**

4. On the Home Screen, press **ENTER** again.

5. You should see **Done** on your calculator screen.

To clear data in L_1 and L_2 only:

1. Press **LIST.**

2. Press the **up arrow key** to move up until you are on top of the L_1.

3. Press **CLEAR.**

4. Press **ENTER** (you should see the L_1 list clear).

5. Use the **right arrow key** to move over to L_2 and repeat Steps 2, 3, and 4 to clear L_2.

Enter your lists, using the following keystrokes (You can scroll up or down your lists using the **up** and **down arrow keys.**):

1. Press **LIST.**

2. Enter the stage numbers 1–8 in L_1. Press **ENTER** after each number.

3. Enter the total number of squares for each stage (1–8) in L_2. Press **ENTER** after each number.

Your calculator screen should look like the following illustration.

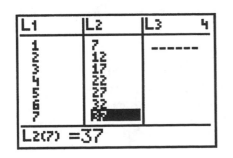

To create a scatter plot to display your data on the TI-73, use the following keystrokes:

1. Choose **2nd PLOT** and press **ENTER**.
2. Choose **#1 Plot 1**. (Be sure Plots 2 and 3 are OFF.)
3. Press **ENTER** on **ON**.
4. Arrow down to **Type**.
5. Arrow over once to the scatter plot icon and press **ENTER**.
6. Arrow down to **Xlist**.
7. Press **2nd STAT** and choose L_1.
8. Press **ENTER**.
9. Arrow down to **Ylistz**.
10. Press **2nd STAT** and choose L_2.
11. Press **ZOOM** and choose **#7 ZoomStat**.

Your scatter plot should look like the following illustration.

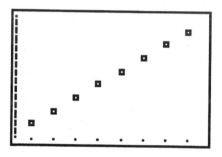

Press **TRACE** and use the **right** and **left arrow keys** to see the coordinates of each point in your scatter plot, as illustrated here.

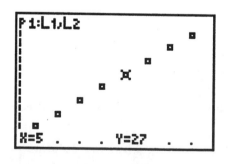

Ask questions about both values in the lists and points on the graph to be sure students understand their meanings and the connections between these representations and those they have previously explored with this pattern. For example, "How does the graph show the same information as your T-chart?" or "How does the graph show different information about this pattern than your rule?"

Extra features of the calculator that you may incorporate into the lesson include the following (see TI-73 manual for directions):

- You can name a list (e.g., name L_1 **Stage** and L_2 **Total**).

- You can use a formula in a list (e.g., use the formula $5 * L_1 + 2$ to generate the values in L_2).

- You can display two scatter plots simultaneously (e.g., use the formula $5 * L_1 + 2$ to generate values in L_3. Set up and display the second scatter plot using L_1 as the **Xlist** and L_3 as the **Ylist**. Choose a different mark. Compare the two graphs.

- Type the function rule $y = 5x + 2$ in the $y =$ screen and compare the graph to the line of points in the scatter plot.

- Discuss adjusting **WINDOW** values to fit specific graphs.

CHAPTER 5

Go Figure!

OVERVIEW

This lesson provides experiences with finding explicit rules for given patterns, using those rules to generate values for any stage of the pattern, and applying the rules to solve a related problem. First, students explore three patterns of figurate numbers. Given the first three stages for square numbers represented by arrays of dots, they produce the next stages for the visual pattern and find an explicit rule to predict the total number of dots needed for any stage. Students explain their thinking, providing their classmates with opportunities to develop new strategies for finding patterns and their rules. Students repeat the procedure they used with square numbers to investigate rectangular and triangular numbers. Finally, they solve a problem involving application of the rules for square, rectangular, and triangular numbers.

This lesson is intended to establish that various strategies may be used to find rules for patterns and that several different forms of a rule may be correct if they are equivalent. It involves substituting any number for the variable in a variable expression to produce the correct value for the expression. Students also use rules involving variables to solve a real-world problem.

This lesson should help students develop understanding of the importance of explicit function rules and provide experience for students in evaluating variable expressions and using such expressions to solve related problems.

BACKGROUND

Being proficient at finding patterns and explicit function rules for patterns requires many experiences for most students. Prior to this lesson, this class of seventh-grade students had limited experience working in groups, in pairs, and alone with a variety of patterns to complete each of the following tasks:

- Produce the next stages for a given geometric or numerical pattern.

- Express an iterative rule for a pattern (e.g., "To get a new term in this pattern, add 5 to the previous term.").

- Try to express an explicit rule for a pattern (e.g., "For any stage in the pattern, the rule is 'The total = 2 more than the stage number.' ")

PREREQUISITE CONCEPTS OR SKILLS

- Experience recognizing and describing, extending, and generalizing visual and numerical patterns
- Experience finding iterative and explicit rules for numerical patterns
- Familiarity with squares, rectangles, and triangles

VOCABULARY

equivalent rules, evaluate (an expression), explicit rule, figurate numbers, iterative rule, rectangular numbers, square numbers, triangular numbers

TIME

The lesson was completed in two sixty-minute classes and individual student reflections were written the following day. If your classes are only forty-five minutes long, we suggest going as far as possible during the first day (the students probably will not complete the investigation of triangular numbers), then attempting to get to the point where students are conferring in pairs about a recommendation for Juan on the second day. On the third day the students can confer in groups of four to share and, if needed, revise their solutions, and then each group of four can present a joint solution to the class. Perhaps individual written reflections can also be written during the last part of that class.

MATERIALS

- *Go Figure!* activity sheets, 1 per student (see Blackline Masters)
- *Go Figure! Investigating Figurate Numbers #1* activity sheets, 1 per student (see Blackline Masters)
- *Go Figure! Investigating Figurate Numbers #2* activity sheets, 1 per student (see Blackline Masters)
- *Go Figure! Investigating Figurate Numbers #3* activity sheets, 1 per student (see Blackline Masters)
- Squares, disks, or cubes for each student (optional)

Finding Rules for Figurate Numbers | The Lesson

Students were presented with the following problem, along with the three activity sheets containing figurate number investigations (see Blackline Masters).

Juan is saving money to give both his mother and his grandmother a very nice box of candy for Mother's Day. The clerk at the candy shop tells Juan that the store packages candy in certain square, rectangular, or triangular boxes (see the figurate number investigations on your activity sheets). Juan has decided the following:

1. He will buy the same number of pieces of candy for his mother and his grandmother.
2. He can afford up to fifty pieces of candy each for his mother and his grandmother.
3. He wants the two boxes to be different shapes.

After completing the investigations about square, rectangular, and triangular numbers, write a paragraph to recommend to Juan the shapes and sizes of boxes you think he should buy. Be sure you explain your mathematical thinking.

This problem was chosen in part because it involves evaluating variable expressions. Too often in mathematics classes prior to Algebra I, students seldom, if ever, encounter problems for which evaluating several variable expressions is part of solving a problem. Instead, they see substituting values in variable expressions as isolated drills unrelated to any real situation they might encounter. While middle school students often enjoy and learn much through exploring patterns for which the students see no direct application, I feel it is important to impress upon students as early as possible that finding patterns and rules for patterns is often an essential step in solving more complex problems. Moreover, I have found that students who have successes and see the value of variables in problem solving have a more positive attitude toward working with variables and abstract mathematics in general.

The reason the problem was introduced to the students at the beginning of the lesson was to provide motivation for students to explore figurate numbers. While there are many mathematical and real-world applications for figurate numbers, the topic does not automatically appeal to some middle school students. Except for limited exposure to square numbers, the students in this class had never heard of figurate numbers. Given a problem for which knowledge of such numbers was apparently required, all the students in this class seemed interested in tackling the investigations. This technique of introducing a problem that requires students to have knowledge of a new mathematical skill or concept in order to solve it can provide a strong motivation for students to learn the needed skills or concept. Certainly, that happened in this class. Immediately after hearing the problem read aloud by a classmate, Kathleen asked, "What are figurate numbers?"

A short discussion followed, during which Celina offered, "It looks like a figurate number is one where dots can be made into a shape in geometry—a square or triangle or something like that."

John added, "For each kind of these figurate numbers, there seems to be a whole group of them that follow a pattern."

Satisfied that the students had the general idea of what the term *figurate numbers* means, I told them to start Investigation #1, about square numbers. I asked the students to investigate the square numbers first for several reasons: many of the students had some familiarity with square numbers, students usually find the explicit formula for square numbers more easily than the ones for rectangular and triangular numbers, and the visual image of square shapes is easier for most students to link to the rule in words and in symbols. Because they had done several similar activities prior to this one, the students worked alone on this part of the lesson. However, they were free to consult with each other whenever they were stuck or wanted verification of their thinking. Manipulatives were available for the students to use, but most made T-charts or went directly to drawing stages of the pattern on their papers.

Many students first determined the iterative pattern and rule. Emmanuel made a chart showing the first few square numbers and how he found them (see Figure 5–1).

Emmanuel expressed his rule as, "Add the number you added before and two more to get the next square number." When asked to show how to use his rule to find the tenth square number, Emmanuel continued his chart until he correctly found the tenth square number to be *100*. As indicated in the chart, he added *19* (two more than the 17 used to help find the ninth square number) + *81* (the ninth square number) to get *100*. However, he was understandably frustrated at the idea of extending the chart to find the one hundredth square number.

When working with middle school students who have little or no experience finding rules for patterns, I find that they often think iteratively. I feel it is important to validate iterative rules but also to make students aware of the limitations of such rules. Emmanuel discovered this for himself when he realized how tedious it was going to be to find the hundredth square number, since he would need to find the value of each square number up to the ninety-ninth to produce his answer. He declared that he could not find another rule.

Since several other students were also unable to find an explicit rule for finding any square number, I asked whether anyone had a hint to offer that

FIGURE 5–1   Emmanuel's first chart

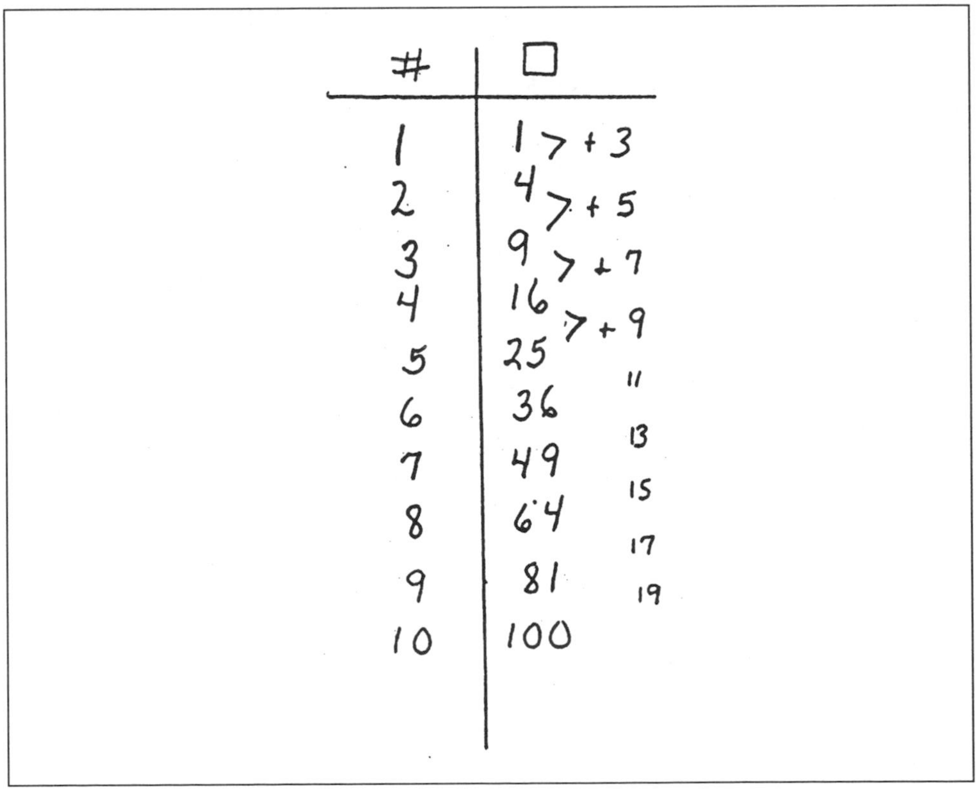

would not give away the rule but might help those who were having trouble. Erika offered the following suggestion: "Look at the pictures of the squares you drew and the lengths of their sides."

Emmanuel studied his drawings, smiled, and furiously made a new chart expressing the total number of candies (dots) as the product of the numbers of candies along two sides (see Figure 5–2).

Thus, Emmanuel's explicit rule was "To get the total number of candies in a square box, multiply the number of candies on one side of the box by itself." When asked to find the hundredth square number, he quickly multiplied 100×100 and got the answer 10,000. Emmanuel then helped several other students who were having trouble finding an explicit rule.

Erika's advice to look back at the drawings not only helped Emmanuel and others find the rule for square numbers but seemed to help many students more easily find the rules for rectangular and even triangular numbers in the subsequent investigations. Once again I was reminded that using manipulatives or drawings is often the key to students' discovering patterns and their rules as well as tackling problems of many other kinds.

Many students completed the investigation of square numbers with little difficulty. One rule, derived by Amma, is typical of those provided by students who quickly completed the investigation, including an explicit rule. Amma wrote the rule: *Multiply the number by itself.* When asked to explain, she said, "If you want the eighth square number, you just multiply eight times eight. If you want the tenth square number, you just multiply ten times ten."

Since this class of students had very little experience writing rules using a variable, I asked for a volunteer to express the rule "multiply the number times itself" using a variable. Several volunteers raised their hands, and Brook offered, "The rule is n times n." I asked Brook to come to the board and show us step-by-step how his rule worked. (The writing he did is labeled "Notation" and his spoken words are labeled "Comment.") (See Figure 5–3.)

FIGURE 5–2   Emmanuel's second chart

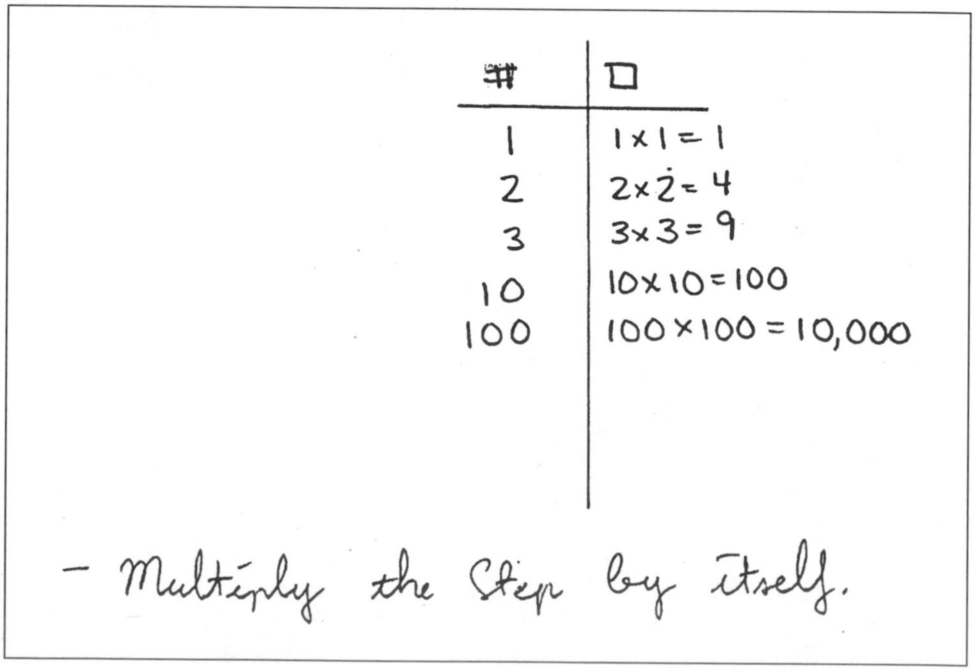

#	□
1	$1 \times 1 = 1$
2	$2 \times 2 = 4$
3	$3 \times 3 = 9$
10	$10 \times 10 = 100$
100	$100 \times 100 = 10,000$

— Multiply the step by itself.

FIGURE 5-3 Brook's explanation

Go Figure! **95**

Notation	Comment
$n \times n$	My rule is *n* times *n*.
5	For the fifth square number, my rule says to use five for *n* (the same number as the square I want to find).
5×5	I multiplied five times five for *n* times *n*.
25	So the fifth square number is twenty-five.

Immediately, several students had the same question: "Is it OK if I used a different letter for my variable?" I confirmed that any variable was fine, but that the same variable should be used twice in the rule, as in $a \times a$ or $b \times b$, since the same number was being used twice as a factor.

I was pleased that Brook substituted the values in his rule and evaluated the expression in columns that clearly showed how the process worked. His actions provided an opportunity to point out to the other students that writing steps in successive rows is a method many people use successfully when evaluating variable expressions.

When I asked if there were further questions, Erin asked whether it was correct to express the rule as n^2. I assured her that n^2 was another way to express $n \times n$ and was certainly correct. I reminded the class that often several forms of a rule are possible and that every correct form of the same rule will yield the same results when the same value is substituted for the variable. To emphasize this point, I asked Erin to go to the board and use her rule to find the fifth square number as Brook had done (see Figure 5–4).

Since there were no further questions, I asked the students to start Investigation #2, about rectangular numbers. The students worked alone or in pairs as I circulated about the classroom, listening to their comments and observing their work. I was pleased that students who were having trouble seemed quite comfortable voluntarily moving to work with another student. I also noticed that I did not hear a single student simply asking another student for the solution. I believe this is true partly because students in this class know that when it comes time to share their thinking, each child may be asked to do the following: (1) give his or her answer and (2) explain his or her thinking. Establishing an atmosphere in the classroom where every student feels capable and responsible for his or

FIGURE 5-4 Erin's explanation

Notation	Comment
n^2	My rule is *n* squared.
5	For the fifth square number, my rule says to use five for *n*.
5^2 5×5	Since five squared means five times itself, I multiplied five by five for *n* squared.
25	So the fifth square number is twenty-five.

her own learning is very important to me. I am convinced that, given the support he or she needs, every middle school student *can* be successful in mathematics, and I believe in sharing both the effort and the responsibility with each student.

Working alone or in pairs, most of the students found the pattern and the rule fairly quickly. Their explanations revealed that many followed Erika's suggestion and focused on the visual images to help them find the pattern and the rule. Most students expressed the rule somewhat like Marissa, who stated, "Multiply the number of the rectangle by the next higher number. For example, the sixth rectangular number is six times seven, or forty-two."

Harold had trouble finding a pattern for the rectangular numbers (see Figure 5–5).

Harold had simply added another row of four dots to the third rectangular number to get the fourth and, similarly, another row of four dots to the fourth rectangular number to get the fifth. His chart was also inaccurate, indicating an increase of four dots for each successive rectangular number. His rule was "For any rectangular number, multiply four times the number." This fit numerically with some of the stages in his chart (3, 4, and 5) but not with Stages 1 and 2. Harold noticed that he had a problem but could not find his error. Further, he said he wanted to solve the problem himself. When most of the other students had finished the investigation and it was clear that Harold was getting more and more frustrated, I asked Harold if he would mind explaining his thinking to me, pointing out that when I am having trouble I use this technique, and I sometimes find my own errors. I explained that I would just listen and maybe ask a question. Harold agreed. He began to explain the way he viewed the third rectangular number. I asked him to start at the beginning. When he started there, he said (refer to Figure 5–5): "I see the first rectangle as one row of two dots, so that gives a total of two. The second rectangle is two rows of three dots, so that gives a total of six. The third rectangle is three rows of four dots, so that gives a total of twelve. Since I was just adding four new dots each time, I added four dots for the fourth rectangle, so I got a total of sixteen and four more for the fifth rectangle for a total of twenty."

I said, "You were adding four dots each time? Show that to me in your chart."

He looked back and exclaimed, "Oh, no—there's my mistake. There are six dots added between the second and third rectangle. I added wrong!" He

FIGURE 5–5 Harold's first drawings and chart

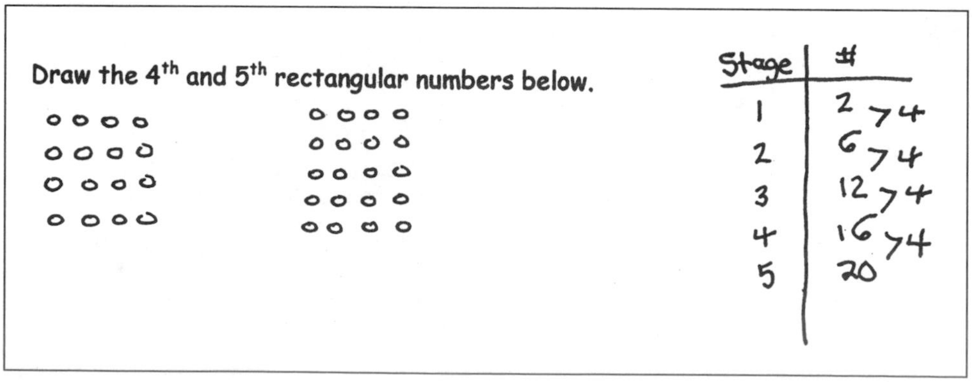

got excited. "So if I added four dots, then six dots, I should add eight the next time, but how can I do that?"

I covered up his fourth and fifth rectangles and said, "Look back at these first three rectangles. Can you describe them for me?" As he refocused on the drawings, he described them as one row of two dots, two rows of three dots, and three rows of four dots. He concluded that the next figure should be four rows of five dots.

He made a new chart reflecting the total numbers of dots in each stage that his pattern now contained and was thrilled when the fifth rectangular number fit his pattern, and his rule (the rectangular number × one more than the rectangular number) also matched up with his visual interpretation of the rectangles (see Figure 5–6). In this case, it seems clear that Harold moved to a numerical chart too quickly and a simple arithmetic error caused him to get off track. Hopefully, he will remember the value of starting over at the beginning when nothing else seems to be working.

The students had a harder time expressing the rule for any rectangular number using variables. Lindsay explained her dilemma this way: "For the tenth rectangular number I know I can multiply ten by eleven, and so forth for the other rectangular numbers, so I know the rule for any rectangular number is 'n times the number one bigger than n,' but how do I write that without words?"

When none of the students could help her, I wrote the following list on the board:

3

1 more than 3

n

1 more than n

I asked the students to give a mathematical expression (no words) for each row. With prompting, they answered as follows:

Prompt	Response
3	3
1 more than 3	$1 + 3$ or $3 + 1$
n	n
1 more than n	$1 + n$ or $n + 1$

FIGURE 5–6 Harold's revised drawings and chart

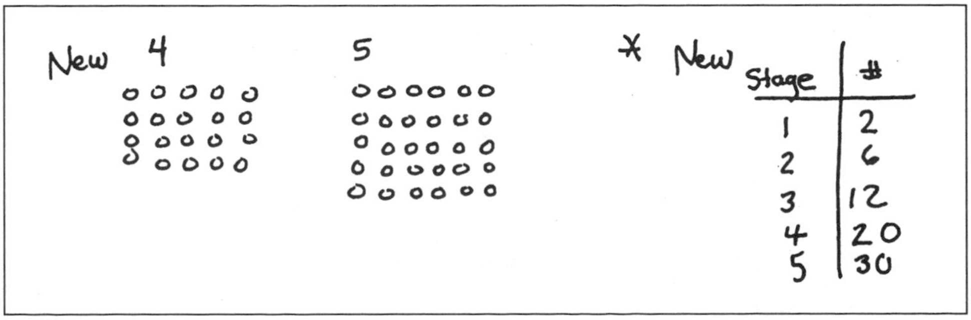

Then Nick said, "I got it, I got it! For our rule, we can say *n* times (*n* plus one)."

Several students nodded but some looked unconvinced. I asked Nick to go to the board and show how the rule worked in a way similar to that used by Brook and Erin earlier (see Figure 5–7).

Several other students used the rule to verify that *n*(*n* + 1) yielded the same results as in their charts and were satisfied that they had found the rule.

Then Erin volunteered that she had seen the pattern a different way and had a different rule. She drew the diagram shown at the left here:

Erin explained that the diagram illustrated the way she viewed each rectangular number. "For the third rectangular number, I see a three-by-three square and another row of three. That gives me a total of twelve candies. For the fourth rectangular number, I see a four-by-four square with another row of four, for a total of twenty candies. Those are the same numbers that everyone else is getting, so I think my rule works, but I'm not sure how to write the rule using a variable."

When asked to write her rule using words, Erin replied, "For any rectangular number, take that number and multiply it by itself. Then add the number you started with to your answer." She called on Erika to help her express the rule with a variable. I encourage my students to use this technique of calling on a classmate when they need a little help.

Erika offered, "I think your rule is *n* times *n* plus *n*, or as I would say it, *n* squared plus *n*."

I asked for a volunteer to evaluate Erin's rule as students had done for the other rules. Alex volunteered, and his explanation is shown in Figure 5–8.

I again reminded the class that often several forms of a rule are possible and that every correct form of the same rule will yield the same results. Then I asked the students to do the triangular numbers investigation.

As I expected, the triangular numbers challenged the students more than the square or rectangular numbers. Actually, it has been my experience that most middle school students have quite a difficult time finding the explicit rule for triangular numbers if this set of numbers is not introduced immediately after rectangular numbers (not many Gausses out there!). In this class, several students found the iterative rule fairly quickly and shared it with the other students. Alex expressed it this way: "For each triangular number, you add that number to the triangular number before it." He drew a T-chart and explained further, "So for the fifth triangular number, you add

FIGURE 5–7 Nick's explanation

Notation	Comment
n × (*n* + 1)	My rule is *n* times (*n* plus one).
5	For the fifth rectangular number, my rule says to use five for *n* (the same number as the rectangle I want to find). Also, *n* plus one must be six, since five plus one equals six.
5 × (5 +1)	I multiplied five times (five plus one), or five times six, for *n* times (*n* plus one).
30	So the fifth rectangular number is thirty.

FIGURE 5–8 Alex's explanation

Go Figure! 99

Notation	Comment
$n \times n + n$	The rule is n times n plus n.
5	For the fifth rectangular number, use five for n since that is the number of the rectangle we want to find.
$5 \times 5 + 5$	Multiply five times five plus five, or twenty-five plus five, for n times n plus n.
30	So the fifth rectangular number is thirty.

five to the fourth triangular number. Since the fourth triangular number is ten, you get ten plus five, or fifteen, for the fifth triangular number." (See Alex's chart in Figure 5–9.)

Tara added, "What Alex says goes along with the drawings. For each new triangle you just add another row of dots—the same number of dots as the new triangular number."

Finding an explicit rule went more slowly. I let the students work for a while and finally said, "Has anyone made an observation that you think can help us find the explicit rule?" I use this technique when no one seems to be making progress toward a solution and the frustration level of the students seems high.

Eloise offered the following: "I found a rule that works for the tenth triangular number and almost works for some others." The other students

FIGURE 5–9 Alex's T-chart

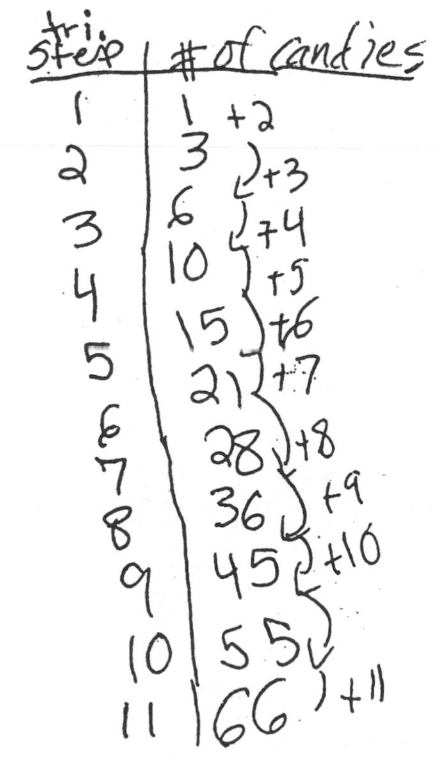

were eager to hear the rule. "Well," she said, "the rule is (n times n) divided by two, plus five. So for the tenth triangular number I did (ten times ten) divided by two, plus five, which gave me one hundred divided by two plus five, then fifty plus five, then fifty-five. Fifty-five is correct from our iterative rule for the tenth triangular number, but the rule doesn't quite work for any other stages." Visually, Eloise's rule and first two expressions look like this:

$$\frac{n \times n}{2} + 5 \qquad \frac{10 \times 10}{2} + 5 \qquad \frac{100}{2} + 5$$

4

4

Students tried her rule for various other stages and noticed that the further they got from the tenth triangular number, the more the values failed to match those generated by the iterative rule.

Lindsay raised her hand. "I'm trying something else, but I need help."

She went to the board and drew the fourth square number (shown at left).

"I noticed that half of each square number is a triangle, but the dots down the middle mess me up," she explained as she drew a diagonal in her square (shown at left).

"The dots on my dividing line mess me up. I need to count them to make my total come out right, but the number (ten) isn't really half the square number, so I can't quite get a rule."

"Wait a minute!" Celina said. "What Lindsay just said made me notice something about Eloise's rule. Look back! For the tenth triangular number, Eloise got (ten times ten) divided by two, plus five. But the five is half of ten! So maybe that's what we need to finish Eloise's rule—n times n, divided by two, plus half of n." I asked Celina to come to the board and demonstrate using her rule (see Figure 5–10).

The students were excited, but Tara pointed out, "Uh oh, I think we're in trouble on the odd ones." I asked her to come to the board and show what she meant. She went through the substitution process for the ninth triangular number and pointed out that $9 \times 9 \div 2$ yields 40.5. "We can't have half a number in our answer," she said. I encouraged her to continue. She next divided 9 by 2, got 4.5 and added that to 40.5. She and the rest of the class were pleased to see that the result was forty-five, the same value for the ninth triangular number that their iterative rule produced.

FIGURE 5–10   Celina's explanation

Notation	Comment
$n \times n \div 2$ + half of n	The rule is **n times n, divided by two, plus half of n**.
10	For the tenth triangular number, we use ten for **n**.
$10 \times 10 \div 2 + 5$	First we multiply ten by ten (one hundred) and take half (**fifty**). Then we add half of ten (**five**).
50 + 5	That gives us **fifty plus five** . . .
55	or **fifty-five**.

Emmanuel pointed out that the rule still included some words, but he suggested $\dfrac{n \times n}{2} + \dfrac{n}{2}$ as the final form of the rule. To no one's surprise, Erika pointed out that the rule could also be written as $\dfrac{n^2}{2} + \dfrac{n}{2}$. The students all nodded.

I challenged the students to find another form of the rule. They groaned a little but began to work again. Soon Lindsay said, "I got it! I got it!"

She went to the board and explained her new version of the rule. "Remember, a while ago, I was trying to divide square numbers in half, but I didn't know what to do with the dots on the dividing line. Well, I can use the rectangular numbers instead!"

She drew on the board (right), saying, "This is the third rectangular number. When I divide it in half and count the dots on one side of the line, I get the correct number for the third triangular number. The same thing happens for any rectangular number."

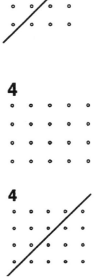

Noticing confused looks on several faces, I asked Lindsay to show another example. She drew the fourth rectangular number on the board (right), explaining, "This is the fourth rectangular number. If I divide it in half using a diagonal line [as she added the line—right] and count the dots below or above the line, I get the right number of dots for the fourth triangular number. So each triangular number is half the same rectangular number!"

Keyonna added, "And the top half looks just like the other triangular numbers, so that fits the geometry pattern, too."

I asked whether anyone could express Lindsay's rule using words, and Erin said, "Each triangular number is the same as half the rectangular number with the same number. So to get the tenth triangular number, you can just find the tenth rectangular number and divide by two" (see Figure 5–11).

Then I asked the students to express the rule for triangular numbers using variables. The children worked quietly until most indicated they had a rule. Then Erika volunteered, "The rule is just n times n, plus one, divided by two." When asked to put it on the board, she wrote $n \times (n+1) \div 2$. I asked whether anyone wrote the rule differently and these forms were added:
$$\frac{n(n+1)}{2} \quad \text{and} \quad \frac{1}{2} \times \left[n \times (n+1) \right].$$
I repeated for the students that these were forms of the same rule and would all work.

I wrote all the forms for the rules for square, rectangular, and triangular numbers that the students had discovered on the board. I asked Tara to

FIGURE 5–11 Erin's explanation

Notation	Comment
10 × 11	The tenth rectangular number is n times (n plus one), or **ten times eleven**.
10 × 11 = 110	Its value is **one hundred ten**.
110 ÷ 2	For the tenth triangular number, just divide one hundred ten in half.
110 ÷ 2 = 55	That gives fifty-five, so the tenth triangular number equals **fifty-five**.

reread the problem they were to solve aloud. After she did this, I asked the students what they would like to do next to help determine their recommendations for Juan. Brook suggested that they should use the rules for square, rectangular, and triangular numbers to make a list of the values of each of the three types of those figurate numbers that were less than fifty. I told the students that we would begin with that task the next day in class.

Using Figurate Numbers to Solve Juan's Problem

I started class the next day by reminding the students that they had decided the next step in solving Juan's problem was to use their rules to list all the square, rectangular, and triangular numbers less than fifty. I asked, "Who would like to show the class how to use a rule you found to make the list of square numbers?"

Erika volunteered and presented the example shown in Figure 5–12.

"Does Erika's explanation make sense to everyone?" I asked.

Most of the students in the class nodded, but Harold asked, "Can I use *n* times *n* as the rule for square numbers? I like it better and you have to multiply to get the answer anyhow."

I assured Harold and the rest of the class that they could use any of the equivalent forms of the rules (which were still on the board from the day before) to generate their lists. Next I asked whether anyone needed an example of using the rule for rectangular or triangular numbers before they started to work.

Marissa raised her hand and said, "I think I understand, but can you help me start the triangular number list?"

Suspecting that several pairs might have trouble evaluating the rule for triangular numbers, I encouraged Marissa to come to the board, assuring her that another student or I would help her if she needed it (see Figure 5–13).

I asked for a volunteer to help Marissa, and Eloise suggested, "Marissa, just put a one in place of each *n* in the rule and then do the math. When you want to find the second triangular number, just use twos instead of ones, and so on." (See Figure 5–14.)

For some classes of middle school students, I would skip these reminder demonstrations of how to substitute values for variables into ex-

FIGURE 5–12   Erika's explanation

Notation	Comment
n^2	I like to write the rule for square numbers as *n* **squared**.
$n = 1$	To find the first square number, I would use one for *n*.
1^2 1×1	Since *n* **squared** means *n* times itself, I multiply one times one for *n* **squared**.
1	So the rule gives the first square number as one—even though I could do that one in my head. Then I would use two for *n*, then three for *n*, and so on until my answer was above fifty and I could stop.

FIGURE 5-13   Marissa's explanation (Part One)

Go Figure!   **103**

Notation	Comment
$\dfrac{n \times n}{2} + \dfrac{n}{2}$	I like this form of the rule for triangular numbers.
	So to find the first triangular number, I do something with one,

FIGURE 5-14   Marissa's explanation (Part Two)

Notation	Comment
$\dfrac{n \times n}{2} + \dfrac{n}{2}$	So, for the first triangular number, I use one for **n**.
$\dfrac{1 \times 1}{2} + \dfrac{1}{2}$	That means I write one times one over two and add one over two to that. Uh oh—fractions.
$\dfrac{1}{2} + \dfrac{1}{2}$	One times one is just one, so I have one-half plus one-half.
1	That's easy (thank goodness). I get one for the first triangular number. And I know that's right from yesterday!

pressions. However, I find that most middle school students need to be shown the steps for evaluating an expression that contains variables in more than one lesson before they are comfortable doing it on their own—even when they derived the expressions or rules themselves. Certainly, the questions about variables that came up earlier in this lesson indicated that this class included students who needed these examples before using the rules to generate their lists of figurate numbers.

When all the students indicated that they were ready to begin, I reminded them to use any form of the rules that they had determined the day before to generate a list of the values for the square, rectangular, and triangular numbers less than fifty. I emphasized that each pair should choose the form of the rule that made the most sense to them for each of the three kinds of figurate numbers they had explored. Then each pair was to reread and discuss the original problem and write a recommendation for Juan.

It was encouraging to see that most pairs chose to use the following forms of the rules (in each case, n = successive whole numbers):

- For square numbers, n^2

- For rectangular numbers, $n(n + 1)$

- For triangular numbers, $\dfrac{n(n + 1)}{2}$

These choices indicated to me that many of the students in this class were listening to and understanding the explanations of their classmates. Moreover, by choosing to use more efficient forms of the rules, the students implied that they recognized the value of such efficiency. I never force a student to use a particular algorithm or form of a rule until he or she is comfortable doing so, but it is nice when this process of becoming more mathematically sophisticated happens naturally, without the nudging I otherwise eventually employ.

Many pairs of students made small errors during this part of the exploration. Several pairs made errors using the rules to calculate the square, rectangular, and triangular numbers with values less than fifty. Brook and Celina, for example, calculated the eighth triangular number as thirty-seven and the ninth as forty-seven. The errors in calculation may have caused them to ignore one of the parameters of the problem (different-shaped boxes) when formulating their recommendation (see Figure 5–15).

Marissa and Alex also incorrectly calculated the triangular numbers. Using the iterative rule (add two, then three, then four, etc., for successive terms), they missed every triangular number after the second because of an addition error. Apparently, since they found no numbers the same in any of their three lists of figurate numbers, they reinvented the problem and came up with another creative recommendation (see Figure 5–16).

Emmanuel and Erika, on the other hand, made a different kind of error. They generated a correct list of the values less than fifty for each of the figurate numbers but seemed to have slightly misunderstood the problem (see Figure 5–17). It appeared they misread the problem to mean that Juan could afford a *total* of fifty candies—and they recommended he buy one box of six for the mother and one box of six for the grandmother.

Kathleen and Keyonna also generated accurate lists for all three groups of figurate numbers but apparently failed to get all the details of the problem straight (see Figure 5–18). These girls recommended different numbers of candies for the mother and the grandmother, thereby ignoring one of the requirements indicated in the problem.

FIGURE 5–15   Brook and Celina's recommendation

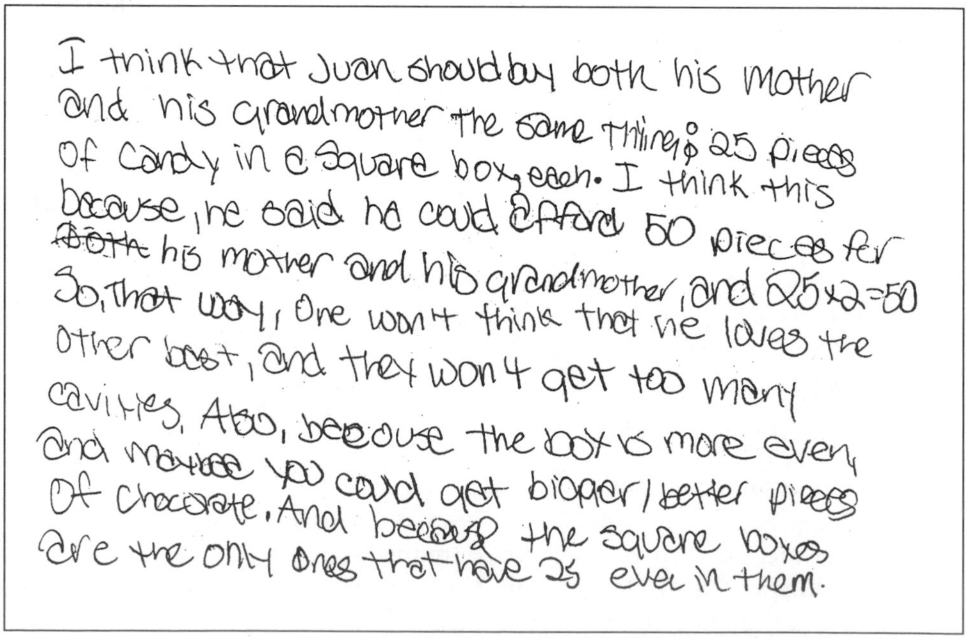

I think that Juan should buy both his mother and his grandmother the same thing: 25 pieces of candy in a square box each. I think this because, he said he could afford 50 pieces for both his mother and his grandmother, and 25×2=50 So, that way, one won't think that he loves the other best, and they won't get too many cavities. Also, because the box is more even, and maybe you could get bigger/better pieces of chocolate. And because the square boxes are the only ones that have 25 even in them.

FIGURE 5–16 Marissa and Alex's recommendation

I think Juan should buy one square box with 25 pieces of candy for his grandmother, then a rectangle box with 20 pieces of candy ance a triangle box with 5 pieces of candy for his mom. To get an exact amount of 50 and an equal amount for both of them I could only do by giving one of them more then one box of candy.

FIGURE 5–17 Emmanuel and Erika's recommendation

Juan, I think you should take one triangular box of 6 candies and one rectangular box of 6 candies. I think this because you stated that you want the same amount of candies for your grandmother and for your mother, but you also said you could only afford 50 candies and you also said that you wanted 2 different shaped boxes for the candies. One triangular box of 6 and a rectangular box of 6 is the only option you can have if you want different shapes and you can only afford 50. Of course there are other options that match for these 2 shapes but they add up to more than 50 wich you can't afford.

FIGURE 5–18 Kathleen and Keyonna's recommendation

I would recommend Juan to buy the triangle and square boxes because they have the highest amount of candy without going over 50. I would pick the 7th level of square (49) boxes and the 9th level of triangle boxes (45)

Since in circulating about the class I noticed that various small errors in calculations or in misreading or misinterpreting a portion of the problem had caused several pairs to make inappropriate recommendations for Juan, I changed the plan for the remainder of the lesson. I had intended to allow all pairs to complete their recommendations. Then I would ask one or two pairs to share their recommendations with the class and others to add comments or share their work only if their reasoning was different. I anticipated that a few students would need to revise their work.

Now it seemed that more than a few students were going to end the class with inappropriate recommendations caused by some small arithmetic error or misinterpretation of the problem, without having an opportunity to discover and correct their errors or revise their recommendations. Therefore, I decided to ask each pair of students to join another pair and compare their lists of figurate numbers and recommendations before anyone shared their answers with the entire class.

I felt it was not worth the amount of student time and effort for pairs who had made mistakes to essentially start over to solve the problem *after* hearing the recommendations of their classmates. Instead, I hoped that each group of four students could examine their two solutions together, find and note any errors, and then choose one recommendation (revising it, if desired) for the group to share with the class. By monitoring the groups of four as they worked together, I felt I could assure not only that all students found and noted their errors but also that they could verify a correct solution and agree on an appropriate recommendation, all within a reasonable amount of time.

This plan worked. For example, Amma and John were able to help Brook and Celina find their errors in calculating the triangular numbers and, after rereading the problem together, the four quickly found the solution.

For the future, I made a note to have the whole class share their lists of figurate numbers before setting out independently to use those lists to solve Juan's problem. Unless students have had a significant amount of practice substituting numbers for variables to generate a table of values, this step is advisable. I also will have the students reread the problem together and then list the parameters of an acceptable recommendation.

I feel we teachers need to observe students closely enough to recognize when it would be best to alter the plan for how a lesson in progress should proceed. We also must acknowledge the impact of time requirements and restrictions. I decided an inordinate amount of time would be required for students to rework their problem (essentially from the beginning) because of small errors or misconceptions. I also felt that each student in this class could benefit as much mathematically and more personally by working with others at this point in the lesson to produce a correct solution and quality recommendations.

During this part of the lesson, there was lively discussion among all the groups. It was great to see students defending their ideas and helping each other understand errors without any put-downs. In many situations, I think, the value of students working with other students in a small group cannot be overrated. All the students are empowered when they can find a correct solution they all understand.

Every group was able to find all significant errors and agree on a solution and recommendation. One reason I believe the groups could come to agreement easily and correctly is that the errors students made initially were small ones. I would have revised the lesson in other ways if I had observed students with apparent misunderstandings about finding explicit rules for figurate numbers and evaluating variable expressions—or if the students did not show a basic grasp of the problem and how to solve it.

Most of the final group recommendations were correct and simply stated. Typical of the class was the recommendation by John's group (see Figure 5–19). The students obviously used their table of values to correctly solve the problem.

Some groups offered more expansive solutions. For example, Tara's group included the observation that there was an additional solution (a rectangular and triangular box of six candies each) but explained their preference for the thirty-six-piece square and triangular boxes. (See Figure 5–20 on page 108.)

As the bell rang, I felt the students had accomplished the goals for the lesson. They explored three patterns of figurate numbers, finding iterative and explicit rules for each and relating those rules to the visual pattern as well. Hopefully, through hearing the thinking of their classmates, some developed new strategies for finding patterns and their rules.

By evaluating the variable expressions they discovered, students generated lists of successive square, rectangular, and triangular numbers, illustrating the utility of such expressions and practice with the procedure. This lesson gave students an opportunity to apply the results of their algebraic thinking with patterns and variables to solve a problem. And, finally, the students hopefully got a feeling for the power of variable expressions to help solve such problems.

FIGURE 5–19 Final recommendation by John's group

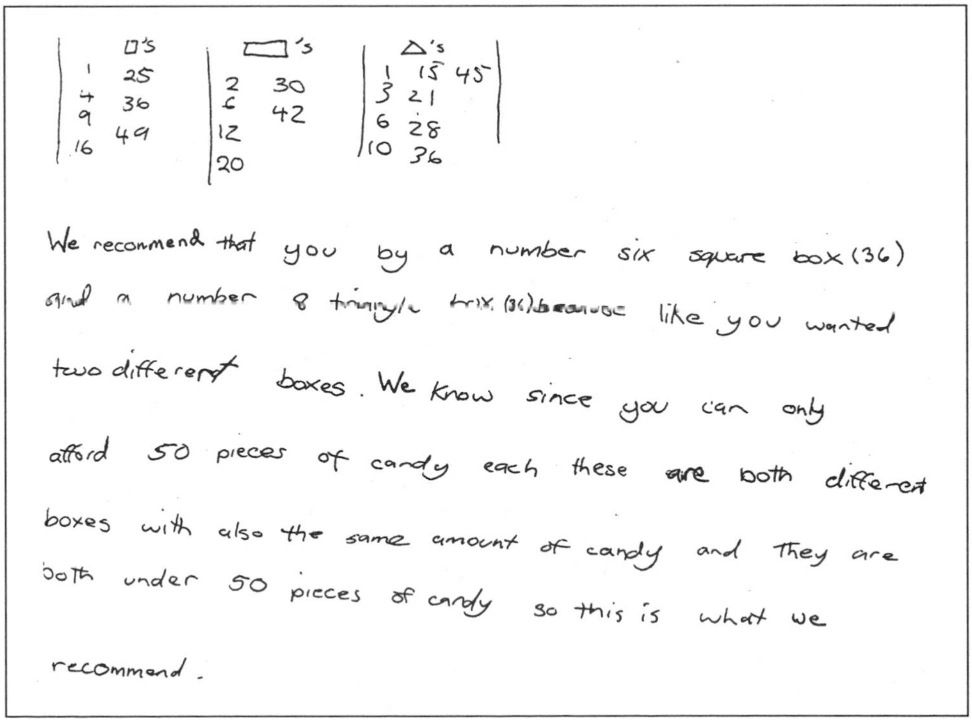

□'s		▭'s		△'s	
1	25	2	30	1	15 45
4	36	6	42	3	21
9	49	12		6	28
16		20		10	36

We recommend that you by a number six square box (36) and a number 8 triangle box (36) because like you wanted two different boxes. We know since you can only afford 50 pieces of candy each these are both different boxes with also the same amount of candy and they are both under 50 pieces of candy so this is what we recommend.

FIGURE 5–20   Final recommendation by Tara's group

Level	Square	Rect.	Tri.	
1	1	2	1	
2	4	6	3	
3	9	12	6	
4	16	20	10	
5	25	30	15	
6	36	42	21	
7	49	56	28	
8	64	72	36	
9	81	90	45	
10	100	110	55	

We think he should buy the square box and fill the box with 36 pieces and a triangle box with 36 pieces because the chart shows that you can fill a square box and triangle box with 36 pieces each.

He should buy a ▭ level 2 for his ma and a △ level 3 for his grandma. they are different shaped boxes, under fifty pieces, and the same number. If he thinks 6 candies each is not enough he should by ▭ level 6 for his ma and △ level 8 for his grandma Like before, they are different shaped boxes, under 80 pieces and the same number of candy. (36)

The 13 Nights of Halloween activity is appropriate for a lesson that involves many of the same concepts and skills as *Go Figure!*

The book *The 13 Nights of Halloween*, by Rebecca Dickinson (1996), offers a nice connection between children's literature and mathematics. The story is much like that described in the song "The Twelve Days of Christmas" in that a goblin gives his girlfriend a set of gifts each night for thirteen nights of Halloween. Thus, there are many opportunities for data gathering, finding and expressing patterns, and finding rules for those patterns. Both square and triangular numbers are evident in some of the patterns.

Read (or have students read) the book *The 13 Nights of Halloween* aloud. Then present them with one or more of the following questions to explore:

- Predict the total number of gifts the goblin gave on the thirteenth night of Halloween.

- Find the number of gifts for each night of Halloween. Look for patterns.

- Estimate the total number of gifts the goblin gave in the thirteen nights.

- Find the total number of all the gifts the goblin had given by the end of each night of Halloween. Look for patterns.

- Find the total number of each kind of gift the goblin had given by the end of the thirteen nights (how many owls, how many toads, etc.). Look for patterns.

- Write the rule for the total number of gifts the goblin gave on the nth day.

- Figure out the probability of choosing a worm if all the gifts are in a pile.

The most obvious connection to the *Go Figure!* lesson is that the total number of gifts on the nth night equals the nth triangular number.

Possible Questions for Extensions for *The 13 Nights of Halloween*

- Write your own version of *The 13 Nights of Halloween*. Include math questions about your story.

- Suppose the story was *The 30 Nights of Halloween*. What can you predict about the answers to questions like 1–7 above?

At least two other books offer the same kinds of patterns. They are *The 12 Circus Rings*, by Seymour Chwast (1993), and *My Little Sister Ate One Hare*, by Bill Grossman (1996). Of course, "The Twelve Days of Christmas" could be used as the basis for such an activity as well.

Cannonballs (Tetrahedral Numbers) | Extension Problems

Often there are piles of old cannonballs found at historic forts. Usually the cannonballs are stacked in the shape of a tetrahedron (triangular pyramid), with one cannonball on the top layer, three on the second layer, six on the third layer, and so on, as shown in the illustration at left. Notice that each layer is centered on top of the layer below it. You may want to build a model using Ping-Pong balls or other spheres, but you will probably need tape or sticky putty to hold the balls in each layer together. (Marshmallows might work better than exact spheres!)

Give students the following problem:

Find the total number of cannonballs in a pile 10 layers high and then in one 15 layers high. Try to find a rule, in words or using a variable, for the total number of cannonballs needed for such a pile with any number of layers.

Few middle school students will be able to express any but the iterative form of the rule—"Total cannonballs in a pile with *n* layers equals sum of *n* consecutive triangular numbers"—but they will enjoy finding the triangular numbers in a real-world context. Also, this is a perfect scenario for students to experience the power of a spreadsheet! The explicit rule for total cannonballs in a pile with *n* layers is:

$$\frac{n^3 + 3n^2 + 2n}{6}$$

Middle school students enjoy and can benefit from substituting values for *n* to check their own results for stacks of cannonballs with a specific number of layers.

Stack of Oranges

Sometimes grocers will make a display of oranges by stacking them in a pyramid shape. Usually the oranges are stacked with one orange on the top layer, four on the second layer, nine on the third layer, and so on, as shown in the illustration at left. Notice that each layer is centered on top of the layer below it. You may want to build a model using Ping-Pong balls or other spheres, but you will probably need tape or sticky putty to hold the balls in each layer together. (Marshmallows might work better than exact spheres!)

Give students the following problem:

Find the total number of oranges in a pyramid 10 layers high and then in one 15 layers high. Try to find a rule, in words or using a variable, for the total number of oranges needed for such a pyramid with any number of layers.

Few middle school students will be able to express any but the iterative form of the rule: "Total oranges in a pile with *n* layers equals sum of *n* consecutive square numbers." This is a perfect scenario for students to experience the power of a spreadsheet! The explicit rule is:

$$\frac{2n^3 + 3n^2 + n}{6}$$

Again, middle school students enjoy and can benefit from substituting values for *n* to check their own results for stacks of oranges with a specific number of layers.

Related Problem

The *Condo Challenge* lesson (Chapter 9) can be used following *Go Figure!* However, if *Condo Challenge* is used immediately after *Go Figure!*, your students are unlikely to produce the variety of interpretations for the growing pattern shown in Chapter 9. Instead, they most likely will simply interpret each of the four wings for any stage as the sum of counting numbers and employ the rule for triangular numbers as the basis for their explicit rule. Therefore, we suggest waiting at least several weeks between the two lessons.

Technology Connections

If graphing calculators are available, the equivalent forms of the explicit rule for each kind of figurate number explored in the *Go Figure!* lesson can be entered in the *y* = menu and the tables can be viewed. The tables (shown below and on page 112) can be compared to verify that equivalent forms of a rule produce the same results for any stage and to show values for large stage numbers.

Square Numbers

```
Plot1  Plot2  Plot3
\Y1=X*X
\Y2=X²
\Y3=
\Y4=
```

X	Y₁	Y₂
1	1	1
2	4	4
3	9	9
4	16	16
5	25	25
6	36	36
7	49	49

X=7

Rectangular Numbers

```
Plot1  Plot2  Plot3
\Y1=X(X+1)
\Y2=X²+X
\Y3=
\Y4=
```

X	Y₁	Y₂
1	2	2
2	6	6
3	12	12
4	20	20
5	30	30
6	42	42
7	56	56

X=7

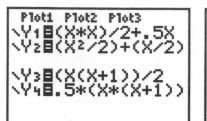

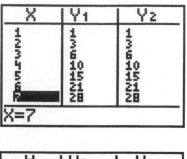

If you feel it is appropriate for your students at the time of this lesson, the calculators can also display scatter plots that can verify in a visual way that equivalent forms of a rule produce the same results. Directions for creating such scatter plots using TI-73 calculators can be found in the "Technology Connections" section of the *Personalized Patterns* lesson.

CHAPTER 6

Bulging Backpacks

OVERVIEW

In this lesson students estimate and find the actual weight for each of their backpacks. The class constructs a scatter plot to display some of the data, then each student creates a personal scatter plot. The students then superimpose a set of points on each scatter plot to represent perfect estimates. The class discusses the equations for the graphs of the perfect estimates and also those for consistent over- and underestimates. Finally, students are asked to reflect on their own performance, both interpreting their own scatter plots and evaluating their estimates.

This lesson gives students experience plotting points on a Cartesian plane and interpreting those points in terms of a real-world situation. More important, for the first time students consider a set of points on a graph as a representation of the relationship (or lack of it) between two variables.

This lesson also introduces the students to the graph of the function $y = x$ and the real-world meanings for points above and below that line, all within the context of the backpack lesson. Students learn that a set of points clustered about a line indicates a relationship and that a function rule can be written when the points fall on a single line. Over time, with numerous similar experiences, students develop an intuitive understanding of functions and correlation.

BACKGROUND

This class of sixth-grade students had limited experience working with patterns. They had produced the next stages in a series and found iterative rules for numerical and geometric patterns. They had been introduced to the x- and y-axes and graphed isolated points in the first quadrant on the Cartesian plane, but they had not graphed scatter plots.

PREREQUISITE CONCEPTS OR SKILLS

- Finding iterative and explicit rules for patterns
- Graphing points in Quadrant I (optional)
- Scaling axes appropriately for specific data

VOCABULARY

axis, axes, Cartesian plane, coordinate grid, coordinates, function, function rule, origin, plot (a point), Quadrant I, scatter plot, variable, x-axis, y-axis

TIME

The lesson was completed in one ninety-minute class. If your classes are only forty-five to sixty minutes long, we suggest going as far as possible during the first day (the students probably will not get to graph their personal scatter plots). On the second day, you should be able to finish the lesson. If needed, students could write their reflections outside of class or on a third day.

MATERIALS

- Bathroom scale
- Student backpacks
- 1 sheet of 1-inch square grid paper
- Colored stick-on dots in three colors (for class scatter plot), one dot of each of two colors and a few of a third color per student
- 1 sheet of graph paper per student
- Colored pencils, one or two colors per student (optional)

The Lesson

Bulging Backpacks

I introduced this lesson by asking students how good they thought they might be at estimating the weights of their backpacks. Most expressed that they had no idea how well they might do with such estimating. I explained that this lesson would give them the opportunity to get some experience with estimates and comparing those estimates with the actual weights. Then each person could determine how good an estimator he or she was during this activity.

I continued, "Each of you will estimate the weight of each student's backpack and then we will find the actual weights, using a bathroom scale. Next the class will work together to create a kind of graph known as a scatter plot. Then each of you will create a personal scatter plot using your own estimates and the actual weights for the backpacks. Finally, you will interpret your scatter plot. During this lesson you will be introduced to some important mathematical ideas that may be new to you."

I always like to give the students an overview of the lesson to provide motivation for the activity and to focus their attention on the specific objectives of the lesson.

Next I posed a question to the entire class: "Do you have any suggestions for how we might estimate and find the actual weights of the backpacks, then record the information?"

Through a brief discussion the students designed the following plan:

- Each student makes a table and records his or her own data. The table has three columns, with the names of all the students in the class in the first column, personal estimates in the second column, and actual weights in the third column.

- The students make estimates for only three backpacks, then find their actual weights, to help students get some general idea of how much backpacks weigh.

- Students use the bathroom scale (conveniently on the table in the front of the classroom!) to weigh each of the three backpacks to the nearest half-pound.

- The students continue to make estimates and subsequently find weights to the nearest half-pound for the rest of the backpacks.

Following the plan the students designed, I asked three students, Daniel, Alice, and Jack, to put their backpacks on the table at the front of the classroom. Each student in the class lifted each of the three backpacks and recorded an estimate for the weight of each backpack to the nearest half-pound in his or her personal chart. Next, Daniel put his backpack on the scale; it weighed 10.5 pounds, to the nearest half-pound. I asked the students to share their estimates for Daniel's backpack, and many were not even close to the actual weight: estimates were as low as 4 pounds and as high as 26 pounds. Then Alice and Jack weighed their backpacks, and the students recorded the actual weights (14.5 pounds for Alice and 22.5 for Jack).

I asked the students what they had learned about their ability to estimate the weights of backpacks from the data they had so far. A few students, like Nashalie, were pleased. She stated, "My estimates are all close to the real weights, and so I think I'm doing good. I should keep going like I am."

A larger group consistently overestimated, like Marianna, with over-estimates of 15, 20, and 30 pounds for the three backpacks. As she explained, "I need to lower my guesses so the rest of my estimates will be closer to the real weights."

Sergio, with estimates of 9, 11, and 15 pounds, respectively, said that he needed to "think heavier" since he had underestimated all three backpacks.

I reminded the students that they should consider this first part of the activity as simply the opportunity to make "guesstimates" of backpack weights and to obtain some values to use as references for the rest of the activity. I told them that they would show these first three results in a different way than they would show all the rest of the results in their scatter plots. I did this because I hoped to later be able to point out the value of benchmarks with any kind of estimating. I also wanted the students who had made very poor estimates for the first three backpacks to feel like they were about to get a fresh start.

Next, eight more students brought their backpacks to the front of the room to be estimated and weighed. Each student in the class estimated all eight backpacks before knowing what any of them actually weighed. However, any student was free to lift any of the eight backpacks or relift any of the first three backpacks to reestablish a physical benchmark in order to better estimate the remaining backpacks. I allowed this relifting because I have observed that most middle school students have had few, if any, experiences related to establishing benchmarks for measurements of any kind—weight, height, distance, and so on. I believe such benchmarks are important if we want students to be able to use mathematics to make sense of their world.

When all the students had finished entering their estimates into their tables, I had each of those eight students weigh his or her own backpack and announce the result to the class. A few had to be reminded that the entire backpack (including all straps) should actually be on the scale. There were many comments when students correctly estimated the weight of a backpack and more than a few groans when their estimates were not close to the actual weights.

Then the last group of students in this small class brought their backpacks forward and the class repeated the estimating and weighing process. (**Note:** I have used this lesson successfully with classes of more than thirty students, as well.) After all the actual weights had been recorded, I asked, "Looking at your results, how many of you would consider yourself a good estimator of backpack weight?"

Vito replied, "Yes, I think I am good at it. I don't think a person needs to be close every single time to be a good estimator, just a reasonable guesser most of the time. I was close to the right weight for most of the last two sets of backpacks."

I indicated that I agreed with Vito's conclusion, and several students smiled. I believe that it is important to reinforce to students the idea that even a good estimator will not always be close and that a general trend is more important than one, or even a few, examples. Confidence in estimating, like everything else, is partially a result of experience and success, and I try to provide opportunities for both whenever possible.

I told the students that they would now begin to make scatter plots of their results to help them determine how well they had estimated—this time from the graph of their results. Kevin immediately asked, "What's a scatter plot?" This question opened the way for me to explain that a scatter plot is simply a kind of graph that shows information about two variables at the same time. I also explained that a scatter plot can help a person decide whether there is a relationship between the two variables that are graphed.

This class had some experience graphing coordinates on a Cartesian plane, but it soon became clear that they made few, if any, connections between plotting isolated points and applying the skill of plotting such points to create a scatter plot. I taped a large, blank sheet of one-inch square grid paper on the board at the front of the room. I then repeated that each point in a scatter plot shows information about two variables (values that change), and the overall graph gives a visual representation of how changes in those variables are related or not related to each other. I asked whether anyone could tell us what the variables for this lesson might be. When no one volunteered, I asked, "Well, what two values do we have for each backpack?"

Rudi volunteered, "The estimate and the real weight."

I nodded and then posed the question, "So if Christy's backpack weighs twenty pounds and you estimated it weighed fifteen pounds, how can we show that on this scatter plot?" Again, no one volunteered.

I quickly reviewed plotting a point from two coordinates on a graph. Then I explained that in order to graph points to represent the class's data about backpacks, the numbers along the axes should represent the range of values for the weights and estimates of the backpacks. I polled the class and found that all weights and estimates were less than 30 pounds and then elicited that each axis should be numbered from 0 to 30 so all the values obtained by the class could be shown on the scatter plot. Also, I told the students they should employ the same scale on both axes, using the horizontal, or x-, axis for the actual weights of the backpacks and the vertical, or y-, axis for the estimates.

I selected these two characteristics of the scatter plot for specific reasons. I asked the students to use the same scale and numbers on each axis because I wanted the graph of $y = x$ (to be plotted later in the lesson) to bisect Quadrant I so the students would have a visual image of that benchmark function. I wanted the actual weights along the x-axis and the estimates along the y-axis because this configuration would create a nice visual image of the relative accuracy of the estimates. That is, the point for any *under*estimate would fall *below* the $y = x$ line, and the point for any *over*estimate would fall *above* the $y = x$ line. I did not explain this to the students at this point in the lesson because I wanted them to observe this characteristic themselves after the scatter plots were complete.

"Let's create a practice scatter plot first," I suggested. So the students set aside their blank scatter plots and began to construct the class scatter plot together. I pointed out to the students that the class scatter plot would not look exactly like anyone's personal scatter plot, but it would be used to practice plotting data points and demonstrate the procedure each of them would use in making his or her personal scatter plot. Two students drew, numbered, and labeled the axes 0–30 on the large grid paper, and I explained that each student would graph the point for one backpack on this practice scatter plot using stick-on dots.

I suggested that each student graph the actual weight and the estimate each had made for her or his own backpack on the class graph. Daniel went first and quickly placed a yellow stick-on dot at (10.5, 10) by moving one finger up from 10.5 on the x-axis and one finger right from 10 on the y-axis, then placing his stick-on dot where his fingers met. Alice, however, said she did not know where to put her dot. I asked her to choose someone to help her, and she chose Christy. After they conferred quietly, Alice explained, "My backpack weighed fourteen and a half pounds, so I need to move along the bottom line to fourteen point five. My estimate was six pounds, so I move up six and put my dot here," as she pointed at the correct intersection for (14.5, 6).

I affirmed Alice's response and asked whether anyone could explain once more what Alice had done to plot her point. Piero went to the front of the room and pointed appropriately to the graph as he explained, "Alice found the actual weight of her backpack on one axis [pointing to the x-axis] and her estimate [pointing to the y-axis] on the other axis. She placed the coordinate where those two lines intersect [tracing the imaginary lines with his fingers until they met]."

I asked the original group of three students for whose backpacks the class first made estimates to circle their points in red. I explained that I asked Daniel, Alice, and Jack to do this because those estimates were made with no prior experience, so I wanted to separate them from the overall impression the scatter plot might indicate about the relationship between the estimates and actual backpack weights.

Despite their confident indications, some students had trouble when it came their turn to graph. Nashalie, for example, switched the x- and y-coordinates, and more than one student was confused about the exact placement of the dot until another student traced the appropriate lines for them from the axes to their intersection. Thus, I feel that the creation of the class scatter plot is an important part of this lesson unless the students have had a lot of experience plotting points from lists of data.

Once the class scatter plot was completed (see Figure 6–1), I asked a few questions to check the students' understanding of information displayed by the graph. For example, pointing at the dot at (13, 16), I asked, "What does this point tell you?"

Without prodding, Terrence was able to explain, "For a backpack that weighed thirteen pounds, the estimate was sixteen pounds." I repeated this question for several other points. Then I asked for a volunteer to show me the point on the scatter plot for a backpack that weighed 20 pounds and was estimated to weigh 18 pounds. Mary quickly identified the correct point, as did several other students from similar descriptions of other points.

I then asked whether the graph indicated that there was a trend or a general relationship between the estimates and the actual weights. The students agreed that there seemed to be a general trend. As Hector put it, "The scatter plot mostly shows small estimates for the light backpacks and

FIGURE 6–1 Class scatter plot #1

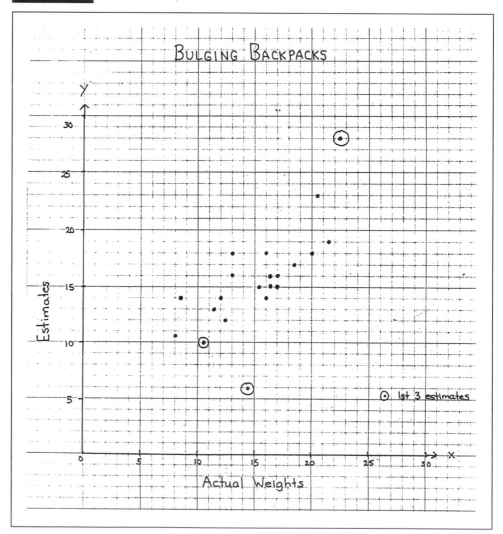

big estimates for the heavier backpacks. At least that happens for most guesses and backpacks."

I augmented Hector's conclusion by explaining that two variables are considered to be *correlated* when there is a strong general trend that connects them. In this case, there was a correlation between the estimates and the actual weights because, in general, as the actual weights increased, the estimates also increased. Both the numerical data and the scatter plot showed this trend. When explaining a concept in words seems just beyond the students' grasp, I think it is appropriate to help them formulate their mathematical definitions by supplying a simple, correct way to express the concept. As in this lesson, I then follow up by giving the students another opportunity to provide their own definitions.

Next each student constructed a personal scatter plot to display his or her own estimates versus the actual weights of the backpacks. As they began to work, I asked, "When you are finished, will all the personal scatter plots look exactly alike?"

A few frowns told me the answer was not obvious to some of the students, but Luis quickly said, "Of course not! My estimates are different, at least sometimes, than other people's."

"Is Luis correct?" I asked.

Mary confirmed, "Yes, everyone's actual weights will be the same, but their estimates will be different—at least sometimes."

I also reminded the students to circle the points that represented the weights and estimates for Daniel's, Alice's, and Jack's backpacks in red on their scatter plots.

As I circulated among the students, most proceeded with confidence, but a few had trouble. Nashalie asked to be shown again how to graph a point. Also, two students had trouble when the coordinates included a number other than a whole number (e.g., Hector's backpack weighed 14.5 pounds). Those two students were uncomfortable placing a point anywhere except at the intersection of two lines on their graph paper. This small problem was quickly cleared up by asking them to recall the bathroom scale that we used for weighing the backpacks and how the arrow for the actual weight settled halfway between the marks for 14 and 15 pounds. That reminder led them to conclude that they should plot the point halfway between 14 and 15 on the graph.

When all the scatter plots were completed, I asked each student to interpret his or her personal scatter plot. First I had each student answer the question "What does my scatter plot show about my estimates for the weights of the backpacks?"

Sergio volunteered, "My scatter plot shows that I was a good estimator." He went on to explain that most of his y values (estimates) were close to his x values (the actual weights).

"So how does that affect the way the scatter plot looks?" I asked.

He replied, "When you look at my scatter plot, the points are not all over the page. They are sort of a group of points that go from the bottom left to the upper right of the graph."

Owen frowned as he stated that he really couldn't tell much from looking at his scatter plot. "Some estimates are close," he said, "but others are not so close." Several other students agreed that they also found it difficult to evaluate their performance by looking at their personal scatter plot.

When asked whether they could identify more accurate estimates, all students agreed that they improved after the first three, as evidenced by "how far the first three points [for Daniel, Alice, and Jack] are from the rest of the others, which are sort of bunched up," as Jack expressed it.

In answer to the question "Where are the points for low estimates?" Leah replied, "Low on the graph."

Similarly, when asked how to identify high estimates, Vito answered, "Higher on the graph than other points close to them."

So I returned to the question "How do you recognize on the graph an estimate that is close to the actual weight?"

Daniel volunteered, "The point is about the same distance to the right as up."

I interpreted these answers to indicate that many of the students had good intuition about how the location of points on the graph indicated the accuracy of the estimates, but I wanted deeper understanding. Thus, I asked, "What would the graph look like if every single estimate matched the actual weight?"

Reid offered an interesting response. He said, "Each point would be a corner of a square." When asked to explain what he meant, Reid hopped up, went to the class scatter plot, pointed to 14 on the x-axis and 14 on the y-axis, traced up and across with his fingers and said, "See, the point would be at the corner of a square that is fourteen on each side." This answer was not what I was expecting, but I tried to refocus Reid by saying, "Yes, and where would all the points (or corners of all those squares) appear on your scatter plot?"

Reid frowned a bit, then smiled. "They would make a line," he said.

Knowing that some students did not follow Reid's explanation, I suggested, "Let's all try this together." Then I had each student who had made a perfect estimate for his or her own backpack place another dot of a different color (blue) on top of the one they originally plotted. I repeated that each new blue point had a y-coordinate (estimate) that matched the x-coordinate (actual weight) on the class scatter plot. It was obvious that many of the students were surprised to see that the points all fell on a line that went diagonally up to the right from the origin (see Figure 6–2).

I asked the students what they noticed about the new set of points. Nashalie stated, "There is a diagonal line of dots when every estimate matches the actual weight."

I wanted to help the students further examine and express the rule for perfect estimates, so I asked a few clarifying questions. First, I added the point (0, 0) to the class scatter plot and asked, "Will this point fall on the line of perfect estimates?" Then I added, "What does this point mean in our backpack experiment?"

Piero answered, "For a backpack that weighed nothing (an air pack!), the estimate was also zero—a perfect guess, so the point is on the line of perfect guesses."

"And for this new set of points, for a forty-pound backpack, where would the point be?" I inquired.

Julie volunteered, "The point would be at (forty, forty) and on the line (but off our page!) because the estimate was the same as the actual weight."

Finally, I asked, "Can anyone give a rule for the set of all points that would be *on* this line [pointing to the new set of points]?"

Ryan stated, "The graph is the line of points when each estimate exactly matches the actual weight."

"Exactly," I affirmed. "Since the x values are along the horizontal axis and the y values are along the vertical axis, can anyone give a function rule for the line?"

FIGURE 6-2 Class scatter plot #2

Bulging Backpacks   **121**

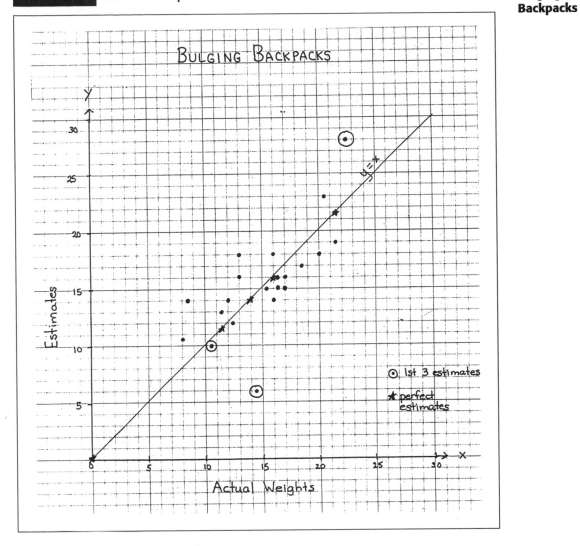

Marianna slowly said, "The estimates equal the actual values."

I wrote Marianna's statement on the board and asked, "Who can state that rule using variables?" No one volunteered. "Remember that function rules just express the same ideas as words except they use variables. Does that help?"

With that comment, several hands went up, and Leah said, "I think it would be y equals x."

"Is that what you had in mind?" I asked, and the other students nodded. "So the function rule for this line," I stated, pointing to the line of blue dots on the class scatter plot, "is y equals x [$y = x$]?" All the students nodded. I suggested that it would be a good idea to make a mental picture of this graph and try to remember it because that image could serve as a benchmark for thinking about a lot of function graphs from now on.

I think it is important for students to have benchmarks for the graphs of functions so they can compare new functions they encounter to those benchmarks. For example, in a later lesson or grade, students can quickly develop a strong sense of slope if they compare the graphs of $y = 2x$, $y = 3x$, $y = -2x$, and so on, to the familiar graph of $y = x$. I also have found that most students will not recognize these benchmarks for themselves and will not remember them without several experiences to reinforce the visual image so that they can use it as a reference. Thus, one of my primary objectives for this lesson was to begin to establish such an image for the graph of $y = x$.

I also briefly revisited the ideas of relationship, correlation, and function in the context of the backpacks and the new $y = x$ line on the class graph. I pointed out that, of course, there was a relationship between the x and y variables for the points shown on the line; in fact, there was a perfect correlation between those x and y values: each estimate equaled the actual weight. I further repeated that any time a rule can be written that produces a correct y value for each x value, a function exists. The rule *estimate* = *actual*, or $y = x$, works for every point on that line and, therefore, is the function rule.

To expand the idea of linear function rules and their graphs, I suggested, "Now let's look back at our class scatter plot. What is the meaning of this dot in our backpack lesson [pointing to the dot at (16, 18)]?"

I called on Nashalie and she stated, "The real weight of a backpack was sixteen pounds and someone guessed eighteen pounds."

I affirmed her answer, glad to see that Nashalie seemed to have eliminated her confusion with x- and y-coordinates. "Now, how is this point [indicating (12, 14)] like that one [pointing back to (16, 18)]?"

Ryan answered that, in both cases, the estimate was two pounds more than the actual weight. "Are there any other points like these two?" I asked.

"What do you mean?" Daniel asked.

"Are there any other points for which the estimate is two pounds more than the actual weight?" I asked. Everyone agreed that there were no more on the class scatter plot.

"Well, suppose I wanted to make a function rule for all the estimates that were two more than the actual weight. What would that function rule be?"

"I can tell you in words," Jack said. "The estimate is two more than the actual weight."

I wrote those words on the board, saying, "Yes, so who can think of a way to write the function rule?"

Christy blurted, "I know, I know—y equals x plus two."

"Yes," I answered, "and what would the graph for y equals x plus two look like?"

No one answered immediately. "A line?" Marianna asked tentatively.

"How many of you agree that the graph would be a line?" I asked. When almost all hands were raised, I asked, "And can you tell me anything else about the graph?"

Luis said, "I think the line would be higher than our y equals x line."

Then Daniel added, "Yeah, it would be two above the other line."

"Well, let's see," I replied. "In this new set of points, what would the y value be for our function if x equaled ten?" Christy offered the answer 12 pounds and plotted the point in a third color (green). Students plotted several more points for estimates that were two above the actual weights until it was clear that they formed a line (see Figure 6–3).

"So were your predictions correct?" I asked, and the students verified that every point that satisfied the rule "Estimate = actual weight + 2" fell on the same line and that the line for $y = x + 2$ was two units above the graph for $y = x$. I reminded them once more that any time a rule can be written that produces one correct y value for each x value, a function ex-

FIGURE 6-3 Class scatter plot #3

Bulging Backpacks **123**

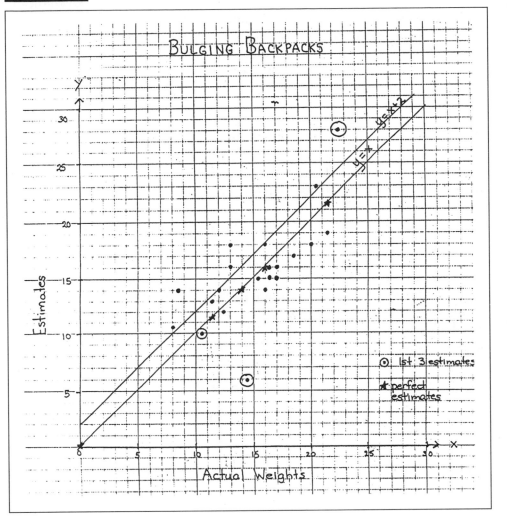

ists. Thus, the function $y = x + 2$ was represented on the scatter plot as the line of green dots.

"OK, let's think about another set of estimates," I suggested. "Talk to the person next to you about what the graph would look like for estimates that were three pounds less than the actual weights of the backpacks."

After the students had a minute or two to discuss the new function, I asked, "Who can tell one thing about the graph that would show that each estimate was three pounds less than the actual weight of the backpack?" Students gave the following responses:

■ The points would form a line.

■ The line would be three units below the $y = x$ line.

■ The function rule would be $y = x - 3$.

■ Every time an estimate was 3 pounds less than the actual weight, the point for that event would fall on the line $y = x - 3$.

This last observation was one that I had failed to elicit when considering the $y = x + 2$ function earlier in the lesson. Actually, the reason I used this "Who can tell one thing about . . . ?" technique is that when I do, students often observe something I forgot or did not think of at all, so I use the question often. Of course, the technique also gives more students the chance to share a variety of responses. Once again it paid off!

Also, when a student *does* observe something mathematically new to the class, I try to ask a follow-up question to make sure other students understand the new information. In this case, I asked, "So who can tell us how Vito's observation applies to the function y equals x plus two [pointing to that line on the scatter plot], which we were looking at earlier?"

Owen stated, "Any time an estimate for a backpack was two more than the actual weight, the point would be on the line for y equals x plus two.

I nodded and offered one last question: "What if every single estimate were seven pounds? No matter what the backpack looked like, the estimate was seven pounds. What would be the function rule?"

Without a moment's hesitation, Vito said confidently, "It would be a straight line across at seven."

I asked Vito to explain his thinking. He came up to the class scatter plot and said, "If the backpack weighed five, the point would be (five, seven) [pointing to that place on the graph]. If the backpack weighed ten, the point would be (ten, seven) [pointing to that place on the graph]. If the backpack weighed any number of pounds, the point would be at (something, seven), so there would be a horizontal line of points right here [sweeping his hand across the scatter plot at $y = 7$]."

"And what would the rule for those points be?" I ventured. No one spoke up. "What is it in words?"

Vito answered, "For every actual weight, the estimate is seven pounds."

And, with prompting, Reid added, "So the rule is y equals seven."

For the last part of the lesson, I asked each student to go back to his or her personal scatter plot and add points for perfect estimates (the $y = x$ line). I asked that they use a different color or kind of mark for each of these points than they used for their first set of points. Then each student should see whether he or she could add to the earlier interpretation of the personal scatter plot and what it showed about what kind of estimator of weights of backpacks he or she was.

When everyone had added the new line of points to his or her own graph, I asked, "So what do you notice?" Several hands shot up.

Callie offered, "If you were a good estimator, the points of your original graph should be close to the new line. And, except for the first three points, mine are!" As Callie held up her scatter plot, the students indicated agreement with her statement. I asked Callie to pass her scatter plot around the room for her classmates to view (see Figure 6–4).

As the scatter plot was passed around, several other students commented that most of their estimates were also close to the $y = x$ line.

Ryan commented, "Almost all my points are below the line." (See Figure 6–5.)

When I asked Alice what this told her about Ryan's estimates, she replied, "I think it means Ryan mostly estimated too little for the weights of the backpacks." Ryan agreed, and I asked him to pass his scatter plot around.

As the two scatter plots were passed around the room, Jack stated, "Well, my points are mostly above the line, so I guess that means I estimate too high." Again, Jack's observation was affirmed as his scatter plot was passed among his classmates (see Figure 6–6 on page 126).

FIGURE 6–4 Callie's scatter plot

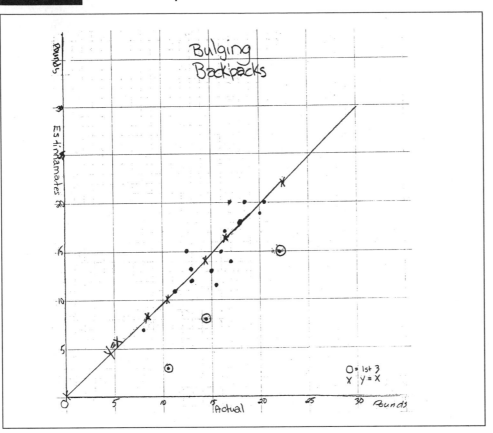

FIGURE 6–5 Ryan's scatter plot

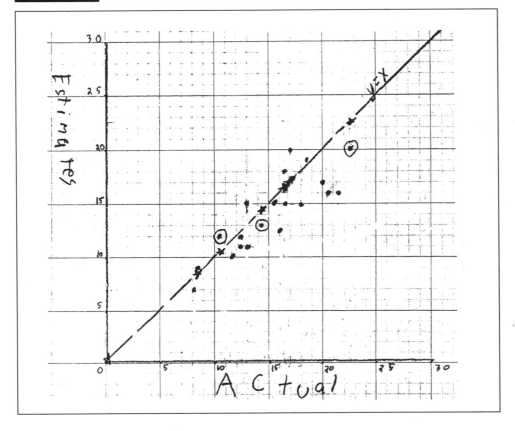

I asked the students to summarize what an informed observer might conclude from the appearance of the various scatter plots. Marianna volunteered. "First," she said, "if the points are close to the 'matching line,' you are a good estimator. Next, if most of the points are below the line, you estimate too low. And, finally, if the points are mostly above the line, you estimate too high."

Leah raised her hand and added, "Also, if the points are spread out all over the page, you didn't do a very good job estimating the weights."

"Anything else?" I asked. No one volunteered. "What does the scatter plot tell you about the correlation of the actual weights and the estimates?" I asked.

Several hands went up. Luis said, "Your estimates are correlated with the actual weights if the points on the scatter plot are clumped around the y equals x line we graphed." When I asked if Luis's statement was correct, everyone gave the "thumbs up" signal.

In order to learn about what each student understood, I wrote the following three questions on the board and asked the students to respond to each of them in writing.

1. What should a person know by looking at your original scatter plot?

2. What should a person know by looking at the points and line you added later to your scatter plot?

3. What are the main things you learned from this activity?

FIGURE 6–6 Jack's scatter plot

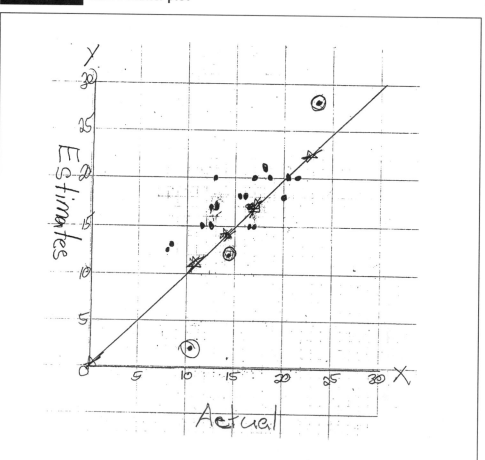

I hoped the students' answers would reflect some understanding of the concepts introduced in the lesson. I also expected that I would find a few misunderstandings that had not come out in the class discussion.

The answers to the first question indicated that most of the students had gained the basics of what a scatter plot is and how to create such a graph. First, in their own words, students described how a scatter plot shows information (see Jemma's response in Figure 6–7).

Thus, Jemma and other students in the class seemed to grasp the important idea of how a graph can show the relationship between two variables.

Also, in their answers to the first question, many students indicated that they grasped the basics of how a scatter plot can show correlation. Typical was the statement by Nashalie (see Figure 6–8).

Finally, in their answers to the first question, the students seemed comfortable with the mechanics of creating a scatter plot (see Vito's response in Figure 6–9 on page 128).

Other students mentioned scaling the axes and described graphing a point.

In all these answers the students related their understanding of mathematical concepts to the context of the backpack activity. I believe these real-world associations will help students recall and internalize those mathematical concepts and, ultimately, be able to apply them in new situations.

However, one written response to the first question implied that the student had made an incorrect conclusion (see Figure 6–10 on page 128).

Although Mary's error in thinking surprised me, her writing gave me the opportunity to revisit the conclusion with her in an individual conference. This is an important advantage of having each student explain her or his thinking in sentences or paragraphs: teachers can find out about errors in

FIGURE 6-7 Jemma's response

> They could see that you can graph two things by using this type of graph. You can show your estimate and the actual answer for a backpack with just one dot as they should notice.

FIGURE 6-8 Nashalie's response

> In a scatter plot you can tell whether there is a correlation between the two things you are graphing. In my scatter plot there seems to be a correlation between actual and estimated weights (ha, ha) because, not to brag, the dots are close to the imaginary matching line, as anyone can tell.

FIGURE 6–9 Vito's response

> They can tell the two coordinates for each point are found along the x-axis and the y-axis. The x part represents how much our backpacks weigh and the y part represents the estimate.

FIGURE 6–10 Mary's response

> When looking at the scatter plot they should know that the higher points are the heavier backpacks and the lower points are the lighter backpacks.

thinking before they solidify in a student's mind and perhaps serve as the foundation for further misunderstandings. In her answers to a few questions that I asked Mary about her scatter plot, she concluded that a "high point" in the plot showed a large estimate instead of a large actual weight. She also noted that such estimates were given more often for the heavier backpacks and therefore "appeared mostly in the right half of the scatter plot."

The answers to the second question ("What should a person know by looking at the points and line you added later to your scatter plot?") were much more detailed. The students' writing indicated that graphing the $y = x$ line really helped them clarify some mathematical ideas and establish a benchmark for graphs of related situations. Typical of the responses was the one by Hector (see Figure 6–11).

Students focused on different details. Brigit, for example, included both a verbal and a pictorial description for the graph of $y = x$ (see Figure 6–12).

Few of the students gave many details about the function $y = x$. However, the writing of the class as a whole indicated that the students seemed to have gained at least a beginning level of understanding about the benchmark function and how it might help them interpret a scatter plot of this sort.

Several of the students, like Hector, wrote responses that articulated a deeper understanding than I expected (see Figure 6–13).

For the final question ("What are the main things you learned from

FIGURE 6–11 Hector's response (Part One)

**Bulging
Backpacks**

129

> When I added the y=x line to the scatter plot it was much easier to figure out how good I guessed and were the guesses too high or too low. With this line a person could figure out if you are a high or low guesser and if you had any perfect guesses.

FIGURE 6–12 Brigit's response

> If your guess and actual answer were the same then your dot would be on a diagonal line 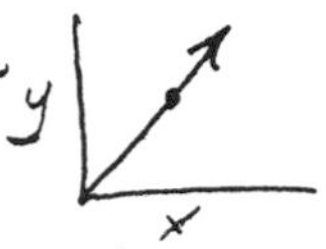
>
> This line is called y = x and helps you see perfect guesses. It also divides the estimates that were too high from the ones that were too low.

FIGURE 6–13 Hector's response (Part Two)

> I also learned that you can make rules for some points on this kind of graph. If you had all perfect guesses, the rule is estimate = actual weight and if you were 2 pounds too high on every one, then the rule is estimated weight = actual weight + 2 or y = x+2.

this activity?"), student answers were quite varied. Many wrote several paragraphs that included a wide range of observations. In varying proportions, the students described the activity, discussed their personal results, and explained the mathematics involved. In general, the writing left the impression that all the students had gained new understandings through the lesson. Leah's answer gives the flavor of most responses (see Figure 6–14 on page 130).

As usually happens, the student writing expressed some thinking I didn't expect. One of the most powerful mathematical ideas related to this lesson was expressed by Terrence (see Figure 6–15 on page 130).

I had Terrence share that part of his answer with the class and rein-

FIGURE 6–14 Leah's response

> I learned what a coordinate is and what a scatter plot is. Also that you can tell what type of guesser you are by how close your points are to the line of perfect guesses, y=x. The line of perfect guesses goes from zero diagonally up where the two parts of the point (coordinates) are the same. The first three estimates were way off because we didn't know how to do it. I think my scatter plot tells I'm a pretty good guesser because my points are pretty close to the line of perfection.

FIGURE 6–15 Terrence's response

> I learned how to tell how good a guesser I was by using dots or pairs of coordinates. I think that having a drawing or graph shows the same information as the numbers, but in a different way, and it can help you understand what the numbers really mean.

forced his observation that a graph can often make interpreting data easier. I had not really verbalized this point during the lesson. Thank you, Terrence!

I also think it is important that only Daniel wrote *I learned to estimate weights better in the future.* While many students noticed that they got better at making guesses for the weights of backpacks during the activity, only Daniel mentioned applying this learning in future situations. Since one of my objectives was to help students establish benchmarks for estimating the weights of objects, Daniel's writing was a signal to me that I need to do a better job with this part of the lesson in the future.

The student writing also provided ideas for ways I could increase the effectiveness of the lesson. And, as is often the case, the student writing provided a springboard for me to help students clarify their thinking. For example, Marianna's paper included the paragraph shown in Figure 6–16.

This answer indicates that Marianna's mathematical thinking was very sound in some important ways: she recognized the connection between the numerical and visual representations for points on a graph, and she had a strong sense of how to interpret the real-world meaning for each kind of point on her scatter plot. At the same time, however, she did not grasp how $y = x$ could be a rule for exact estimates.

In Marianna's case (and similarly with other students), a follow-up conversation with her would most likely add significantly to the mathematics she gained through this lesson. She simply didn't connect the $y = x$ line to the rules she had made for herself. Without the writing, I most likely would not have been aware of this slight, but significant, gap in her understanding.

These paragraphs and others by the students in this class reminded me of the importance of getting written feedback from every student as often as possible. The information we as teachers can gain from such writing is invaluable in assessing our teaching, as well as the learning that is going on, and in highlighting incomplete or inaccurate ideas students have.

I believe that this lesson fostered the development of algebraic thinking.

I am confident that, over time, students will develop an intuitive understanding of correlation and functions through numerous similar experiences.

FIGURE 6–16 Marianna's response

I don't agree that there is a 'rule' for perfect guesses. There were all kinds of backpacks and all kinds of books inside. I did notice the connection between the numbers and the graph. For example, I made the following rules for myself:

① far to the right and high = accurate
② far to the right but low = low estimate
③ far to the left but high = over estimate
④ far to the left but low = accurate
⑤ middle and low = low estimate
⑥ middle and middle = accurate
⑦ middle and high = over-estimate

Using these rules made it easier for me to read my graph.

Students can do investigations similar to the *Bulging Backpacks* lesson to compare estimates and actual values for many different situations, including the following:

- Numbers of candies in bags
- Lengths of pieces of string
- Heights of people

In each such investigations, the following strategies may be appropriate:

1. When all students have completed their scatter plots, ask them to analyze the graphs. Be sure the following questions are answered:

   - Did you estimate the correct amount at least once? If so, describe the location of the coordinate(s) on the scatter plot.
   - Was your estimate too large at least once? Too small? Describe the location of the coordinate(s) on the scatter plot.
   - Overall, did you do a good job of estimating? How does the scatter plot reflect your answer?
   - (If appropriate) What does it mean if there are several coordinates in a horizontal line? A vertical line?

2. Now ask students what the scatter plot would look like if someone accurately estimated every actual value. If the students are graphing by hand, have them use a different color to plot those points, then elicit the function rule for the line $y = x$. If they are using calculators, elicit the function rule for the line, then have them enter it in the $y =$ menu and graph it on the screen along with the scatter plot. If students have difficulty stating the function rule, the following questions may help:

   - Do the new coordinates you just graphed form a line? Describe that line in relation to the x- and y-axes. (A diagonal line, equidistant from the axes, that bisects Quadrant I.)
   - For each value of x, how does the corresponding y value compare? (The same value.)
   - If one of your estimates was too high, where is the coordinate for that point in relation to the line we just plotted? (Above the line.)
   - If one of your estimates was too low, where is the coordinate for that point in relation to the line we just plotted? (Below the line.)

3. Relate the graph of $y = x$ to a discussion of benchmarks. Explain to students that they will want to remember what the graph of $y = x$ looks like when they are analyzing or predicting the graphs for other similar functions.

4. If appropriate, follow up with questions similar to the following:

   - In relation to the $y = x$ line, what do you know about the location of the coordinate in this activity for a person whose estimate was two more than the actual value? (Two units above the line.) What is the function rule for the set of coordinates for all estimates that are two larger than the actual value? ($y = x + 2$)

- In relation to the $y = x$ line, what do you know about the location of the coordinate in this activity for a person whose estimate was three less than the actual value? (Three units below the line.) What is the function rule for the set of coordinates for all estimates that are three less than the actual value? ($y = x - 3$)

Of course, students should investigate some sets of data for which there is no linear relationship, as well.

More patterns appropriate for use in lessons similar to *Bulging Backpacks* can be found in *Navigating Through Algebra in Grades 6–8* (Friel et al. 2001, 10–12) in the section "Growing Patterns."

The Carnival Game | Extension Problem

The Carnival Game

In the carnival game, you are asked to drop coins into a vase from a distance that is at least 18 inches above the vase. To win a prize, your coin must land inside the vase. You notice that very few people are winning prizes. Conduct an experiment to investigate this type of situation.

Work with a partner. Find a vase with a small opening at the top. One person measures the height above the vase while the other drops the coins. Use any coin and drop the coin from 6 inches, 8 inches, 10 inches, and so on, up to 24 inches above the vase, trying to make the coin land inside the vase. Do ten trials at each height and then swap roles with your partner. Make a table and record the total number of times out of twenty that the coin lands in the jar for each height. Graph your data. Be prepared to report and explain your findings to the class.

Materials

- Vase with small opening
- Yardstick or meter stick
- Coin
- Paper for recording data and graphing results

In this lesson, students' scatter plots should show a negative correlation between the x variable (height in inches) and the y variable (number of coins that land in the vase).

Students should compare results for different coins as well as those for different vases. Finally, they can compare and contrast the results to those found in the *Bulging Backpacks* lesson.

POSSIBLE FOLLOW-UP

It is challenging for students to design the height from which the coin should be dropped for a "fair" game of this sort and defend that design to their classmates.

Graph the Estimates and Actual Weights in the Class Scatter Plot with a TI-73

There is much controversy about the weight of student backpacks. Recent research indicates that a student's backpack should not weigh more than 10 percent of a student's body weight. You can visit the Web site *www.learningspace.org/teach_learn/lplan/library/Muse* to find a lesson relating to this recommendation. Several related Web sites are listed there as well.

After the *Bulging Backpacks* lesson, students are often interested in comparing the estimates they made with the actual weights of the backpacks in a different way. This can be done in several ways. One way is to use a graphing calculator to create two box-and-whisker plots, one for estimates and one for actual weights.

Clear any data in the lists (L_1 and L_2) you wish to use, using the following keystrokes:

To clear data in ALL lists:

1. Press **2nd MEM.**

2. Choose **#6 ClrAllLists.**

3. Press **ENTER.**

4. On the Home screen, press **ENTER** again. You should see **Done** on your calculator screen.

To clear data in L_1 and L_2 only:

1. Press **LIST.**

2. Press the **up arrow key** to move up until you are on top of the L_1.

3. Press **CLEAR.**

4. Press **ENTER.** You should see the L_1 list clear.

5. Use the **right arrow key** to move over to L_2 and repeat Steps 2, 3, and 4 to clear L_2.

Enter your lists using the following keystrokes:

1. Press **LIST.**

2. Enter the estimates in L_1. Press **ENTER** after each number.

3. Enter the actual weights in L_2. Press **ENTER** after each number.

4. You can scroll up or down your lists using the **up** and **down arrow keys.**

Your calculator screen should look somewhat like the following illustration:

L1	L2	L3 3
11	8	------
14	8.5	
10	10.5	
13	11.5	
14	12	
12	12.5	
	13	

L1(7) =16

To create two box-and-whisker plots to display your data on the TI-73, use the following keystrokes:

1. Press **2nd PLOT.**

2. Choose **#1 Plot 1.**

3. Press **ENTER** on **ON.**

4. Arrow down to **Type.**

5. Arrow over once to the **box-and-whisker icon** 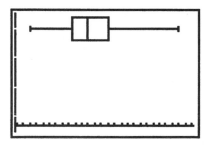 and press **ENTER.**

6. Arrow down to **Xlist.**

7. Press **2nd STAT** and choose L_1

8. Press **ENTER**

9. Be sure **Freq** is set to 1.

10. Set the viewing **WINDOW** or press **ZOOM** and choose **#7 ZoomStat.**

Your box-and-whisker plot for estimates should look somewhat like the following illustration:

Press **TRACE** and use the **right** and **left arrow keys** to see the values for each quartile, as shown:

Repeat the steps above to display the actual weights (L_2) in a box-and-whisker plot in Plot 2 (use #2 **Plot 2**). Display both plots as shown:

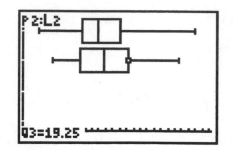

As in this case, students' estimates will often have a significantly larger range than the actual weights of the backpacks. You can also graph a modified box-and-whisker plot to check for outliers and compare the statistics for estimates and actual weights with the calculator. (See TI-73 manual for these directions.)

Who Finishes When?

OVERVIEW

In this lesson students solve a problem using different strategies. They share their solutions and explain their thinking, providing their classmates with opportunities to become more comfortable with multiple representations. Then the students work together to find a graphic solution for the problem and compare that solution to their other representations.

This lesson is intended to increase students' facility with multiple representations. It also should help them develop an understanding of the connections between them; for example, how a graph displays the same information as a table. Hopefully, they can begin to see points on a graph as representing a relationship or function, not just as individual points. In addition, by comparing multiple representations students should begin to internalize the meaning of such concepts as *intercept* and *slope*.

BACKGROUND

The students in this eighth-grade class had substantial experience solving nonroutine problems using different strategies. They had shared their solutions and their thinking. However, they had not focused on the links between the multiple representations in their solutions. Nor had they solved such problems using a graph. They had studied functions primarily as generalized rules for patterns, not as representations of real-world situations. They had not been introduced to intercept or slope.

PREREQUISITE CONCEPTS OR SKILLS

- Recognizing and describing, extending, and generalizing visual and numerical patterns
- Finding iterative and explicit rules for patterns
- Working with linear functions and their rules (optional)
- Graphing on the coordinate plane (Quadrant I only)

VOCABULARY

coordinates, dependent variable, equation, explicit rule, function, independent variable, intercept, linear function, multiple representations, scatter plot, slope

TIME

The lesson was completed in one ninety-minute class. If your classes are only forty-five to sixty minutes long, the students will likely only be able to find individual or paired solutions for the problem and create appropriate graphs on the first day of class. Interpreting their graphs and finding connections between the graphs and other representations will probably require a second day, with some groups able to complete their individual paragraphs. Alternatively, students can offer alterations or extensions of the problem during the second day and write the individual paragraphs at home.

MATERIALS

- *Who Finishes When?* activity sheets, 1 per student (see Blackline Masters)

- 1 sheet of graph paper per student

- Blank transparency film and pens

The Lesson

Who Finishes When?

Students were presented with the following problem:

Who Finishes When?

Alice's walking rate is 2.5 meters per second. Her younger brother, Mack, walks 1 meter per second. Because Alice's rate is faster than Mack's, Alice gives Mack a 45-meter head start in a 100-meter race. What happens in the race?

Explain your strategy for solving this problem and give evidence to support your answer.

I chose a problem that I felt would not be threatening to any of the students and that might be solved in a variety of ways. I hoped all of the students in the class would produce at least a partial solution so they could increase their confidence and expand their thinking during the later parts of the lesson. I also worded the problem in an open-ended manner in order to encourage solutions involving multiple representations. This was important because I wanted to help students establish the relationships between the different representations for this problem and, hopefully, help them begin to generalize those findings. I find that an essential part of the success of many lessons is carefully choosing a context or problem that will accomplish the specific objective I have in mind while providing a rich mathematical experience for the students as well.

Students were allowed to collaborate in solving the problem if they wished. I offered the students no guidance about how they were to solve the problem because I wanted as many different strategies and representations as possible for the students to compare later in the lesson. I circulated around the room to answer student questions, but almost all the students were engaged in finding a solution on their own or with a partner.

The majority of the students drew a diagram to help them solve the problem. Essentially, many drew and marked off a horizontal or vertical number line to represent 100 meters, designated starting positions for Alice and Mack, and depicted in some pictorial manner the details of the race. Even most of the students who relied primarily on another method to solve the problem started with a rough sketch of the problem situation. As they were working, students noticed and commented that using a diagram generally took more time than other methods used by their classmates. When later asked why they chose to use a detailed diagram despite the extra time required, students indicated that they were more comfortable with this strategy. They were very willing to corroborate their answer by using a different approach, but clearly had more confidence in using a visual depiction of the problem on which to base their solution. I have found this preference to be common among middle school students, perhaps because they have had little experience using tables, equations, and graphs. It is one of the reasons I have students share solutions—so they can gradually become comfortable with what are often more efficient problem-solving strategies.

During this part of the lesson, only one group asked for help. They were trying to use two TI-Explorer calculators to simulate the problem but were uncomfortable with the solution they got, even when they repeated the process a second time. I asked to watch and listen while they worked through the process again and Casey willingly began to demonstrate. The students had used the constant functions on the calculators, one set at +1 for Mack and the other at +2.5 for Alice. Casey explained that they chose those numbers because Mack went 1 meter per second and Alice went 2.5 meters per second. I nodded. "We set their starting points and pressed the constant key on both calculators at the same time until someone got to one hundred. We get that Alice won the race in forty seconds but Mack was right behind her at ninety-five meters, and that doesn't seem right because she was going about twice as far as he was and more than twice as fast."

I indicated that their strategy was sound, but agreed with their conclusion that Mack seemed a little too close behind Alice at the finish and asked them to start once more. "Tell me every step," I said. They gave the following demonstration:

Comment	Display on Calculator #1 (Mack)		Display on Calculator #2 (Alice)	
Since Mack went one meter per second, we set the constant on this calculator at **plus one**.	CONS +	1		
Since Alice went two and a half meters per second, we set the constant on this calculator at **plus two and five tenths**.			CONS +	2.5
Since Mack started at fifty-five meters, we entered his starting value as **fifty-five**.	CONS +	55		
Since Alice started at the starting line, we entered her starting value as **zero**.			CONS +	0
Then we pressed the constant key on both calculators at the same time over and over (forty times!) until the calculator for Alice showed **one hundred**.	CONS + **40** **95**		CONS + **40** **100**	

When I saw that the students started Mack at 55 meters, I thought they had confused his head start (45 meters) with the number of meters he had to travel in the race (55 meters). But when I asked, "Why did you use fifty-five as the starting point for Mack?" the students realized they had merely misread the problem. Too many times I have not been patient enough to let students find their own error: it was delightful to let them discover that their number sense and reasoning were sound and their error was only a very minor one!

When everyone indicated he or she had a solution, I asked for a volunteer to present his or her findings using the overhead projector. Claire drew a diagram and explained her thinking (see Figure 7–1).

"First, I found the time it would take for each person to travel one hundred meters. Alice would take forty seconds to walk one hundred meters because she traveled two and a half meters per second. It would take Mack one hundred seconds to go one hundred meters. Since Alice gives Mack a

FIGURE 7–1 Claire's solution

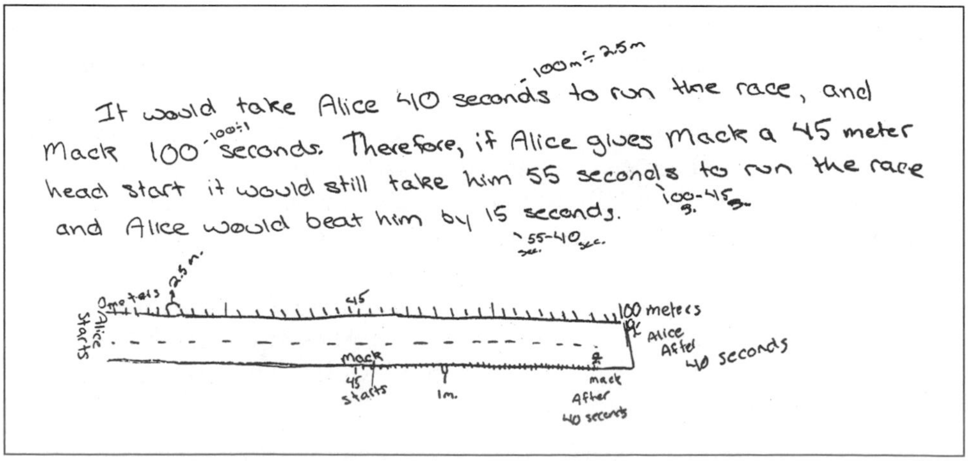

forty-five-meter head start, it would take him fifty-five seconds to run the race and Alice would beat him by fifteen seconds (fifty-five minus forty)."

All around the room there were nods as students realized that Claire's answer was the same as theirs. Claire's explanation seemed to reflect an understanding of rates, but I felt her explanation was not detailed enough for other students to follow her steps, so I asked her to explain her calculations and the thinking behind them again. She said, "To find the time it would take for Alice to finish the race, I divided the distance she had to go (one hundred meters) by how fast she could go in one second (two and one-half meters), and that gave me forty seconds. I did the same for Mack (I divided one hundred meters by one meter per second). Since Mack had to go fifty-five meters, which took fifty-five seconds, Alice would win by the difference (fifteen seconds) in their times." From this expanded explanation, I was satisfied that Claire had solved the problem using a diagram and an understanding of rates. When asked whether she had anything to add, Claire said, "If Mack had a friend who could hold Alice down for more than fifteen seconds, he could have won the race." We all had a chuckle!

Next I asked whether other students worked the problem like Claire did. Most students raised their hands. This poll told me that the students in the class were largely relying on a single method for solving this problem, a numerical method that is hard to generalize into a strategy that works in many situations. At this point, I hoped the students would have the opportunity to see a variety of strategies from their classmates.

Actually, several individuals and pairs used a variation of Claire's method.

Anna and Jose volunteered that their method was slightly different from Claire's. Jose explained, "We noticed that Alice gains one and a half meters on Mack every second. So it would take Alice forty-five meters divided by one and five-tenths meters per second, or thirty seconds, to erase the head start. We knew Alice must win." When asked to compare the two solutions, Jose offered, "We found something out that Claire did not: exactly when Alice caught up with Mack. But we did not figure out how much time Alice would win by, so both methods tell something different."

Pat and Marco used a different variation (see Figure 7–2).

"We worked the problem the same way as Claire, but we also noticed that Alice was walking two and a half times faster than Mack, so she would have needed to walk two and a half times as far just for a tie. Since she didn't walk

FIGURE 7–2 Pat and Marco's solution

Person	Distance to Run	Walking Speed	Time it will take to Finish
Alices	100 meters	2.5 meters per sec	$100 \div 2.5 = 40$ sec
Mack	55 meter	1 meter per sec	$55 \div 1 = 55$ sec

Alicia would win the race because she can run 2.5 times faster then Mack, and even though mack got a 45 meter head start, thats not enough because Alicia would have to run 2.5 times more in distance to just be tied.

that far, she must win." Thus, while Claire used a diagram to support her calculations, Pat and Marco used a different way of reasoning to support their answer. I always encourage my students, once they have found a solution, to work a problem in a different way to be sure they get the same result. I feel it is a good way to confirm or check their answers, and it promotes making connections between multiple representations. Also, practically speaking, it gives the students who get a solution quickly a constructive way to use their time while waiting for others to finish. In multistage problems, this technique also helps students avoid using an incorrect answer to the first stage as the basis for the remainder of the problem.

Chessie said she used the same method. "I just wrote mine down a little different," she said. "For Alice, I wrote two point five x equals one hundred, and for Mack I wrote one x equals fifty-five even though I didn't really need an equation for Mack since you know it takes him one second to walk each meter. Each x stands for the number of seconds needed to finish the race. After that, my solution is the same: Alice's x equals forty and Mack's x equals fifty-five, so Alice wins by fifteen seconds." I pointed out that, while their thinking was the same, most people would consider the methods different since Chessie had used equations in her solution. Actually, I was glad someone had used equations since some students initially have difficulty understanding the difference between this kind of equation, $2.5x = 100$, in which the variable represents one value we want to find, and a function rule, $y = 2.5x$, in which the equation represents a relationship and the variable can have different values. If no student had used equations, I would have used questions to elicit appropriate equations for this problem in order to point out this important difference.

I asked for someone who worked the problem a different way to explain his or her solution to the class. Brittany volunteered.

Brittany used proportions to solve the problem (see Figure 7–3). She explained to the class, "To solve this problem you need to figure out how many seconds it takes Alice to walk one hundred meters when she walks two and a half meters per second. You also need to know how many seconds it takes for Mack to walk fifty-five meters (he has a forty-five-meter head start) when he walks one meter per second. To do this I solved proportions with the amount of seconds they walked as x."

FIGURE 7–3   Brittany's solution

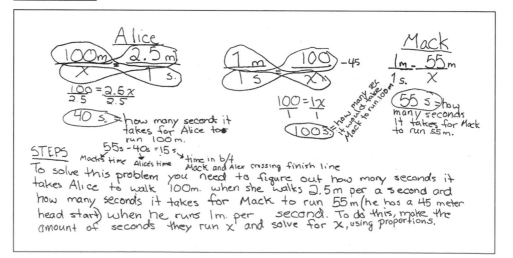

I asked the students whether they remembered how proportions work and they all nodded. Despite this claim, I asked for a volunteer to explain using proportions to solve this problem. I did this because I wanted to be sure students made the connection between the "bare proportions" and the problem situation.

Caroline explained it this way: "We knew Alice walked two and a half meters per second and we knew the total distance she had to travel was one hundred meters, so we could use a proportion—two and a half meters over one second equals one hundred meters over x seconds $\left[\dfrac{2.5\text{m}}{1\text{sec}}=\dfrac{100\text{m}}{x\text{sec}}\right]$ to find the missing time since her rate stayed the same. When we found x, we had the time it took her to go one hundred meters. You could use the proportion one meter over one second equals fifty-five meters over x seconds $\left[\dfrac{1\text{m}}{1\text{sec}}=\dfrac{55\text{m}}{x\text{sec}}\right]$ to find Mack's time for going fifty-five meters, but you don't really need to since you just know that one over one is the same as fifty-five over fifty-five."

The final way that was presented by the students in this class was the use of a table. Chris and Valerie built a table showing the distances that Alice and Mack had traveled at the end of each five-second interval of the race (see Figure 7–4).

Having seen Chris working on a table, I had asked him to transfer it to a transparency for the overhead projector. I have found this an effective way for students to share their work with the class. Student-made transparencies save time, the projected transparencies are often easier to read than charts, and errors can be changed easily.

Pointing to the table Chris had copied onto the overhead transparency, Valerie explained to the class, "We knew that Alice walked two and a half

FIGURE 7–4 Chris and Valerie's solution

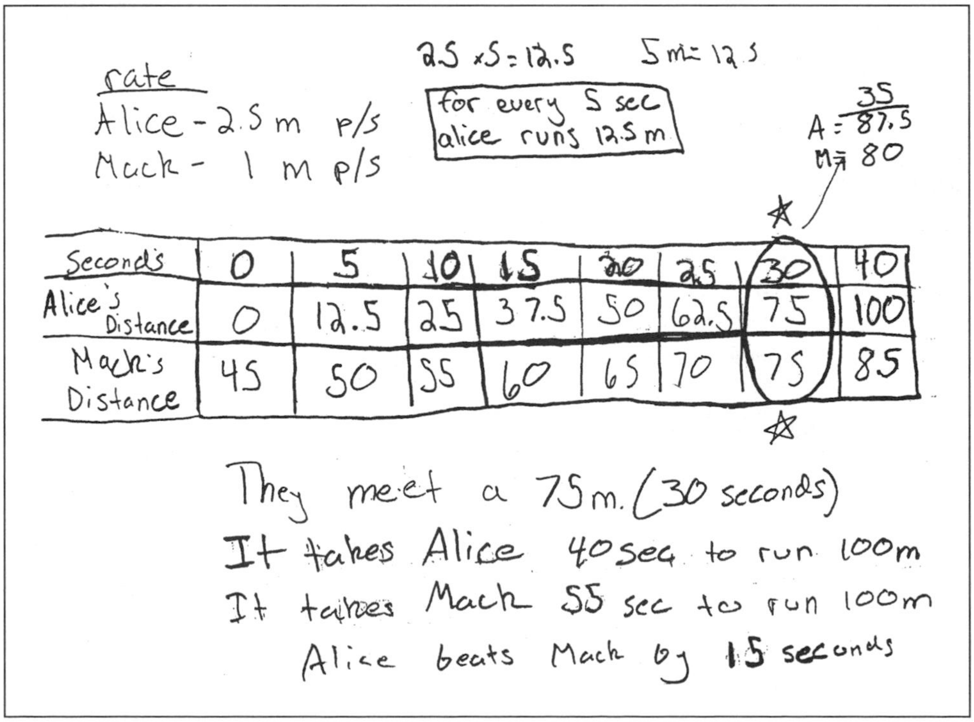

meters every second and Mack walked one meter every second. We decided to make a table to show the total distance each one had traveled after every five seconds. We used five-second intervals because we didn't want the table to be too big. You can see that Alice caught Mack in thirty seconds and that Alice won after forty seconds. You can also tell that it would have taken Mac fifteen more seconds to get to the finish line."

Liz asked, "How can you tell that Mac would need fifteen more seconds to finish?"

Chris explained, "Well, you can see that Mac is at eighty-five yards when Alice wins and, since he runs five meters every five seconds, it would take him fifteen more seconds to get to one hundred meters, the finish line." I asked Chris to extend his table so that it would be clear to everyone what he was saying. He did so and repeated his explanation.

Then I asked, "Liz, what does the sixty-five in Chris's table tell you?"

She answered confidently, "The sixty-five means Mack was at sixty-five yards after twenty seconds in the race." I asked this question to be sure Liz understood how to interpret the table. Often middle school students have difficulty understanding what the values in tables mean or how to connect them to the problem situation they represent.

When the students indicated that they had shared all the methods they used to solve the problem, I asked the class to work together to construct a graph that showed what happened in the race. I passed out graph paper to each student and Gia volunteered to do the drawing on the board. I projected a grid onto the whiteboard using a transparency on the overhead projector.

The students had constructed scatter plots in previous years. Perhaps based on those experiences, they quickly suggested using the x-axis for time in seconds and the y-axis for distance in meters. This group seemed to intuitively understand the idea of independent versus dependent variables, and that distance in this problem depended on time. However, I failed to explore this topic and lost an opportunity to enrich the lesson. Hopefully, next time I will include such a discussion.

On the whiteboard Gia traced over lines on the grid to indicate the axes, then labeled each one in intervals of five. I noticed later that some students chose different scales for their graphs, usually matching the intervals they had used in their original solutions. I asked the class how to show Mack's and Alice's positions at the beginning of the race. Valerie had no difficulty identifying (0, 45) as the point for Mack's initial position and (0, 0) as the point for Alice at the start of the race. When asked how those points fit with the problem, Liz offered, "Mack was at forty-five meters when the race had been going zero seconds and Alice had gone zero meters at zero seconds into the race." I wanted to be sure students who might be silently struggling heard the meaning of those important points linked to the problem situation again.

When Gia asked for a volunteer to call out the coordinates for Mack's progress during the race, Anna pointed out that Chris already had them in his chart, so Chris indicated (5, 50), (10, 55), (15, 60), (20, 65), (25, 70), (30, 75), (35, 80), and (40, 85). As Gia plotted the points on the board, Pat noted that all the points weren't really needed "to get the main idea," but most students included all of them on their individual graphs. Chris then called out the coordinates for Alice: (5, 12.5), (10, 25), (15, 37.5), (20, 50), (25, 62.5), (30, 75), (35, 87.5), and (40, 100), and Gia plotted these points as well (see Figure 7–5).

FIGURE 7–5 Gia's graph (Version One)

Who Finishes When? **145**

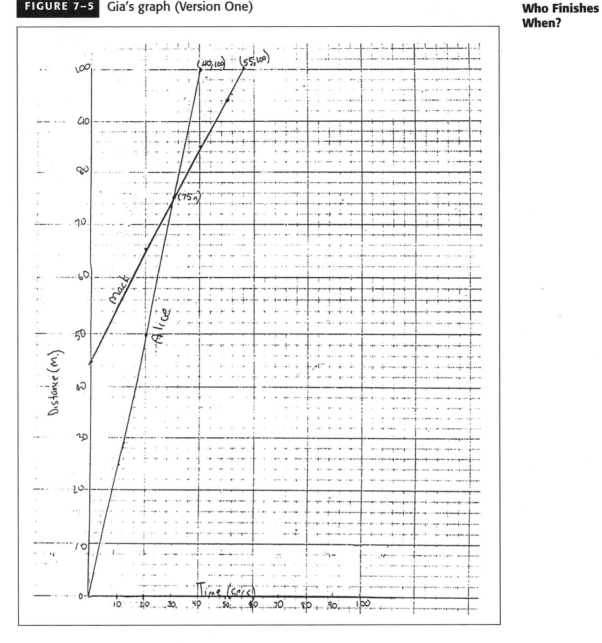

I asked the students to look at the graph, think about the problem they were given, and discuss with another student the answers to the following questions:

- How does the graph show where Mack and Alice started the race?

- What does the point (30, 75) show?

- How does the graph show who won the race?

- Which is steeper—the line for Alice or the line for Mack? Why?

- Is there anything else you notice about the graph?

After allowing a short time for pairs of students to consider the questions, I asked for their conclusions. Volunteers gave the following answers:

Question	Student Answers
How does the graph show where Mack and Alice started the race?	■ Both runners start at 0 seconds, so the points on the *y*-axis are the starting positions. ■ The lowest point for each runner on the graph is where they started. ■ The coordinates for each runner's starting point are 0 followed by the meter line. For Alice the point is (0, 0) because at 0 seconds into the race she was at the beginning, or 0 meters. For Mack the point is (0, 45) because at 0 seconds he was at the 45-meter mark.
What does the point (30, 75) show?	■ The lines cross where Alice caught up with Mack. ■ The lines intersect at (30, 75) because both runners were at 75 meters after 30 seconds.
How does the graph show who won the race?	■ The line for Alice reaches 100 meters (at 40 seconds) before the line for Mack does (at 55 seconds if he finished the 100 meters). ■ That Alice wins is shown by (40, 100), which means that after 40 seconds she crossed the 100-meter mark. Mack was only at 85 meters at that time, as shown by the (40, 85) point.
Which is steeper—the line for Alice or the line for Mack? Why?	■ Alice's line is steeper because she was going faster. ■ Alice's line is steeper because she went faster (2.5 meters/second) than Mack (1 meter/second).
Is there anything else you notice about the graph?	■ Mack would get to 100 meters 15 seconds after Alice, as shown by his final point being (55, 100) when hers was (40, 100). ■ The graph shows the same information as the table but it also shows a picture of what happened.

I was surprised that it seemed so easy for the students to interpret the graph, but I have repeated this lesson with several other groups of students and they, too, have seemed to have little difficulty at this point in the lesson understanding how the graph relates to the problem situation. My primary reaction was and is, "If only all algebra students came to us with this background!" I believe from my own experience and those I have read or heard about from other teachers that, in general, students who hear multiple solutions and representations for a particular problem find each subsequent method or representation relatively easier to understand. Thus, this class of students correctly viewed the graph as simply one more way to present the solution to the problem, with which they were quite familiar by this time.

Besides checking on students' initial understanding of the graph as it related to the context of the problem, I also asked the questions given previously in order to help students develop concepts associated with functions and their graphs. I believe working with real-world problems helps students view function rules and, later, algebra in general, as a way to help explain the world. Instead of abstract mathematical ideas that have little appeal to many students, I hope that our students will view functions and algebra as a language that can help them understand and explain things that happen in their everyday lives. Dealing with graphs based on a familiar situation helps students view functions as a representation of a relationship, in this case the relationship of time passed to the number of meters traveled. Concepts directly associated with graphs, like intercept and slope, are also built over time. By examining where the distances of the two walkers in meters appear on the graph at time zero, students had an initial experience with intercepts. By comparing the steepness of the two lines on the graph and thinking about what this aspect of the graph reflects about the problem it represents, students could begin to develop an understanding of slope.

Finally, with numerous experiences like this lesson, students can learn to reason about the quantities in many situations and how they relate to each other. They can learn to see the connections between different forms of representations—diagrams, words, tables, graphs, and symbols. They are able to picture the graph from the equation or the table, and vice versa. They think algebraically!

At this point in the lesson, because I was so impressed with the understandings about the graph that the students seemed to have, I decided to see how far the students could go. I asked the students to alter or add to the problem in some way and provide a solution for their new question. I explained that not everyone was required to get an answer for this extension, but I urged each student to try. As expected, not all students were able to offer an extension in the amount of time available, but selected answers are given in the following table.

Question	Solution
What if there were no head start?	Liz pointed out that Mack would have walked only 40 meters when Alice won if they had both started at 0 meters.
How long would it take Alice to erase the head start?	Pat showed the following calculation: $$\frac{45m}{1.5m \text{ gained/sec}} = 30 \text{ sec}$$ He pointed to the intersection of the two lines on the graph.
How can you make the race closer?	Nicholas concluded, *Mack could start somewhere between 45 and 60 meters for the race to be closer but Alice still to win.* He made a new table to show Mack starting at 50 and 55 meters.
How can you make the race a tie?	Gia added a simple statement to his original solution: *To make the race a tie, Mack should get a head start of 60 meters.* He added and labeled the line for this change on his graph and wrote *The lines are parallel on the graph because Mack has the same rate.* (See Figure 7–6.)

FIGURE 7-6 Gia's graph (Version Two)

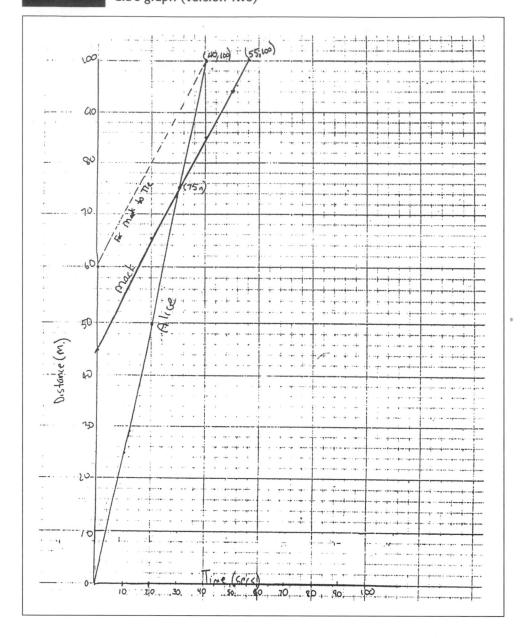

It is often tough to decide when to end a lesson. In this case, some of the students seemed to really be excited about the problem and had offered comments on their own about changing the problem situation. To support my position that "What if . . . ?" questions are invaluable learning opportunities, I took a few minutes to let students share ideas they had. When appropriate, I have students suggest such questions the next day; other times such questions are offered as out-of-class extensions.

As a culmination of the lesson, I asked each student to write a paragraph to explain how her or his own initial solution compared to the graphic solution. Generally, the students' writing revealed that they understood the connections between their initial solution and the graph. In most cases, they found aspects of the graphic solution that were not evident in their representation.

Eamonn wrote out his solution in words and drew a simple diagram (see Figure 7–7).

FIGURE 7-7 Eamonn's comparison

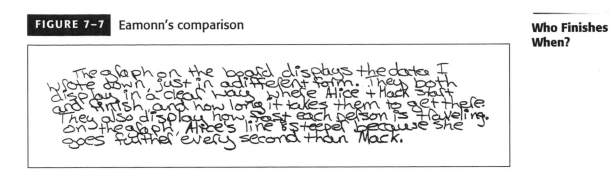

Eamonn wrote, *The graph on the board displays the data I wrote down, just in a different form. They both display in a clear way where Alice and Mack start and finish and how long it takes them to get there. They also display how fast each person is traveling. On the graph, Alice's line is steeper because she goes farther every second than Mack.* While Eamonn did not provide the reasoning behind his calculations in his paragraph, he did indicate an understanding of the common elements of the two solutions. Valerie pointed out that his original solution did not indicate in any way when or where Alice passed Mack. Eamonn countered that, while Valerie was correct, he believed his paragraph was a clearer explanation—that a person would have to know more to figure out the same things on the graph that he explained in his paragraph.

Anna showed her calculations for determining how many meters each racer covered in ten seconds and then she drew an elaborate diagram, showing the progress of the race every ten seconds (see Figure 7–8 on page 150).

Anna wrote, *I included the exact same information in my diagram as in the graph. For example, my diagram and the graph both show that at 30 seconds Mack and Alice are tied at 75 meters.* She omitted other ways her diagram and the graph were alike, so the class listed them. But the most interest was generated by the fact that Anna switched the axes on her graph from the way the class did it at the board (she used distance in meters along the x-axis and time in seconds along the y-axis). Several students were surprised when they noticed that the line representing Mack was now steeper than the one for Alice. After consulting with Gia, Anna explained, "On my graph you have to think that the lines show that each distance Alice traveled (moving sideways) compared to the number of seconds (moving up) was more than Mack's. I think the way the class did it gives a person a better picture of what really happened—except for my diagram, of course!"

Brittany used proportions to solve the problem (refer back to Figure 7–3). She made a chart to show the comparison of her solution with the graph (see Figure 7–9 on page 151).

Brittany acknowledged that the graph showed more information, but she said she believed her way was easier to understand for most people.

Chessie had used equations to solve the problem (see Figure 7–10 on page 151). In her paragraph Chessie explained, *The equations I used to solve the problems show up as points on the graph. For Alice, the point (40, 100) shows that she reached the 100m mark after 40 seconds. For Mack, the point (55, 100) shows that he would have reached the 100m mark after 55 seconds.*

Chessie's attempt to connect her equations with the graph gave me the opportunity to compare her equations with the function rules. I asked

FIGURE 7–8 Anna's original solution, graph, and comparison

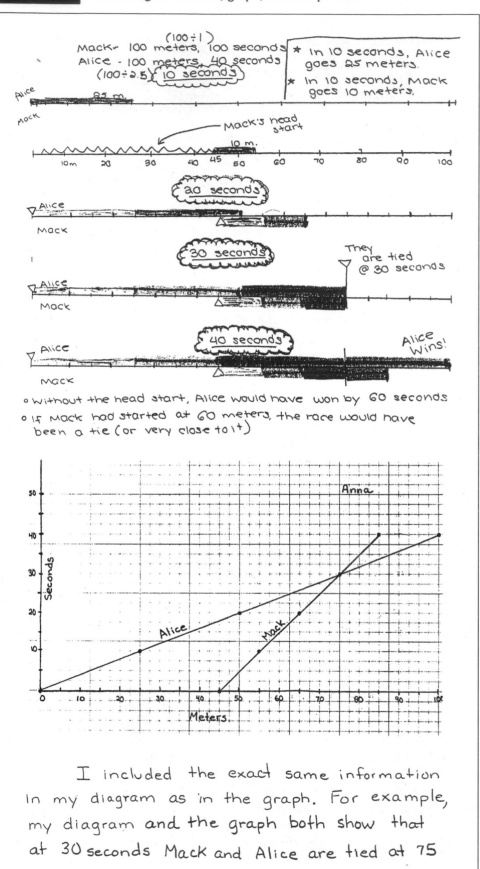

I included the exact same information in my diagram as in the graph. For example, my diagram and the graph both show that at 30 seconds Mack and Alice are tied at 75 meters.

FIGURE 7-9 Brittany's comparison chart

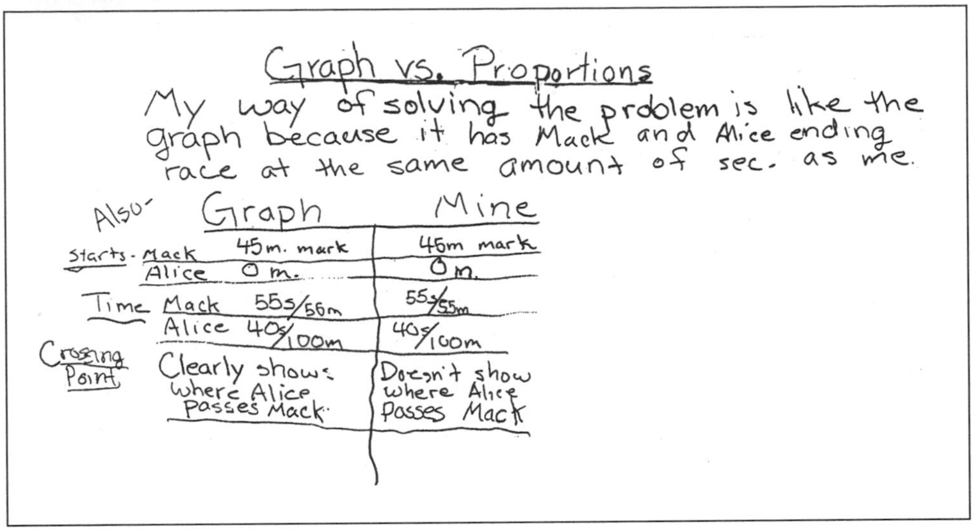

Graph vs. Proportions

My way of solving the problem is like the graph because it has Mack and Alice ending race at the same amount of sec. as me.

Also:	Graph	Mine
Starts - Mack	45m. mark	45m mark
Alice	0 m.	0 m.
Time Mack	55s/56m	55s/55m
Alice	40s/100m	40s/100m
Crossing Point	Clearly shows where Alice passes Mack.	Doesn't show where Alice passes Mack

FIGURE 7-10 Chessie's solution and comparison

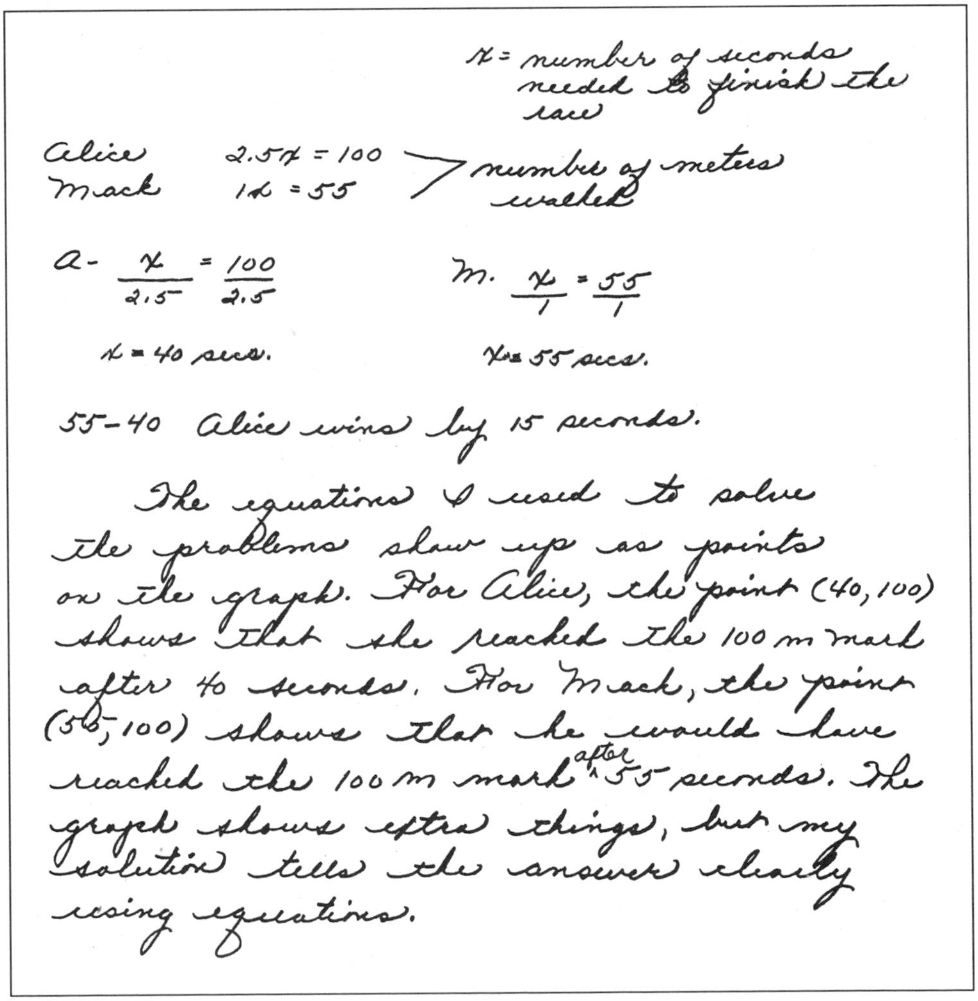

x = number of seconds needed to finish the race

| Alice | 2.5x = 100 | number of meters walked |
| Mack | 1x = 55 | |

a. $\dfrac{x}{2.5} = \dfrac{100}{2.5}$

x = 40 secs.

m. $\dfrac{x}{1} = \dfrac{55}{1}$

x = 55 secs.

55 - 40 Alice wins by 15 seconds.

The equations I used to solve the problems show up as points on the graph. For Alice, the point (40, 100) shows that she reached the 100 m mark after 40 seconds. For Mack, the point (55, 100) shows that he would have reached the 100 m mark after 55 seconds. The graph shows extra things, but my solution tells the answer clearly using equations.

everyone to look back at the line on the graph that showed Alice's progress in the race. I reminded students that the y values for their points represented the number of meters traveled and the x values represented the number of elapsed seconds. I asked whether anyone could use y and x to give a rule that would work for every point on Alice's line. Chessie herself was among the volunteers. She said, "Every y value tells the number of meters that goes with the x value (seconds) for that point."

I acknowledged that what she had said was correct, but again asked for a rule, using y and x, that would work for every point on Alice's line. Pat nearly jumped out of his seat to say, "Y equals two point five x!"

"Yes," I clarified, "for every value of x (number of seconds), the y value (distance) is x times two and a half. And how does that fit with the problem?"

Pat explained, "The number of meters Alice has walked is always two and a half times the number of seconds she has walked."

I elaborated to try to help students realize the important difference in the two equations. "Chessie's equation for Alice was a mathematical statement that enabled her to find one value for x. The equation y equals two and five tenths x shows the rule for each of the points on Alice's line and, more important, the *relationship* between Alice's distance and time." I reminded the students that such a relationship is called a function and that different values can be substituted for each of the variables.

I then asked if someone could provide a similar explanation for the differences between the equation Chessie used for Mack and the function rule for Mack as shown by the graph. Chessie started over several times but finally said, "My equation helped me find one value to know who won the race, but the function rule y equals x works for Mack at any point in the race. His distance traveled is always the same as his time. You can use different values for one of the variables and get the right values for the other variable because they always are paired."

I feel this is one of the most important parts of this lesson. In my experience, students grasp the concept of function best and fastest when working with real-world situations. Further, a grasp of functions is essential to understanding in algebra.

Chris and Valerie used a table to solve the problem (refer back to Figure 7–4.) They wrote the comparison shown in Figure 7–11.

At this point, I asked for a show of hands as to which students thought the table was easier to understand and which thought the graph was. The table method got a few more votes. Actually, I was surprised that the graph got as many votes as it did. I think it is the visual power of a graphical representation that makes it so appealing to students, but we teachers must recognize that most students need many experiences to learn to interpret graphs comfortably. I also think the votes would have been different if the class had not analyzed the graph together so extensively. There is a lot for students to take in when they first start graphing functions—even more so when comparing two functions!

Thus, this problem illustrates that words, diagrams, symbols (equations), tables, and graphs can all represent the same solution. I want my students not only to move freely among representations, but also to know how one representation translates into another. I realize that this objective will not be accomplished easily or quickly by some, but I am convinced that solving problems within real-world contexts and repeatedly using and relating multiple representations can provide the opportunity for all students to develop algebraic thinking.

FIGURE 7–11 Chris and Valerie's comparison

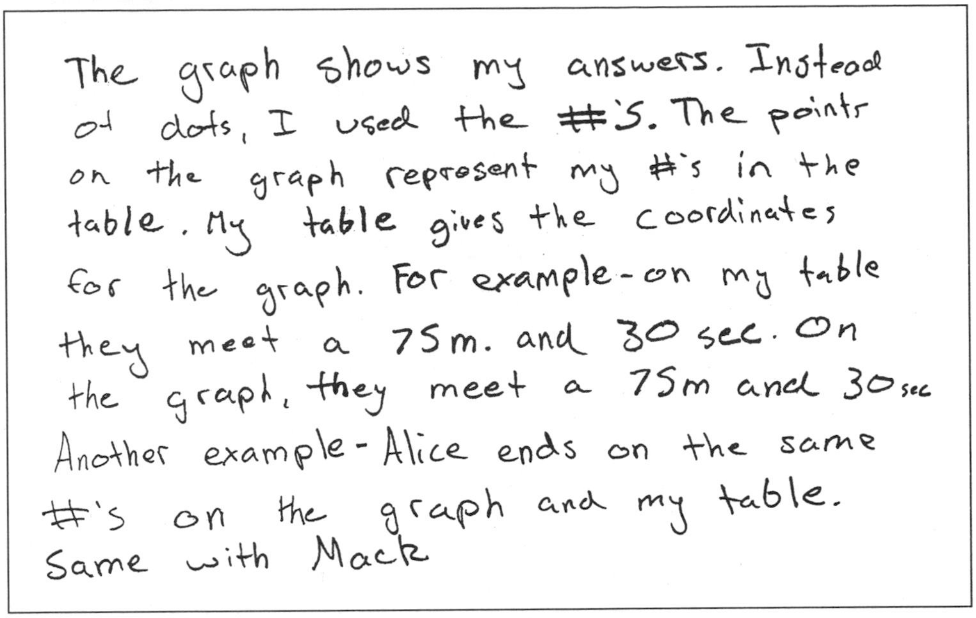

Who Finishes When? **153**

The graph shows my answers. Instead of dots, I used the #'s. The points on the graph represent my #'s in the table. My table gives the coordinates for the graph. For example—on my table they meet a 75m. and 30 sec. On the graph, they meet a 75m and 30 sec Another example—Alice ends on the same #'s on the graph and my table. Same with Mack

What Happens When?

Similar Problem

The following problem is appropriate for a lesson similar to *Who Finishes When?*

> Ann and Steve enjoy biking. Ann usually averages 10 miles per hour, while Steve averages 8 miles per hour. On a trip of 40 miles, Ann gives Steve a 30-minute head start. What happens during the trip?

Be sure students consider the following questions as they share solutions:

- How do the various solutions show the same information?

- How do the various solutions show different information?

- Which solution/representation do you think is the easiest to understand? Why?

- What change(s) could you suggest to make the problem more interesting?

More activities similar to *Who Finishes When?* can be found in *Navigating Through Algebra in Grades 6–8* (Friel et al. 2001). They are "Walking Strides" (25–26), "Stacking Cups" (41–43), and "Walking Rates" (44–45).

What's Going On?

Extension Problem

The following problem is appropriate for a lesson to follow *Who Finishes When?*

Consider the two lines on the following graph. Make up a situation the graph could represent.

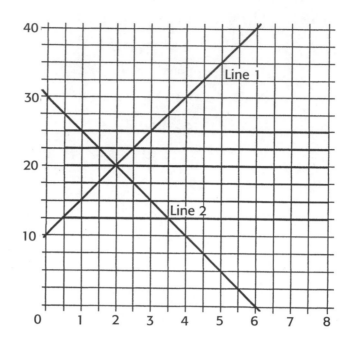

If appropriate, students can be given the following tasks and questions:

- Write a rule for each line.

- What do the rules mean in the situation you described?

- What are the coordinates of the points on the vertical axis?

- What do the plotted points on the vertical axis mean in the situation you described?

- What are the coordinates of the point on the horizontal axis?

- What do the plotted points on the horizontal axis mean in the situation you described?

- What is the point of intersection of the two lines?

- What does the point of intersection mean in the situation you described?

Other activities appropriate for use after *Who Finishes When?* can be found in *Navigating Through Algebra in Grades 6–8* (Friel et al. 2001). They are "Pledge Plans" (46–48), "Printing Books" (56–58), and "Comparing Video Rental Stores" (66–70). All involve emphasis on multiple representations and the connections between them.

Technology Connections

A nice follow-up activity for *Who Finishes When?* is to have the students use a TI-73 or another graphing calculator to create motion plots that match given time–distance plots displayed using an overhead ViewScreen calculator. For this activity, students use a CBR (Calculator-Based-Ranger) and an application that is available on such calculators.

First, students should investigate the effects of each of the following actions on a motion plot:

- Walking versus standing still

- Walking slower versus walking faster

- Walking toward the CBR versus walking away from it

For each round of this activity, a student briefly views a random time–distance plot displayed on the calculator. He or she then tries to walk in front of the CBR to create a matching graph while the CBR tracks and graphs the time passed along the x-axis and the distance from the CBR along the y-axis. Each time–distance plot can be displayed again if the student thinks he or she can better match the graph on a second try.

Example of time–distance plot displayed by CBR and corresponding student motion plot (dotted)

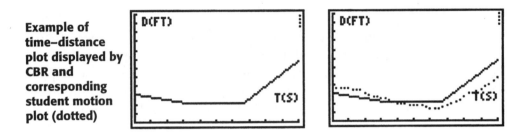

This activity is described in the article "Mission Possible! Can You Walk Your Talk?" by Iris D. Johnson (2000). You can also find this article in the "Readings" section on the CD that accompanies *Navigating Through Algebra in Grades 6–8* (Friel et al. 2001). A slightly different version of the activity is found in *Mathematics and Science in Motion: Activities for Middle School*, by Chris Brueningsen et al. (1997).

CHAPTER 8

Stretching Slinkies

OVERVIEW

In this lesson students set up an investigation and gather two sets of data. They record their data in a table and graph the data. They try to find approximate rules to fit the data sets, then share their rules and explain how they arrived at their answers. Finally, the students analyze, discuss, and write about the various representations and how they reflect what happened in the investigation.

This lesson is intended to provide students with experience with a hands-on investigation involving data gathering and recording, graphing of data, finding approximate function rules, and analyzing their findings. It should help students realize some of the challenges associated with gathering and analyzing real-world data. By comparing multiple representations (tables, graphs, and function rules) and connecting them to a real-world investigation, students should begin to internalize the meaning of such concepts as function, intercept, and slope. Overall, the lesson provides students with a powerful glimpse into how algebraic thinking can be used to describe and predict phenomena in the real world.

BACKGROUND

Prior to this lesson, the students in this seventh-grade class had a significant amount of experience extending visual and numerical patterns and finding iterative and explicit rules for those patterns. However, the patterns they had encountered each had a specific function rule and every value fit the rule exactly. Thus, they had studied functions primarily as generalized rules for consistent patterns, not as representations of real-world situations. They also had experience creating scatter plots, but had not been introduced to intercept or slope.

PREREQUISITE CONCEPTS OR SKILLS

- Recognizing and describing, extending, and generalizing visual and numerical patterns

- Finding iterative and explicit rules for patterns
- Working with linear functions and their rules

VOCABULARY

dependent variable, explicit rule, function, function rule, horizonal (*x*-) axis, independent variable, intercept, iterative rule, linear function, multiple representations, scale, slope, vertical (*y*-) axis

TIME

The lesson was completed in one ninety-minute and one sixty-minute class. Some student reflections were completed the following day. If your classes are only forty-five to sixty minutes long, the students will likely be able only to set up the experiment and gather and record data on the first day of class. Analyzing their data and finding approximate explicit function rules will probably require a second day, with some groups able to begin preparations for their presentation to the class. Group preparation and presentations to the class will fill most of a third day. Written reflections will probably need to be done at home or in class the following day.

MATERIALS

For each group of four students:

- 1 copy of *Stretching Slinkies, Version 1* or *Stretching Slinkies, Version 2* activity sheet per student (see Blackline Masters)

- Yardstick or meter stick

- Ruler

- Small paper cup

- 1 pipe cleaner

- 2 paper clips

- Small Slinky (party favor type—may be cut in half)

- 10 coins each of two different denominations

- 4 sheets of graph paper (1 for each student)

Gathering Data and Creating Multiple Representations | The Lesson

Students were asked to conduct the following investigation:

Set up your investigation as shown below.

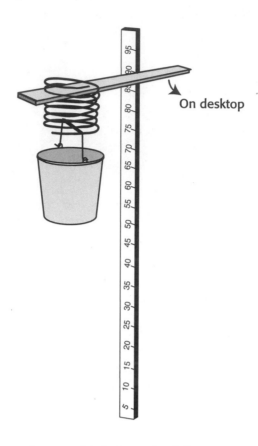

On desktop

As you set up the equipment, think about the following questions:

1. What will happen to the distance from the bottom of the cup to the floor as you add ten coins (for example, dimes) one at the time to the cup?
2. What will happen to the length of the cup plus the Slinky as you add ten coins (for example, dimes) one at a time to the cup?

Choose one of the questions above to investigate. Record your results. Then do the following steps:

1. Repeat your investigation with a different type of coin.
2. Graph the results of your investigations.

Find a rule for each type of coin you used to predict the length of the cup plus the Slinky for any number of coins.

I chose a relatively simple experiment so that students would not be intimidated. I also selected it because the measurements obtained by middle school students doing this investigation rarely provide exact function rules. At the same time, with careful measuring, the results are almost always consistent enough for students to make a reasonable approximate rule for those results. I felt that this lesson could provide students with a valuable experience in analyzing real-world data and with opportunities to practice and grow in their use of algebraic thinking.

Students collaborated in groups of three or four to carry out the investigation. None of the groups had problems with the basic set-up for the investigation. However, I realized that some of the offhand comments I overheard during that process could help standardize procedures. For example, Alex warned his group, "We'll need to be careful that the ruler stays flat on the desktop every time we measure." I heard several of this type of comment and decided it would be a good idea to have students share their ideas for techniques to use during the investigation. I felt this was important to do since I knew the accuracy of their measurements would significantly affect the students' ability to find a rule to coincide reasonably with the data. Thus, I stopped the students after they had spent a few minutes in their groups setting up the equipment, and they had a whole-class discussion. The class decided on the following guidelines for the measurement phase of the investigation:

- The ruler holding the Slinky should be kept flat on the desktop during all measurements.

- The bottom of the yardstick should remain firmly on the floor during measurements and the stick should be perpendicular to the floor ("straight up and down").

- The ruler should remain between the same coils of the Slinky for all measurements.

- The cup handle should remain between the same coils of the Slinky for all measurements.

- The bottom of the cup should be as level as possible for all measurements.

- No measurement should be taken until the cup was completely still (no swinging or bouncing).

- Two people should verify each measurement.

These seemed like good guidelines to me; unfortunately, according to later student comments, the students did not always follow their own guidelines. Still, I think it is important to let students help determine the guidelines for any investigation and to emphasize their importance to the reliability of the conclusions about the investigation.

Once the guidelines were established, each group chose which version of the investigation they would carry out: measuring the distance from the bottom of the cup to the floor or measuring the length of the cup plus the Slinky as they added coins to the cup. Roughly half the class chose each version. Each group also chose the two kinds of coins they wished to compare, and students began to measure. I circulated around the room to identify any problems and to answer student questions.

Most of the groups seemed to be gathering their data carefully. However, two groups were confused about exactly what they needed to measure and record. Paul's group decided to do the experiment measuring the total length of the Slinky and the cup as they added each coin. When I came to their group, the students in the group were discussing whether they were recording the correct information in their table (see Figure 8–1 on page 160).

The initial length of the Slinky plus the cup was 9 inches, and they recorded that length in their table. However, after that initial measurement, the students had recorded only the changes in length as they added coins to the cup. For example, for one penny, they had recorded the length in the chart as 3 inches, which was the difference between the length of the cup and Slinky with no coins and the length after one coin had been added. Af-

FIGURE 8–1 Paul's group's table

Number of Coins	Pennies Length	Pennies Length	Nickels Length
0	9 to 18 = 9"	9	9 >3
1	3	12	12 >3½
2	2 no!	14	15½ >3
3	2	16	18½ >3
4	1½	17½	21½ >2½
5	2	19½	23 >3
6		22 >2½	26 CUP HIT THE FLOOR
7		24 >2	
8		26	
9		26 CUP HIT THE FLOOR	
10		26	

ter the lengths for one through five coins had been recorded in this way, Paul realized that the table should contain the entire lengths of the Slinky plus the cup. His group had a brief discussion during which Paul easily convinced the other students that they were not recording the correct information, and then they constructed a new column and recalculated the values they had obtained thus far, as can be seen in the table. Such false starts are to be expected and students should learn to see them as opportunities to adjust rather than as mistakes. Essentially the same experience happened to the other group that started out recording the wrong information.

These incidents reminded me of one of the strengths of having students work in small groups. Often one of the students in the group realizes an error in procedure, calculations, or thinking as the group is conducting an experiment or working through a problem. Having my students question their techniques or find their own errors is an important goal of my math classes. If students are to become independent thinkers and problem solvers, I feel, it is important that the teacher not point out every mistake as it occurs but rather give the students the opportunity to discover such errors for themselves.

I do not, of course, think teachers should never help students discover mistakes. The other group that made the same error as Paul's group was starting to graph their data when I noticed that those students, too, had recorded only the changes in lengths rather than the total lengths. To help them avoid the considerable amount of time they would have to spend regraphing both sets of data, I simply asked the members of the group to explain what they had done so far. In the middle of explaining their procedure, Emmy exclaimed, "Oh, no . . . we just recorded the difference from the last length each time in our table. we should have written the whole length."

When asked "Why?" by another member of her group, Emmy replied, "When there were no coins in the cup we wrote down the whole length, and so we need to do that for each number of coins so we can see the same kind of thing—the same measurement—for each number of coins." The other members of her group agreed and they constructed a new table, using the changes in length they had recorded to figure and enter the total lengths for each number of coins. Emmy made another insightful comment as they were making the new table. "These changes we recorded in our first table will help us find the rule for each kind of coin," she observed. When no one in her group commented, I bit my tongue and waited for the students to figure out the significance of what Emmy had added. I knew that her observation would certainly come up again when the students were looking for a rule for each kind of coin to represent what happened in the experiment.

Once all the groups had recorded their data in tables (about thirty minutes later), I called the class back together to discuss the next part of the activity, graphing their findings. I asked the class to make suggestions about how the graphs should be constructed. Ron suggested that the "bottom line" should show the number of coins, 0–10, since "that's what we all have alike, and it's what you start with." I affirmed Ron's suggestion, adding that mathematicians usually graph the variable you are given on the horizontal axis and call it the *independent variable*.

Jillian added that the lengths from the floor or the total lengths of the cup plus Slinky should then be plotted along the y-axis. I concurred and added—for those students who might not remember—that the horizontal axis is often referred to as the x-axis and the vertical axis as the y-axis, although any names might be given to the variables in an experiment or problem. I also added that, since each length changed according to the number of coins in the cup, length in this situation would be called the *dependent variable*.

When I asked what else must be considered in constructing the graphs of the results, Heather contributed, "We have to number the axes."

"What do you mean?" I asked.

Heather responded, "The x-axis is easy. Just start at zero and move one or two spaces for each coin. The y-axis is harder. Each group might need to use different numbers. We should each look at our tables and see what lengths we found and fit them along the y-axis."

I felt like Heather needed to clarify her explanation, so I asked, "When you said 'move one or two spaces for each coin' along the x-axis, did you mean you can move over one space from zero to one, then two spaces for one to two, and so on?"

Heather looked horrified and practically shouted, "Oh, no! You have to decide whether you want to move one or two spaces for each coin, but it needs to be the same amount you move for each new coin." Then she added, "You need to do the same for the lengths—decide how to space them out according to the numbers you have, but make the spaces worth the same amount."

I nodded and asked, "What Heather has said is important in constructing graphs that will show a picture of what happened in your experiment. Can someone else repeat what Heather has said in your own words?"

Alex volunteered and stated, "We'll label the x-axis along the bottom with the number of coins, zero through ten, spacing the numbers out evenly. And we'll label the y-axis along the left side with the lengths in inches. Again we'll start with zero and go as high as we need to, but make sure the numbers are spaced out evenly."

"Does anyone know the mathematical term for 'spacing the numbers out evenly' along the axes?" I asked.

"Is it 'using a scale'?" Jason asked.

I affirmed that using a scale, in this case, simply meant spreading the range of numbers in the data evenly along each axis. I asked the students whether there were any further questions they needed to ask before constructing their graphs. Since there were no questions, I instructed them to construct their graphs in their groups and then look at their tables and graphs to find a rule to describe what happened for each kind of coin in their experiment.

I had two purposes for this whole-class discussion. Because these students had not had much graphing experience, I wanted to review the basics to help students avoid spending a significant amount of time constructing a graph incorrectly. I also wanted to emphasize the correct mathematical language that was appropriate for the task. Without making a pointed issue of vocabulary, I wanted to review (or to introduce, for some students!) the terms *x-axis, y-axis, independent variable, dependent variable,* and *scale* in the context of the experiment so that these terms would have concrete meaning for the students. I also led this discussion *prior* to the students making their graphs in order to encourage the use of such vocabulary as they worked together in their groups to construct appropriate graphs.

Students then went to work making their graphs. While they collaborated with their group members, each student made his or her own graph showing both sets of data. I required this because I felt the students in this class needed individual practice, since they had done little graphing on the coordinate plane and none for a situation like this experiment. Most of the students had little difficulty constructing their graphs. Tamara, however, did not look at both sets of data before scaling her *y*-axis, so she had to start over when she began to graph her second set of data because it was data for heavier coins and her graph would have extended beyond the page.

Although the class had not discussed the fact that the graph should indicate in some way which set of points matched which set of data, each group of students realized that this was needed. They chose a variety of ways (using different colors for the two sets of coordinates, using different marks, using written labels close to each set of points, etc.) to differentiate the two groups. I was pleased that the students did this and was reminded that overall class discussions should not limit students' creativity. In this case, I made a note to discuss this aspect of the graphs in the whole-class discussion but not to limit the students to a particular way of doing it.

As the students in each group completed their graphs, I asked each student to exchange with another member of the group to check the accuracy of each other's graphs. A few minor errors were found, but overall the graphs were done correctly. Checking for accuracy of the graphs was an important step before the students tried to find a rule for each set of data because I knew, from past experience, that some students would find their rules more easily from the graphs than from their tables. Inaccurate graphs would certainly impede this process!

Not surprisingly, the hardest part of the lesson for this class was finding the rules for each set of data. As I circulated among the groups I found that every group started by trying to determine how much one coin changed the distance they were measuring. This surprised me because, of course, there were several possible starting points for determining a general rule. I speculated that the students in this class were especially concerned about the amount of change from one step to the next because all of their past experiences with function rules had involved uniform changes. When I later asked the students why they chose to focus on this aspect of their data first, they verified my hunch. As Asad explained, "Whenever we found function rules before this experiment, the tiles or chips or numbers increased the same amount for each step. When we looked at our table, each coin did not change the length exactly the same amount. We knew we needed the amount of change in our rule so we had to decide what to do about that."

Heather explained it a different way. "When we looked at our table for quarters, the distance to the floor was four less inches each time we added a quarter for the first few coins. But some quarters *didn't* change the distance exactly four inches. On the graph, it was the same: for each new point we moved over two spaces, but we didn't always move down the same amount. At first, we weren't sure what to do about that."

It was fascinating to see the different solutions the groups found to this challenge. Some groups wanted to use what they considered a "mathematical rule" (as Keyonna worded it) to determine the values they would use for the amount of change caused by each coin. Alicia's group simply added the change each coin made and then found the mean of that change (see Figure 8–2).

FIGURE 8–2 Alicia's group's table and explanation

Number of Coins	Length of Slinky and Cup	
	Coin 1 Pennies	Coin 2 Quarters
0	15½ in	15½ in
1	17½ in.	21 in
2	19 in	24 in.
3	21½ in	29 in
4	23 in	31 in.
5	25 in	35 in
6	26½ in	36 in (Bottom)
7	28½ in	
8	30 in	
9	31½ in	
10	33½	

For every penny, it moved an average of 1.8 inches and didn't hit the floor. For every quarter it moved an average of 3.9" and it did hit the floor after 6 coins, therefore it could not move for 7th thru 10th coin. We did this by adding up the differences and dividing by the # of coins.

	Penny	Quarter
1	+2	+5½
2	+1½	+3
3	+2½	+4
4	+1½	+3
5	+2	+4
6	+1½	+½
7	+2	19½
8	+1½	
9	+1½	
10	+2	
	18"	

10)18   1.8

5)19 ½   3.9

Notice that this group included the last quarter they added to the cup in their list of changes until Alex pointed out, "It wouldn't be fair to include the sixth quarter because the cup hit the floor before it could go as far as it probably would have gone. You can tell by looking at all the others. We should use just the first five quarters to get our answer." The other students agreed to use the means—1.8 (for pennies) and 3.9 (for quarters)—in their rules.

Paul's group also used a mathematical average that they thought was appropriate to help them form their rules. They looked at all the changes in length (refer back to Figure 8–1) that occurred for a particular coin and decided to use the mode of those changes for their rule. As Keyonna said, "Since more pennies added two inches to the length than any other number, we think the rule for pennies should include 'two inches for each penny in the cup.' "

Some groups simply eyeballed their data to decide on the best value for the amount of change related to each coin. RJ explained his group's thinking: "We noticed that each dime usually made the Slinky (plus the cup) one and a half inches longer, and each quarter usually made the Slinky four inches longer. We just looked at the table and those numbers [one and a half and four] were kind of averages."

Similarly, Ron's group computed a few differences in the lengths from the floor and then, as Annie expressed it, "declared that the distance changed one and a half inches for most dimes and about two inches for each penny." (See Figure 8–3.)

FIGURE 8–3 Ron's group's data

# of dimes	distance from floor	# of pennys	distance from floor
0	22.5 inch.	0	22.5 inch.
1	21 inch.	1	20.5 inch.
2	19.5 inch.	2	18.5 inch.
3	18 inch	3	17 inch.
4	16.5 inch.	4	15 inch.
5	15 inch.	5	13 inch.
6	13.5 inch.	6	11 inch.
7	12 inch.	7	9.5 inch.
8	10 inch	8	8 inch.
9	8.5 inch.	9	6 inch.
10	7 inch.	10	4.5 inch

x	y		x	y	
0	22.5	-1.5	0	22.5	
1	21	-1.5	1	20.5	-2
2	19.5	-1.5	2	18.5	-2
3	18	-1.5	3	17	
4	16.5		4	15	
5	15		5	13	
6	13.5		6	11	
7	12		7	9	
8	10		8	8	
9	8.5		9	6	
10	7		10	4.5	

However, I noticed that Ron's group made separate tables of x and y values for each coin and used these tables to examine the changes in lengths. I was curious why they made a new table and why they chose to use that table when looking for rules. Jason said, "We made the new table so it would be easy to graph and because we could try to think about the variables instead of the coins." The other members of the group were quick to point out that it wasn't really necessary to make a whole new table but they felt it "helped us think about the graph." I immediately suspected that these answers indicated this group was more comfortable using variables than most of the other groups. This was supported by the fact that they had less difficulty than most groups using variables in their general rules.

Jillian's group was even more creative. After looking at their table of values, they chose a few select values to round to the nearest whole number (see Figure 8–4 on page 166). When I asked why the group had chosen to round those particular measurements, Carlos answered, "Mostly, the dimes went down by one and a half inches for each one and the nickels by three inches. We figured we must have messed up on a few of our measurements, so we tried changing a few of them a little and then our list is almost perfect!"

I discussed with the group that I thought their method of adjusting the data to find a good estimate for the "perfect" change in the lengths was appropriate. However, I reminded them that they should always record and report the original, not the altered, data as well as be able to explain their method for making sense of the inconsistencies in their original data.

Emmy's group was the only one that used their graph to examine the difference each coin made (see Figure 8–5 on page 167). Heather explained, "When we looked at our graph for quarters, each time we moved over one quarter [two spaces], the point usually went down four inches [eight spaces]. For the dimes, when we moved over one dime [again two spaces], the point went down about one and a half inches [three spaces]."

I asked Asif to explain how this information could help them make up a rule for any number of quarters or dimes. He said, "Well, from our graph (and tables, too) we know that each time you add a quarter to the cup, the distance to the floor goes down by four inches. And each time you add a dime, the distance goes down by one and a half inches. So our rules should be easy to write."

If only Asif had been correct! As I was circulating among the groups, it quickly became apparent that most of the groups had found some form of iterative rules but were struggling with finding explicit function rules to approximate their results. After a while, I asked the groups to share their iterative rules and their thinking to see whether hearing ideas from other students might help them make the transition to finding the explicit function rules.

We know that most middle school students naturally think iteratively: they build each new stage of a pattern based on the previous stage. I want my students to know that such rules are legitimate and useful in many situations. But I also want them to realize that they have limitations— primarily that you cannot use iterative rules to predict the value for any stage without knowing the value of the stage that immediately precedes it. As mentioned earlier, this class had numerous previous experiences

FIGURE 8–4 Jillian's group's tables

Dimes

# of coins	measurment
0	23. inches
1	21½ inches
2	20½ inches → 20
3	18½ inches
4	17 inches
5	15½ inches
6	13½ inches → 14
7	11¾ inches
8	10 inches
9	8½ inches
10	7 inches
11	5½ inches
12	4¼ inches → 4
13	2½ inches
14	1 inch.
15	floor level

Nickel

# of coins	measurement (floor in inches)
0	23 inches
1	20 inches
2	16½ inches → 17
3	13½ inches → 14
4	10 inches
5	6¾ inches
6	3½ inches
7	1¼ inches
8	Floor level

FIGURE 8–5 Emmy's group's graph

Stretching Slinkies **167**

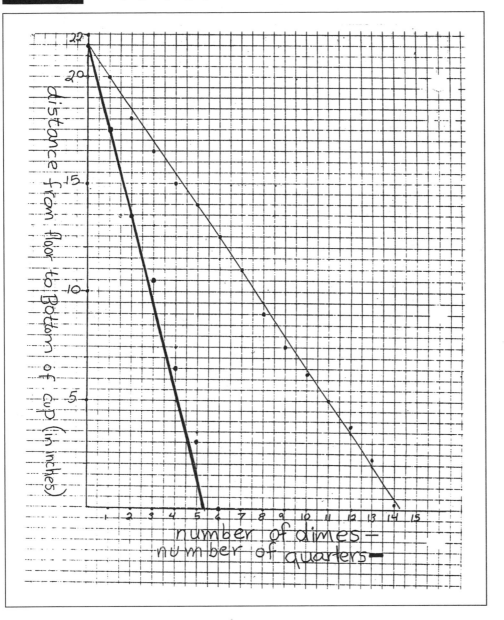

finding both iterative and explicit function rules for simple geometric or numerical patterns. However, in dealing with the real-world data, they seemed to get bogged down in finding a way to express the amount of change between stages in their rules and to be unable to recall the kind of thinking they had used for finding explicit rules in the past. Most groups had recognized some elements of the explicit rules, but none had "put them all together."

I considered dividing the class into two groups for this discussion, combining those who had chosen to measure the total length of the Slinky plus the cup (Alicia's, Paul's, and RJ's groups) and those who had chosen to measure the distance from the floor to the bottom of the cup (Ron's, Jillian's, and Emmy's groups). Instead, I decided to "go for it" and see whether the students could identify the information they needed for their explicit function rules after hearing all the presentations.

I made this decision because I avoid presenting my students with only one kind of problem, or one way a situation can occur, in a lesson or series of lessons. I remember all too well being presented with "mixture problems" as a completely separate entity from "age problems," and so on, and being anxious about trying to remember the "formulas" for "solving" each kind of problem. My primary goal is to help students learn to think mathematically. One way to foster this goal is to constantly offer more than one variation of a situation at the same time to help students recognize important, but perhaps not instantly obvious, similarities and differences—even when I introduce new concepts. With this lesson, the fact that some groups were measuring a length that continued to grow while others measured a length that progressively became shorter could cause confusion. More important to me, it offered variety and, hopefully, gave students an opportunity to distinguish the mathematical impact of that difference.

I asked each group to appoint a spokesperson to write on the board and explain their two iterative rules. I also asked the class to wait until all groups were finished before asking questions or discussing the rules.

The iterative rules (the students' label) reported by each group are listed in the table on the following page.

The students were nearly jumping out of their seats by the time all six groups had reported. I had to remind the class more than once to listen politely until all groups were finished. Still, several students whispered to another person in their group as a new rule was given. Even more students hastily wrote notes, presumably to help them remember a thought for the discussion.

It is not clear to me whether the strategy I used for this part of the lesson was the best one. However, I chose to have all groups present their ideas before discussion was allowed because I take every opportunity I can find to foster the idea of collaboration and its benefits in my classes. Also, I knew there were common elements in the thinking of several of the groups that should become obvious if the class saw all the rules at once.

I asked the class to look again at all the rules on the board and think about iterative and explicit function rules. After a minute I asked, "Are all the rules on the board iterative rules?"

Asad was the first to raise his hand. He noted that two of the sets of rules were not really iterative rules. When asked to explain his thinking, Asad said, "An iterative rule has to use the result of the step before it to find the answer for each new step, but the rules by Alicia's and Ron's groups don't do that."

I asked Alicia's and Ron's groups to respond to Asad's assertion. Alicia said, "I think our rules *are* iterative. We said to keep adding one and a half inches for each new penny and four inches for each new quarter."

Alex cleared things up for Alicia when he said, "I think we just have some extra information in our rules. Iterative rules should just say something like, 'Add one and a half to the previous total.'" He rose to go to the board and change their rules, but I asked him to leave the original versions

Alicia's Group	*Pennies:* Our starting point was $15\frac{1}{2}$ inches. As each penny was dropped into the bucket one by one, the bucket lowered in height approximately $1\frac{1}{2}$ inches each time, so our rule is "$15\frac{1}{2}$ + $1\frac{1}{2}$ + $1\frac{1}{2}$ + $1\frac{1}{2}$, etc." *Quarters:* Our starting point was $15\frac{1}{2}$ inches. As each quarter was dropped into the bucket one by one, the bucket lowered in height approximately 4 inches each time, so our rule is "$15\frac{1}{2}$ + 4 + 4 + 4, etc."
Paul's Group	*Pennies:* Each time you add a penny the total is 2 inches more than the last total. So our rule is "The previous length + 2." *Nickels:* Each time you add a nickel, the total is 3 inches more than the last total. So our rule is "The previous length + 3."
RJ's Group	*Dimes:* Each dime adds 1.5 inches to the total length. Our rule is "For any number of dimes, add 1.5 to the total for the number of dimes before it." *Quarters:* Each quarter adds 4 inches to the total length. Our rule is "For any number of quarters, add 4 to the total for the number of quarters before it."
Ron's Group	*Dimes:* Each dime made the distance from the floor 1.5 inches less, so our rule is "y(distance) $= -1.5x$(# of dimes)." *Pennies:* Each penny made the distance from the floor 2 inches less, so our rule is "y(distance) $= -2x$(# of pennies)."
Jillian's Group	*Dimes:* Every time we added a dime to the cup, it got $1\frac{1}{2}$ inches closer to the floor. So our rule is "New Measurement = Previous Measurement $- 1\frac{1}{2}$." *Nickels:* Every time we added a nickel to the cup, it got 3 inches closer to the floor. So our rule is "New Measurement = Previous Measurement $- 3$."
Emmy's Group	*Dimes:* Each dime made the cup drop $1\frac{1}{2}$ more inches. Our rule for that is "New Distance = Distance before it + $1\frac{1}{2}$." *Quarters:* Each quarter made the cup drop 4 more inches. Our rule for that is "New Distance = Distance before it + 4."

on the board as well as the new ones. He did so. For the new rules he wrote the following:

Pennies: For each penny dropped in the bucket add $1\frac{1}{2}''$ to the length.

Quarters: For each quarter dropped in the bucket add 4" to the length.

Kyle volunteered to add the iterative rules for his group (Ron's). "I think we wrote the explicit rules," he said. I asked him to leave the original versions of his group's rules on the board. He wrote the following iterative rules:

Dimes: For each dime subtract 1.5 from the previous length.

Pennies: For each penny subtract 2 from the previous length.

Next I asked, "Now does everyone agree that there are iterative rules on the board from each group?" Everyone nodded. The period was suddenly over. As the class ended, I asked that each student think overnight about appropriate explicit function rules for the experiment.

Finding Explicit Rules and Connecting Multiple Representations

When the students arrived the next day they gathered into their groups. I had written the rules (all versions) presented by each group the previous day on the board. I instructed the class to *carefully* consider all the information on the board.

> First, think individually, then discuss with your group how each set of rules on the board (original and revised versions) might help you write explicit rules for your findings. Second, concentrating on the experiment you did, work together to write out explicit function rules in words for each type of coin you used. Third, try to write your rules using variables. Finally, each person should be prepared to explain to the rest of the class the rules your group finds and how they go along with what happened in the experiment.

I felt like the students had sufficient past experiences to use the information on the board to jar their memories and help them find appropriate explicit function rules. I always want as many students as possible to think and find answers for themselves, and having the students return to their small groups increased that opportunity.

Again, I circulated among the groups as the students worked together to find explicit function rules. Most of the groups were able to derive their rules without a lot of difficulty. Alicia's and Ron's groups had an advantage, since the class had already identified their original forms of the rules as explicit. In Alicia's group, Alex pointed out that they just needed to reword the rules they had already shared. Writing the rules with variables went quickly after Alicia focused the attention of the group on their table of values from the experiment. Tom's work, shown in Figure 8–6, was typical.

I asked the group to try several values in their rules to make sure they worked and to be prepared to explain how the rules, tables, and graphs described what happened in their investigation. I watched as they substituted 5 for p in their rule to find the total length of the cup and Slinky for five pennies. Kahlin wrote as the other students in the group watched (see Figure 8–7).

When the students looked back at their table, they were puzzled to find that the value they obtained from substituting did not match the one for five pennies in their table. As the other students in the group began to check Kahlin's calculations, Tom interrupted, "Wait a minute! Remember that the one and a half part of our rule was just an estimate; the length didn't change exactly one and a half inches for each penny."

"Oh yeah," Alicia agreed, "and twenty-three is close to the twenty-five that we actually measured and wrote in our table."

"So that's OK?" Kahlin asked as he looked at me.

"What do you think?" I replied.

FIGURE 8-6 Tom's rules

Stretching Slinkies **171**

FIGURE 8-6 Tom's rules

pennies
> The total length of the cup and slinky =
> the starting point (15½) plus 1½ inches for times
> the number of pennies
> total length = 15½ + 1½ (# of pennies)
> $T = 15\frac{1}{2} + 1\frac{1}{2}p$

quarters
> The total length of the cup and slinky =
> the starting point (15½) plus 3 inches times
> the number of quarters
> total length = 15½ + 3 (# of quarters)
> $T = 15\frac{1}{2} + 3p$

FIGURE 8-7 Kahlin's explanation

Notation	Comment
$T = 15.5 + 1.5p$	Total length equals fifteen and one-half, plus one and one half, times the number of pennies.
$T = 15.5 + 1.5(5)$	Put in **five** for the number of pennies.
$T = 15.5 + 7.5$	**One and a half times five** is seven and a half.
$T = 23$	The total length is **twenty-three** inches for **five** pennies.

"I think that's right," Kahlin stated, "but maybe we should try a different number of pennies."

The students substituted in their rule for two pennies and got 18.5 for the total length ($T = 15.5 + 1.5 \times 2$). "That's much better," Tom noted. "We got nineteen total inches when we had two pennies in the cup."

"Yeah," Alex added, "but when you try eight pennies, our rule gives you twenty-seven and a half, but we really got thirty inches when we measured during the experiment. That's getting worse as you go down the table."

"You know," Alicia pointed out, "when we averaged the differences we got from measuring back when we did the experiment, we got one and eight-tenths inches. Maybe we should go back and try that number in our rule—T equals fifteen and one-half plus one point eight p [$T = 15.5 + 1.8p$]."

The other students agreed, and they busily set out to substitute values in the "revived" version of their rule. When I came back to that group a little later, I asked them which rule for pennies they had decided upon and why. Tom spoke for the group: "We decided to go back to the rule T equals fifteen and one-half plus one point eight p because the answers we got when we used that rule were closer to the ones in the experiment than when we used the other rule [including one point five p].”

I explained to the group that they had encountered a situation that often occurs in the real world. Function rules for real-world data commonly have to be tested and refined. “You're doing the work of real mathematicians here. Now, can you see which rule works best for your graph?” I added. They actually looked excited as they turned to compare the two versions of their rule for pennies on the graph. I left them with the promise that I would be asking them to explain their findings and their thinking during their upcoming presentation to the whole class.

I was quite excited. I could not have asked for a more appropriate illustration of working through the challenges of finding explicit function rules for real-world data! (The group members did a great job of explaining it, too!)

Having students substitute values in their proposed function rules had other benefits, too. In Ron's group, the students immediately recopied their original versions of the rules from the board and wrote them as $y = -1.5x$ (for dimes) and $y = -2x$ (for pennies). I reminded these students to try several values in their rules to make sure they worked. They were puzzled when their rules did not produce the values they expected for y. I repeated that the rules should represent what they did and what happened in the experiment. Ron was the first to realize that the rules needed to include the initial distance from the floor. “Remember,” he said, “we started with the cup twenty-two and a half inches from the floor and we subtracted each time to get the new height.”

“Yeah, but that would be an iterative rule,” Jason stated: “y equals twenty-two point five minus one point five, minus one point five, minus one point five [$y = 22.5 - 1.5 - 1.5 - 1.5$].”

“No, no,” Kyle said, “since it got less by one point five inches for each dime, we can write y equals twenty-two point five minus one point five x [$y = 22.5 - 1.5x$]. So for two dimes, we would do y equals twenty-two point five minus one point five times two, or twenty-two point five minus three, which is nineteen point five!”

I was thrilled when the group asked Jason to write and test their rule for pennies. Though he struggled a little with writing the rule (the group helped him), he was able to use it successfully for two pennies ($y = 22.5 - 2x$; $y = 22.5 - 2(2)$; $y = 18.5$). This action was rewarding for me because I try to emphasize to my students that when they work in pairs or small groups it is their responsibility to help everyone in the group understand and agree with the findings and conclusions of the group. I reinforce the importance of this shared responsibility for learning to the students by establishing the policy that each person in the group must be able to explain the results and the thinking of the group to the entire class if called upon.

Jillian's group experienced the same glitch as Ron's group: they forgot to include the starting length in their rules. They were briefly stymied until Carlos noticed that the rules on the board for Alicia's group included the starting measurement. Looking back at their tables and graphs, they were then able to write their rules both in words and using variables. Jillian expressed their rule for nickels (see Figure 8–8).

The group members tested their rules using several values and were satisfied that they were, as Carlos expressed it “close enough—since we know some of our measurements were a little off.”

FIGURE 8–8   Jillian's group's rule for nickels

Stretching Slinkies

173

I got the rule -3x + 23 for nickles because
the graph is decreasing by 3. for each coin and the
graph starts at 23 on the graph
$$y = -3x + 23$$

I believe having the students test their rules by substituting values from their experiment is a vital step in working with rules for real-world data. As illustrated by what happened with virtually half this class, this simple process can help students find their own errors or stimulate thinking about the ways mathematics can be used to predict real-world phenomena.

RJ's group had a different challenge. Asad, one of the students in the group, had made a note to himself during the sharing of iterative rules: *Include the starting value.* He reminded the group of a problem they had worked on earlier in the year that had the rule $y = 2x + 3$. "Remember," he said, "we started with three squares and then increased by two for each step. This experiment is like that. For dimes, we started with twenty and a half inches and increased by one and a half inches for each dime we added."

The group members nodded and wrote rules that were equivalent to Asad's, as shown in Figure 8–9.

FIGURE 8–9   RJ's group's rules

Rules
For the dime it is the
Drop = d + 1.5x the number of coins
in the bucket. I put 1.5
because that is the average
time per drop. d = drop. Then
the rule for the quarter is
Drop = q + 4x number of coins in
the bucket. I put 4 because
that was the average drop
per time. And you always
start at 20 ½ and go up.
$$D = 20 \tfrac{1}{2} + 1.5x$$
$$D = 20 \tfrac{1}{2} + 4x$$

I also reminded this group to try several values in their rules to make sure the values those rules produced were essentially the same as those in the tables and graphs and in the experiment itself.

Emmy's group did the same version of the experiment as RJ's and Ron's groups (measuring the distance from the floor to the bottom of the cup for each number of coins), but they got bogged down in finding their rules. One girl in the group, Heather, modeled her version of the explicit rules from Alicia's group. For the rule relating to dimes, she wrote, *Bottom of the cup = $21\frac{1}{2}$ inches off the floor plus $1\frac{1}{2}$ inches for each dime.* The other students in the group initially accepted her rule and wrote L*(length)* $= 21\frac{1}{2} + 1\frac{1}{2}$d. Of course, when they began to substitute values to check the rule, it did not work. They checked their calculations, reread their rule in words and rewrote the rule using variables, getting the same result they obtained the first time. They tried a similar rule for quarters ($L = 21\frac{1}{2} + 4d$) and then called me over to declare that they were stuck. After hearing what they had done so far, I asked them to look back at the graph that they had used so effectively in finding the amount of change each dime or quarter made in the distance and to describe again what the graph showed. Heather started, "Well, each time we added a dime, the graph shows that we moved two spaces to the right and three spaces down for the next point; that was the same as one and a half inches for each dime."

After waiting for any response and hearing none, I asked, "And what does the graph tell you happened when you added another dime to the cup?"

Jason answered, "The cup dropped about another one and a half inches for each dime." He stopped and obviously was finished with what he was going to say.

"And the distance to the floor—what happened to that?" I asked.

"Wait, wait, I got it," Emmy said, grinning. "The distance to the floor *decreased*! Look at the graph; it goes down. And the numbers in our table go down, too!"

"So?" I prompted.

"So we need to *subtract* in our rule," Emmy and Jason said almost simultaneously.

"Subtract?" Heather asked.

"Yeah," Emmy explained. "We started at twenty-one and a half inches, but the distance to the floor got *less* each time we put in another dime."

"That's right," Heather said. "We need to use *L* [length] equals twenty-one and a half minus one and a half *d* [number of dimes] [$L = 21.5 - 1.5d$]." The group altered their rule for quarters and then tried a few values to check each rule. They gave each other high fives.

Paul's group also had some difficulty deriving appropriate explicit function rules. They had measured the total length of the cup and Slinky but their rule in words for nickels was "The length equals three times the number of nickels. This is because each nickel increased the length by about three inches." Even after describing the investigation to me in detail, they still could not come up with any ideas for changes in their rule.

In answer to the question "What was the length of the cup and Slinky with no coins in the cup?" they dutifully answered, "Nine inches," but failed to indicate any connection that information might have to a rule for predicting the length after any number of pennies was added.

Finally, I asked the group if they would like help from a classmate. When they assented, I asked Asad to come over and have the members of Paul's group explain their experiment. The group agreed that they did not want Asad to tell them the answer, but only to listen and ask them questions. Asad listened and then asked, "So where does the twenty-four inches in your nickels table come from?"

Jana sighed and answered, "Each nickel added about three inches to the length."

Asad said, "OK, and the twenty-four was for how many nickels?"

When Jana pointed to the 5, Asad said, "So going backwards, the length for four nickels was . . . ?" When Jana indicated $21\frac{1}{2}$ inches, Asad led her backward through the table until she answered that for zero nickels the length was 9 inches. "And why is that nine there?" Asad asked.

"Because the Slinky and cup were nine inches long before there were any coins in the cup," Jana answered, sounding exasperated. And Asad, being the excellent facilitator that he was, stared at her with a puzzled look on his face.

"I don't believe it!" Jana exclaimed. "You guys," she said, turning to the members of her group, "we forgot to put the nine inches at the front of our rule!" She went on to explain that the length of the cup and the Slinky was always the original 9 inches for zero coins plus 3 inches for each quarter added to the cup.

The other students in the group had her explain her thinking one more time, and then they set to work and soon produced appropriate rules for both coins in their investigation.

Once again a student in the class had come to the rescue. I was reminded that often another student is a better facilitator than any adult could possibly be.

I asked each group to copy their tables, graph, and rules onto a large sheet of paper or a piece of transparency film to share with the class. In turn, each group was asked to present the two explicit rules they had determined and to relate their rules, tables, and the graph to the investigation they had performed.

From observing and interacting with each group, I had confidence that the students in this class had already learned a lot during the lesson, but I believe such presentations increase the impact of a lesson. I have found that seeing the work and hearing the thinking of other students about experiments helps students grasp the connections among representations much more quickly.

As they see, hear, and discuss several sets of tables, graphs, and rules that represent data from experiments very much like the one they just did, the links between the representations, including the following, become more obvious as they occur over and over:

- As the numbers for length (the dependent variable) decrease in a table, the points in the corresponding graph go downward

- As the graph is steeper (increased slope), the rate of change for the length (dependent variable) in the corresponding table and in the rule is higher.

- When there is a non-zero starting value for length (the intercept) in the function rule, that same value appears on the graph at the point (0, starting length) for zero coins in the cup and in the table, as well in the row for zero coins.

Making connections like these is thus facilitated through the group presentations.

Since I believe that helping students develop proficiency with multiple representations is one of the primary goals of middle school mathematics, I try to target this goal as early and often as possible.

I also believe that group presentations like these serve as an excellent assessment tool. My students know that my evaluations of their learning are measured in part by the quality of these presentations.

Typical of the reports given by this class are the two from Paul's and Emmy's groups. Each student in the group gave part of the report.

Paul's Group (see Figure 8–10)

Function Rule for Pennies

The total length of the Slinky plus the cup equals (the length for no pennies) plus two times the number of pennies: $L = 9 + 2p$

Function Rule for Nickels

The total length of the Slinky plus the cup equals (the length for no nickels) plus three times the number of nickels: $L = 9 + 3n$

Students' Explanation

We measured the length of the Slinky plus the cup. We started with no coins and the length was nine inches. That is the first line in each table and the lowest point $(0, 9)$ on both graphs because that's the beginning for both the pennies and the nickels. We almost forgot that part, but our rules wouldn't work without it. That makes sense, because the nine inches was always part of the length.

In the tables, you can see the total lengths for each number of coins in the cup—pennies in the first column and nickels in the second column. On the graph you find the number of coins along the bottom, or x-axis, and the number of inches along the side, or y-axis. There is one point on the graph for each line in each table. For example, this square [pointing to $(5, 24)$] shows that when we had five nickels in the cup, the total length was twenty-four inches, just like in the table. Dots are used for pennies and squares for nickels.

Our rule for pennies is "Total length equals nine plus two p." That's because the length always had the nine inches before we started adding pennies and most of the pennies made it about two inches longer. That goes with the table. It starts with nine and adds two almost every time. The rule goes with the graph, too. To go from point to point, you go over one space for coins and up two spaces for inches. Since our length kept getting longer, the line keeps going up.

Our rule for nickels is "Total length equals nine plus three n." It's like the pennies because it also starts at nine inches, before there were any coins in the cup. But the nickels add about three inches each time. The length goes up three inches in the experiment, three in the table, and three on the graph each time the number of nickels goes up one.

The difference is that the total for nickels goes up faster than the pennies. It shows on the graph because the line of squares [for nickels] goes up faster than the line of dots [for pennies]. That makes sense with the experi-

FIGURE 8-10   Paul's group's table and graph

Stretching Slinkies   **177**

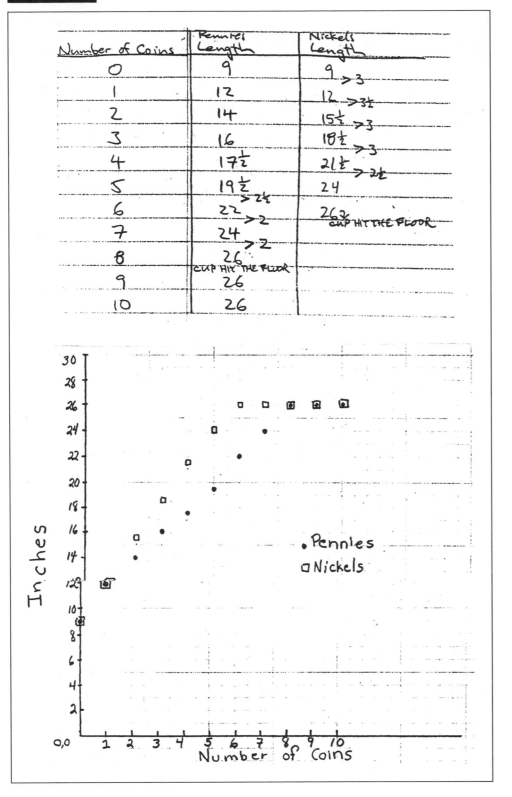

ment, too, because the Slinky and cup got longer faster for the nickels than for the pennies.

P.S. For both our coins, the cup reached the floor before we got to ten coins. You can see that in the table, and it is the flat part of the graph. This would be different if we had started out with the cup higher off the ground.

When this group finished, RJ asked the students, "What about x and y? What are the rules for your graphs?"

Keyonna answered, "The rules are the same. Instead of saying 'Total length equals nine plus two p' for the pennies, you would just say 'y equals nine plus two x' and, for the nickels, 'y equals nine plus three x,' because the coins go by the x-axis and the length goes by the y-axis."

I asked the class, "If the cup had started higher, what would this group's rule predict for ten nickels?" After I waited a few moments so each student could try the substitution independently, Kathleen volunteered to do the work at the board (see Figure 8–11).

FIGURE 8–11 Kathleen's explanation

Notation	Comment
$L = 9 + 3n$	In their rule, the total length equals nine plus three times the number of nickels.
$L = 9 + 3(10)$	Use **ten** for the number of nickels.
$L = 9 + 30$	**Three** times **ten** equals thirty.
$L = 39$	Nine plus thirty equals thirty-nine, so the total length would be **thirty-nine** inches for ten nickels.

Emmy's Group (see Figure 8–12)

Function Rule for Dimes

The distance from the bottom of the cup to the floor equals $21\frac{1}{2} - 1\frac{1}{2}$ times the number of dimes: $y = 21\frac{1}{2} - 1\frac{1}{2}x$

Function Rule for Quarters

The distance from the bottom of the cup to the floor equals $21\frac{1}{2} - 4$ times the number of quarters: $y = 21\frac{1}{2} - 4x$

Students' Explanation

We measured the distance from the bottom of the cup to the floor. After we set up, that distance was twenty-one and a half inches. As we added dimes or quarters one by one, the distance got less and less. You can see those numbers in our tables.

If you look at the table for dimes, you can subtract and see that each one caused the cup to go down about one and a half inches. We think it is easier to see on the graph because when we added one number to the dimes on the x-axis, the next point moved down one and a half inches each time. Even though it wasn't always exact, you can see by the line we drew for our rule (y equals twenty-one and a half minus one and a half x) that the rule tells pretty good what happened in the investigation.

The quarters worked basically the same way. You can subtract the numbers in the table and see that each quarter made the cup drop about

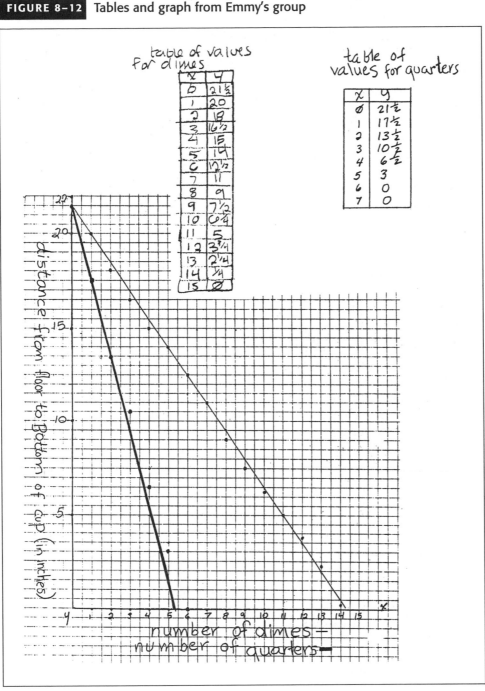

four inches, but again we think it is easier to see on the graph, where every time there is one more quarter, the distance to the floor goes down by four inches. We made our rule (*y* equals twenty-one and one half minus four *x*) and drew the dark line, and it is a good picture of what happened with the quarters.

Our quarters also made the cup hit the floor, so after four quarters the line is flat, like what happened for Paul's group.

Alicia asked the group to explain again why the points and lines on their graphs went down. "I don't get that part," she admitted. (Alicia's group had measured the total length of the Slinky plus the cup, so their graphs had positive slope.)

Emmy jumped in. "That gave us trouble at first. But we weren't measuring the same thing you did in our experiment. We measured the distance from the floor to the bottom of the cup, so the number of inches kept getting *smaller*, not larger like for your group. See the table? And that meant we had to *subtract* in our rule, too (not *add* to the length), so the points and the lines for the each rule moved down each time we added another coin."

Alicia nodded. I asked, "Do the lines on your graph show what really happened in your experiment?"

Asif answered, "We drew the lines on our graph to show what our rules would look like in graph form. The dots are from the numbers in our tables; they show exactly what happened during our experiment. We think the lines show that our rules go with the experiment really well."

"What do you mean, 'go with'?" I asked.

"Well, if the rules and the experiment were exactly the same, I think all our points would be *on* those lines. They [the points] are close, but things just didn't work exactly according to a rule," Asif ventured.

I affirmed that Asif was partly correct: if each number of coins had caused the measurements to be just as their rules predicted, then all the points would fall on the two lines. I asked the students whether that statement made sense to them. Most nodded.

"But," I added, "there is another way in which the lines on the graph do not show exactly what happened in this group's experiment. Can anyone explain how the lines are not a representation of what actually happened during the experiment?"

No one volunteered. After a few moments I added, "Would a *line* show what actually happened in any of your experiments?"

"I get it! I get it!" Alex chimed in. "You have to use points, not lines, on a graph to show what happened in our experiments. The lines make it seem like you had something to measure for things like two and one half dimes or three and one quarter nickels, but we could only measure for whole numbers of coins, so the points show what really happened."

I confirmed that what Alex had said was correct and mathematically important. I explained that it is important to think about the real-world context of a graph (whenever there is one) in order to make decisions about what values make sense to include. After a brief, lively discussion the students agreed that, for this problem, the points on their graphs should not be connected.

When all the groups had finished their presentations, I gave the students the following questions to answer in writing. I tried to choose questions that would do more than require the student to summarize what had happened during the lesson. I wanted to try to determine what the students now understood about multiple representations of data and about function rules in the real world.

1. List the rules your group found in this investigation. Explain each rule in words and how it relates to the investigation and to your table or graph. Most of the answers to this question were quite similar to the ones in the reports mentioned earlier. As might be expected from students learning new concepts, some of the explanations were terse, and none included all the possible connections. In general, the students gave stronger explanations about the relationship of the table and rule to the experiment than that of the graph. I find that this is typical of students in middle school. More experiences will help the students become proficient at finding and explaining explicit rules and making the connections among multiple representations.

2. Is the point (0, 0) a point in the data on your graph? Explain why or why not. Most students' answers to this question reflected understanding of why the origin was not a point on the graph. Typical are the answers shown in Figure 8–13.

FIGURE 8–13 Answers to question #2

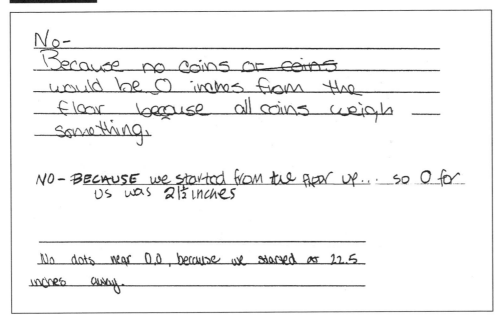

> No–
> Because no coins or coins
> would be 0 inches from the
> floor because all coins weigh
> something.

> NO – BECAUSE we started from the floor up... so 0 for
> us was 2½ inches

> No dots near 0,0, because we started at 22.5
> inches away.

3. Why are the changes in the x values steady and even on your graph while the changes in the y values are not as exact? While many of the student answers were not exactly what I expected, most students gave answers that indicated they understood how their graphs reflected the primary difference between the characteristics of the two variables in the experiment (see Figure 8–14 on page 182).

4. How are your graphs different from those of some other groups? What do those differences tell you about this lesson? Many students answered this question with clear understanding (see Figure 8–15).

Some students had trouble with this question, so I asked students who had written exemplary answers to share them with the class. We then had another short discussion about how the graphs reflected the two versions of the experiment.

5. Use your results to predict the distance for twenty coins of each type. Explain your thinking. Almost all students were able to use their rules to predict the distance they would get for twenty coins. Many added comments like those in Jana's response (see Figure 8–16).

FIGURE 8–14 Answers to question #3

a) Why are the changes in the x values steady and even on your graph?

- because you are using coins. Coins can't come in halfs!

- because it grows by one thing each time

- BECAUSE you use exactly ① coin at a time - not a quarter and a half

- because the changes are even - one by one

b) Why are the changes in the y values are not as exact?

- because the measurements aren't exact

- because of the bouncing of the cup, measuring might be off

- BECAUSE of the bouncing of the cup, measuring might be a little off. paper clip might be twisted, and also the position of the coins in the cup may tilt

- because the coins might not weigh exactly the same

In general, I was pleased with the students' answers to the questions. Although there were some incomplete or weak explanations that showed only partial understanding by some students, I feel that the lesson as a whole was very successful. This class completed a hands-on investigation involving data gathering and recording, graphing of data, finding approximate function rules, and analyzing their findings. Students experienced some of the challenges associated with gathering and analyzing real-world data. They compared multiple representations and connected them to their investigations. Through this lesson, students had an initial experience in deriving explicit function rules for real-world situations and connecting multiple representations of data. I hope they began to develop practical meaning for the concepts of intercept and slope. Finally, I believe this lesson provided a concrete introduction to how algebraic thinking can be used to describe and predict phenomena in the real world.

FIGURE 8–15 Answer to question #4

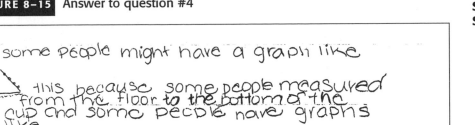

some people might have a graph like

this because some people measured
from the floor to the bottom of the
cup and some people have graphs
like

this because they were measuring
from the desk top to the bottom of
the dixie cup

and while the people who had graphs like

this inches are going up the people w/
graphs like this ⎧⎩ inches are going
down.

FIGURE 8–16 Jana's response to question #5

Our rule for pennies was $T = 9 + 2p$, so for
20 pennies, the length would be $T = 9 + 2(20)$ or
$T = 49$. This could not work for us because the cup
would hit the floor. If we started higher off the floor,
49" would be close to the real length for 20 pennies.

Leaky Faucet　｜　Similar Problem

The following problem is appropriate for a lesson similar to *Stretching
Slinkies*.

The Leaky Faucet Problem

Students design an experiment to model a leaky faucet and determine the
amount of water wasted by the leak. Making a hole in the bottom of a
small paper cup using a thumbtack, then filling it with water works
nicely. The students produce a table and a graph and write an approximate function rule.

The students then use their rule to make predictions about the amount
of water that would be wasted over a longer time or by a large number of
leaks. Finally, each group presents its findings and conclusions and the class
discusses them.

Another activity, "Bouncing Tennis Balls," which deals with some of the same concepts as *Stretching Slinkies*, can be found in *Navigating Through Algebra in Grades 6–8* (Friel et al. 2001, 21–24).

Extension Problem	Disappearing Ms

This problem is appropriate for a lesson to follow *Stretching Slinkies*. Students should discover a nonlinear function while working with M&M's candies. Give each pair of students a bag containing more than sixty-four candies.

Students work in pairs to conduct the following experiment:

1. Pour the M&M's from your bag onto the tabletop. Discard any candy that does not have an M on exactly one side.

2. Place 64 M&M's back in the bag.

3. Pour the M&M's now in your bag onto the tabletop. Examine the candies and remove the M&M's that do not have an M showing.

4. Record the results of the trial in the following table.

5. Repeat Steps 3 and 4 until there are no remaining M&M's.

Our Pair's Results

Trial Number	Number of M&M's with an M showing
0	
1	
2	
3	
4	
5	
6	
7	
8	
9	
10	

6. Collect data from the entire class. Calculate a measure of central tendency (mean, median, or mode) and construct a table showing the average values. Choose the average that you determine best reflects what typically happened in the experiment. Describe any patterns you see in the table.

Class Results

Trial Number	Number of M&M's with an M showing
0	
1	
2	
3	
4	
5	
6	
7	
8	
9	
10	

7. Graph the class data as a scatter plot. Describe any patterns you see in the table.

8. Write a function rule that approximately fits the data for the class results.

Iterative Rule: Number of M&M's after any trial = number of M&M's after previous trial ÷ 2.

Explicit Rule: y (number of M&M's after any trial) = $64 \div 2^x$ when x = number of trials completed.

Technology Connections

A nice follow-up activity for *Stretching Slinkies* is to have the students use TI-73 graphing calculators to create scatter plots for one or more of their data sets and then find the manual line of best fit for that data. The equation found by this method can then be compared with the function rule derived by the students.

Directions for entering lists of data and creating a scatter plot on the TI-73 can be found in the "Technology Connections" section of the *Personal-*

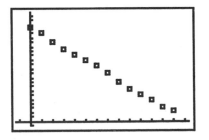

Student-derived function rule: $y = 21\frac{1}{2} - 1\frac{1}{2}x$

ized Patterns lesson. Shown here is a scatter plot of the data gathered for the distance from the Slinky to the tabletop as dimes were added to the cup (*x* = number of dimes in cup; *y* = distance to tabletop).

Equation for line of best fit

Scatter plot and graph of manual line of best fit

To use the calculator to help find a manual line of best fit, use the following keystrokes:

1. Clear any rules in the **y** = menu.

2. Go to the Home Screen by pressing **2nd QUIT.**

3. On a blank line, press **2nd STAT** and choose **#3Manual-Fit** from the **CALC** menu.

4. Press **2nd VARS** and choose **Y1** from the **YVARS** menu. Y1 should appear next to Manual-Fit on the Home Screen. Press **ENTER.** You should be back in the scatter plot with a blinking cursor.

5. Use the **arrow keys** to move to a point you think will be on the line of best fit for your scatter plot. Press **ENTER.**

6. Use the **arrow keys** to move to another point you think will be on the line of best fit for your scatter plot. Press **ENTER.** You should see a line appear through your scatter plot.

7. You can adjust your line to fit your data better by using the **arrow keys** if you wish. When you position the line as best you can, press **ENTER.** The calculator will redraw the line in the scatter plot and paste the equation for that line into the **y** = menu. The equation should be close to the function rule you derived.

8. Use **TRACE** and the **arrow keys** to compare your rule with the manual line of best fit.

CHAPTER 9

Condo Challenge

OVERVIEW

This lesson is intended to help students use physical models to find numerical patterns and to establish connections between geometric and numerical patterns in a variety of ways. The lesson provides experiences with finding a pattern for a series of three-dimensional models and deriving a general rule to predict the number of cubes needed to build any stage of the pattern.

First, the students were given a picture of a condominium model made from cubes, with six cubes forming the center column. They were asked to work in a small group to find the total number of cubes needed to build the model. They were then asked to find how many cubes were needed to build a similar model with twelve cubes in the center column. They were asked to explain their methods and thinking and to try to find an explicit function rule to predict the number of cubes for a model with a center column of any height. Each group of students made a presentation to the entire class. In these presentations each group explained their thinking, thereby providing their classmates with opportunities to develop new ways of connecting concrete models with numerical patterns and their rules.

Students often view physical models in several different ways. They therefore also describe the growth pattern of a series of such models in different ways. This lesson is intended to make students more aware that such diversity of interpretation exists and that various strategies are equally valid and can produce equivalent results.

This lesson should help students develop new ways of searching for, finding, and expressing the rules for patterns, both geometrically and numerically. It should demonstrate that many forms of a function rule can be correct and equivalent. These understandings should help students develop algebraic thinking and become better problem solvers.

BACKGROUND

Becoming proficient at finding patterns and deriving function rules for patterns requires many experiences for most students. Prior to this lesson, this class of eighth-grade students had worked in groups, in pairs, and alone with a variety of patterns to complete each of the following tasks:

- Produce the next stages for a given numerical or geometric pattern.

- Express an iterative rule for a pattern (e.g., "To get a new term in this pattern, add five to the previous term.").

- Express an explicit rule for a pattern (e.g., "For any stage in the pattern, the rule is 'The total equals two more than the stage number.' ").

They used manipulatives, drawings, and tables to help them, and they shared their thinking, methods, and results with the rest of the class.

PREREQUISITE CONCEPTS OR SKILLS

- Experience recognizing and describing, extending, and generalizing visual and numerical patterns

- Experience finding iterative and explicit rules for numerical and geometric patterns

VOCABULARY

equivalent rules, explicit rule, iterative rule, variable

TIME

The lesson was completed in a ninety-minute class and student reflections were written the following day. If your classes are only forty-five or sixty minutes long, it will be necessary to have the group presentations on a separate day. Also, we have found that groups of students who are less experienced with this kind of problem require longer than one forty-five-minute class to find a solution and prepare for their presentations to the class.

MATERIALS

- *Condo Challenge* activity sheets, 1 per student (see Blackline Masters)

- Multilink cubes for each group of four students (preferably 66 or more)

- Large chart paper or transparency film

- Markers

The Lesson | Condo Challenge

Students were presented with the following problem:

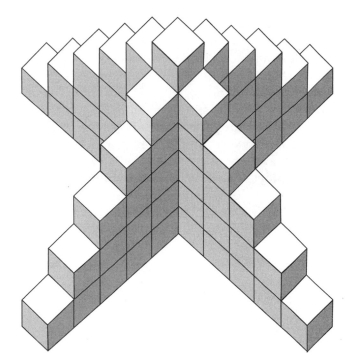

Building planners are designing a new condominium. They are not sure yet how tall they want the building to be.

1. How many cubes are needed to build this 6-high model of Clearview Condos?
2. How many cubes would be needed to build a 12-high model?
3. Explain how you got your answer for Question #2.
4. How many cubes would be needed to build a model of any height? Explain your thinking and make a rule, using a variable if possible.
5. How could your findings help the builders of Clearview Condos?

I chose this problem because students nearly always see it in a variety of ways and find many versions of the solution. I am always looking for rich problems to reinforce for students that for many problems several equally valid solutions can be found, or, if there is one correct answer, there are several equally appropriate approaches to solving such problems. I also like to expose students to ways of interpreting and solving problems that are different than the ones they find on their own in order to help them expand their own problem-solving skills. Finally, I know that having students explore and formalize patterns, share their thinking about them, and eventually generalize and symbolize those patterns will give them a head start on some important components of algebraic thinking.

Students worked in small groups to solve the problem. Copies of the problem, multicolored cubes, chart paper, overhead transparency film, and markers were available. I asked the students to record any patterns that they noticed on the charts they created. Finally, if they determined a general rule—whether iterative or explicit—the students were to write it, using a variable. I circulated around the room as the students worked.

Two of the groups in this class were unable to find an explicit function rule for the problem. Both of these groups approached the problem in basically the same way: they viewed the model for each stage as a combination of four wings and a center column. They were able to discover and describe patterns, find an iterative rule that would give the total number of cubes for any stage, and explain a process that would yield the total number of cubes for any stage; however, they were unable to express that process as an explicit function rule using variables.

Valerie's group, for example, started by building models for the first few stages of the pattern (see Figure 9–1). When I observed the group shortly after the students began to work, they had built models for Stages 1–6 and were making observations about patterns they noticed.

"The number of blocks in the center part is the same as the step number," CJ commented.

"That's good," Leroy noted, "because we can probably use that in our rule."

FIGURE 9–1 Valerie's group's solution

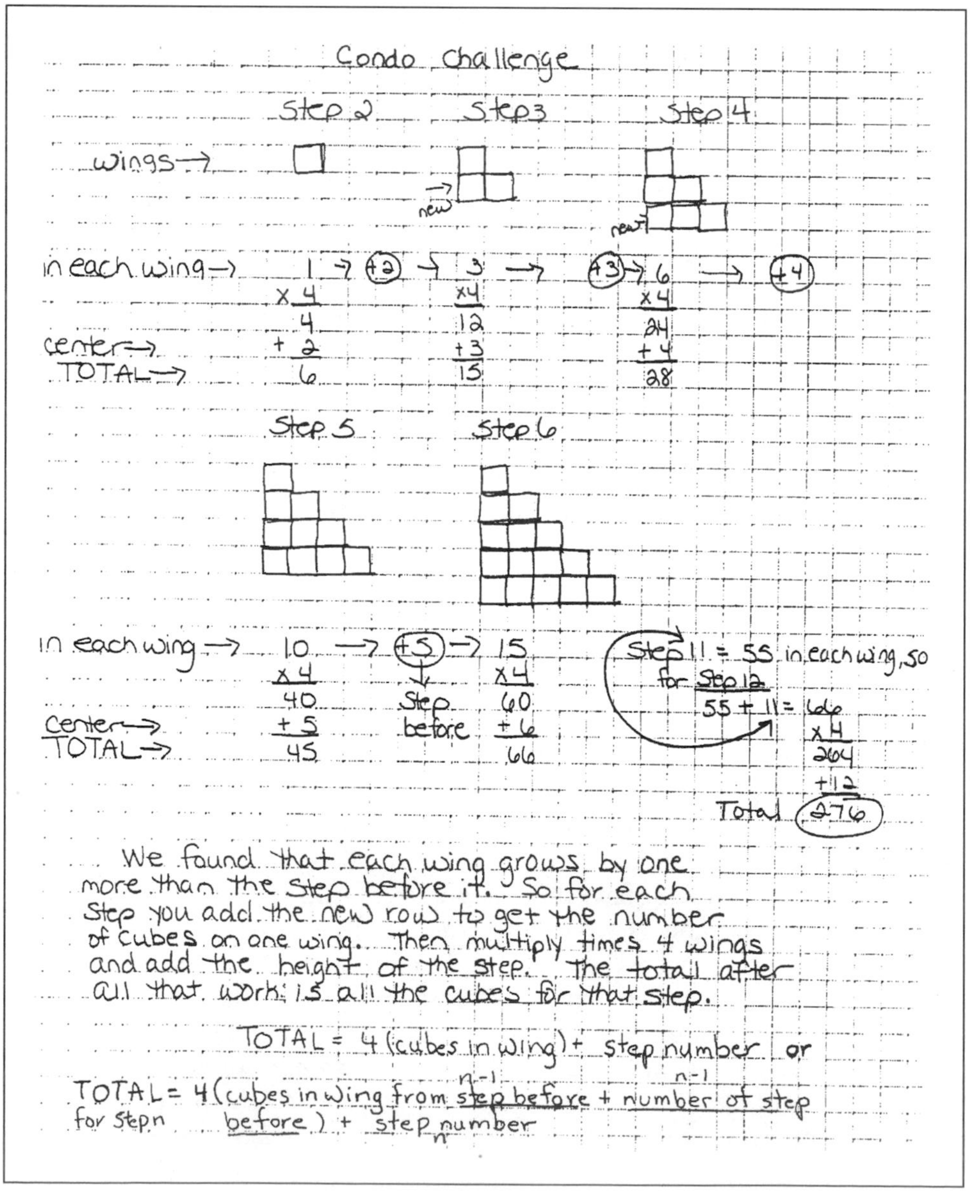

"All four wings have the same number of cubes," Jeff added. "That is reasonable since the models are symmetric."

"You have to add one more cube to get to the next step for each wing," Valerie commented.

"What do you mean?" CJ asked.

"Well," Valerie explained, "when you go from Step Two to Step Three, each wing in Step Three has two more cubes than in Step Two. But when you go from Step Three to Step Four, each wing has three more cubes than Step Three."

"I still don't get it. Show me," CJ requested.

Valerie took the models and showed CJ how each wing in Stage 2 contained one cube, each wing in Stage 3 contained three cubes (two more than for Stage 2), and each wing in Stage 4 contained six cubes (three more than for Stage 3). "So, when you go to each new step you add one more cube for each wing than you did when you moved up to a new step the last time."

CJ nodded. "OK, I get it."

Student interactions such as this are examples of an important way in which collaborative student problem solving has changed my teaching. When I taught primarily through lecture, students seldom had the opportunity to explain and talk mathematics to each other. In pairs and small groups they seem much more willing to ask questions, and they gradually develop ways to express their mathematical ideas more clearly. I am convinced that such interchanges accelerate the acquisition of mathematical understanding, including the ability to think more abstractly and symbolically.

Despite this conviction, and all the positive results of this approach to teaching that I have experienced, my students do not always achieve the mathematical objectives I have in mind for a particular lesson. Valerie's group, for example, as well as another, ran into trouble when they tried to formulate an explicit function rule. I suggested that they draw sketches and write down words for the patterns they had noticed so far, then see whether new ideas grew from their findings.

Later, when I returned to Valerie's group, they had organized their thoughts and had written them down using illustrations and brief numerical explanations. I asked the students to explain their thinking.

"Well," Jeff began, "we think the logical way to view each model is as four wings and a center. We can quickly get the total number of cubes needed for a step as long as we know the total number of cubes needed for the step before it."

"That's because we noticed something new," Valerie added. "The 'growing number' [that's what we called how much bigger each wing is than the one in the previous step] is the same as the number of the step before."

I asked for an example. The students chose Stage 10 and did a few calculations, then CJ spoke. "We got thirty-six cubes in each wing for Step Nine and four times thirty-six (the wings) plus nine (the center), or one hundred fifty-three total cubes for Step Nine. That means for Step Ten, each wing will have thirty-six plus nine (the previous step number), or forty-five cubes, so the total number of cubes for Step Ten is four times forty-five plus ten (the center), or one hundred ninety cubes."

"We worked this out for a lot of stages and the numbers always match what we count in the model. And since it makes sense from the pictures and models, too, we are confident of our rule," Valerie concluded.

"Can you do Step One Hundred?" I asked.

Grinning, CJ readily admitted, "Not unless we have a whole lot of time, because we need to know the total cubes in Step Ninety-Nine!"

"So, what kind of function rule have you found?" I probed.

The students agreed that their rule was iterative but were not the least bit concerned. I indicated that they should use the remaining time to rewrite their rule using a variable and try to look at the models in a different way—as something besides four congruent wings and a center.

When I returned to Valerie's group near the end of class, the students had incorporated another observation into their rule. As Jeff explained, "We made our rule better. We noticed that the number of new cubes in one wing as you go from one stage to the next is the same as the old step number. So all we have to know to find the total number of cubes for a new step is the total number of cubes from the step before it. We also used variables!"

I asked for an example, and CJ wrote the explanation shown in Figure 9–2. (The writing she did is labeled "Notation" and her spoken words are labeled "Comment.")

I encouraged CJ to include her explanation in the group's presentation to the rest of the class. Although the group did not rewrite their solution, CJ did include an example of this additional finding in their presentation.

Steve's group viewed the models in the same way that Valerie's did: a center column, N, which had the same number of cubes as the stage number, and four wings, each of which contained the first $[N - 1]$ counting numbers. But the process through which Steve's group derived that rule was different and somewhat humorous (see Figure 9–3).

Jonathan explained, "First we noticed that each wing started with one block and went up to the stage number of blocks. Not thinking too sharp, we multiplied the numbers one through six together and multiplied that by four since there were four wings. Of course, when we saw the answer, two thousand eight hundred eighty, we knew that was way too big. Looking

FIGURE 9–2 CJ's explanation

Notation	Comment.
$T = 4[\text{cubes in wing in Step}$ $(n - 1) + (n - 1)] + n$ $T = \mathbf{45}$ for Stage 5	Say we know the total number of cubes for Step Five equals **forty-five**. You start by working backwards.
$45 - 5 = \mathbf{40}$	Taking away the center column of five (which is always the same as the step number), you have **forty** cubes for all four wings in Step Five.
$40 \div 4 = \mathbf{10}$	Since forty divided by four wings equals ten, there are **ten** cubes in each wing of Step Five.
$10 + 5 = \mathbf{15}$	Our new rule says, for any step, add the number of the previous step to each wing, so each wing in Step Six has ten plus five, or **fifteen**, cubes.
$T = 4(10 + 5) + \mathbf{6}$	So, for Step Six, you multiply four by fifteen and add **six** (the step number or the number of cubes in the middle stack).
$T = \mathbf{66}$	The total cubes needed for Step Six is **sixty-six**.

We added up all the numbers from 1-11. We then multiplied that the sum by 4 because there is 4 wings. Then the product of that we added 12 to it. While adding 1-11 we noticed it came out to the answer of 66 which is the previous answer (question no 1). When we saw this we realized there is probably a pattern which is:

$$(N! - 1)(\times 4) + N \qquad (N-1)*(\times 4) + N$$

$$\text{start} \text{ counting}$$
$$(N - 1 + \text{all no. smaller than that \#})$$
$$\times 4 + N$$

For Stage 12 -

$$(1+2+3+4+5+6+7+8+9+10+11)(4) + 12 = 276 \text{ or } (66 \times 4) + 12$$

back at the model, we figured out two things: first, we should *add*, not multiply, the numbers together, and second, it would be better to stop the wings at one through five and add the center column separately since there was only one center part that high. This gave us fifteen cubes in each wing times four plus six [the center column], or sixty-six cubes for Stage Six."

Carrie added, "We worked Stage Twelve the same way and wrote our rule for any stage like this [pointing to $(N - 1)! \times 4 + N$ on her paper]." In words the rule is this: "For any Stage N, start with $N - 1$ and add all the smaller numbers than that number, multiply the answer by four, and then add N."

When I asked Carrie to explain the "$(N - 1)!$" in their rule, she said, "That means you start with one less than the stage number and then add all the numbers below it down to one."

"Do the rest of you agree?" I asked. No one commented, so I asked the group to look up the meaning of "*n*!". After finding that *n*! or $(n - 1)!$ was not what they wanted to include in their rule, the students wanted the name for adding a number and all the counting numbers less than that number. When I told them there was no such name or symbol for that procedure, they decided to name it "N*".

I find that students often like to give a name to a mathematical procedure or shortcut they discover. Often they name these discoveries after the student who first suggested the idea, for example, "Joe's Corollary." These eponyms seem to help the students remember the idea, give them a way to refer to the idea quickly, and help them feel ownership and pride in the mathematics they are doing.

I asked whether the group had made any progress toward finding an explicit function rule. Steve pointed out, "No, we don't have an explicit function rule, but we want to investigate something we found. One wing in a Stage Twelve model has the same number of cubes as a whole Stage Six model. We want to see whether that always happens—the total for one model is the same as one wing for the model for the stage twice as high."

When I came back to Steve's group later, they were excited to show me their findings (see Figure 9–4). "We were right!" Steve exclaimed, then continued: "See, if you know the total for any stage, then you know the total of one wing for the stage that is twice as tall. The total cubes for Stage Two is six and one wing in Stage Four has six cubes; the total cubes in Stage Three is fifteen and one wing in Stage Six has fifteen cubes. So if you are asked to find a stage with a large number, you can take one-half of the stage number and start there."

I asked him to give an example. His explanation is shown in Figure 9–5.

The performance and behavior of Valerie's and Steve's groups illustrate a dilemma all teachers sometimes face in our classrooms. The students in both groups found several patterns and could express an iterative function rule to find the total number of cubes using words. They did some solid mathematics, felt good about their results, and were not interested in going further. My usual response is to acknowledge the accuracy and validity of their thinking, then prod them to continue (e.g., incorporate a variable in their rule) and to explore in a different direction (e.g., try to view the models or drawings in a different way). Usually this prodding results in more effort, as in this class.

Still, a particular student or group may not accomplish one or more of the objectives of the lesson. When this happens, I wait until all the groups have made their presentations, then ask that each group look back at their work and make any additions or corrections they feel are important. Often the students can use information or methods they hear in other groups' presentations to expand their own thinking. However, we must realize that

FIGURE 9–4   Steve's group's solution

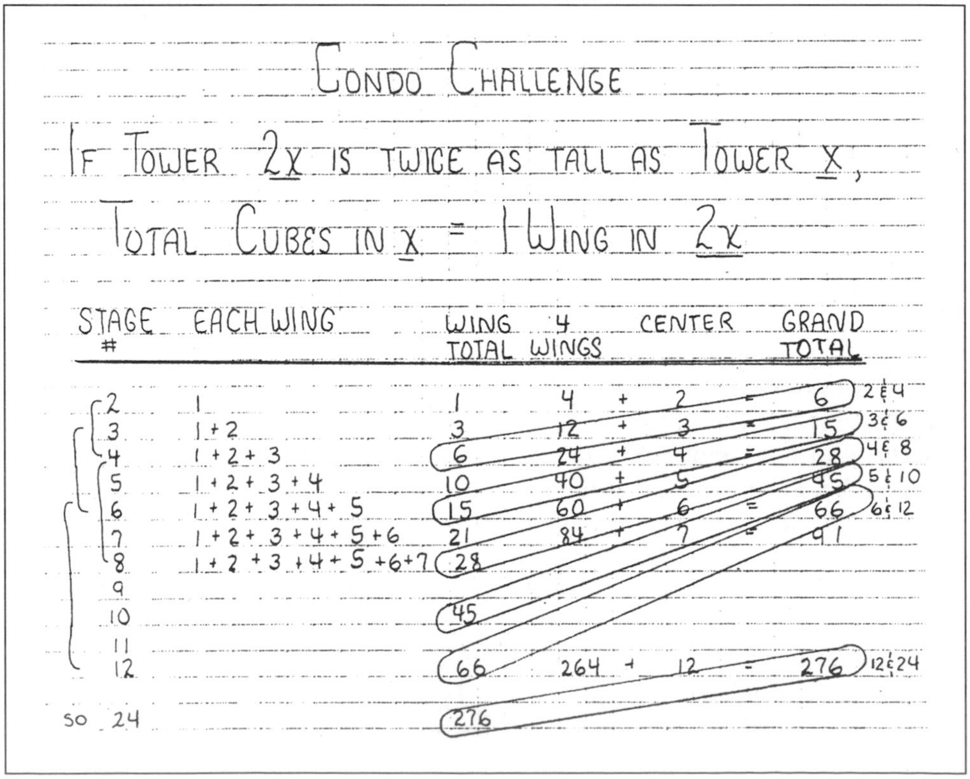

FIGURE 9–5 Steve's explanation

**Condo
Challenge**

195

Notation	Comment
Total for Stage 4 = **28**, so each wing in Stage 8 = **28**	If you are looking for the total for Stage Eight, half of eight is four, so you go back to Stage Four. The total number of cubes for Stage Four is **twenty-eight**. That means each wing in Stage Eight also has **twenty-eight** cubes.
Total for Stage 8 = 28 × 4 + 8, or **120**	If there are twenty-eight cubes in each wing, there are four times twenty-eight, or one hundred twelve, cubes altogether in the four wings. Then just add the center, eight, since the center is always as high as the stage number, and you get **one hundred twenty** cubes.
Always works!	This method works anytime you know the total for a stage that is half the height of the one you want to find.

sometimes students are simply not ready to accomplish all the objectives of a particular lesson. When this is the case, I leave the problem and later introduce one that can be solved using similar thinking, after the students have had some additional experiences that may have prepared them to be more successful. In fact, I decided to use another lesson involving triangular numbers with this class soon.

Dan's group solved the problem in a different way. When I first asked these students to tell me about their progress, Susanna explained, "We have been trying to look at the four wings and a center part of each model to find patterns. We could see that the wings were all the same but we couldn't find a rule—except an iterative one—to work for the total number of cubes. Finally, Dan said we should try to look at the model as two triangles like that [pointing to two wings and the center put together to form one triangular shape]. We're making a table and finding some patterns, and we think this way will work." (See Figure 9–6.)

When asked to explain their thinking, Maria pointed to the partially completed table on her paper (see Figure 9–7 on the following page). "We

FIGURE 9–6 Dan's group's Stage 6 model

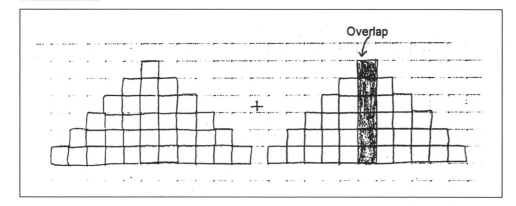

FIGURE 9–7 Maria's table

Stage	Cubes in 1 Triangle	Sum	Total Triangles	Final Total
6	1+3+5+7+9+11	36	72	66
12	1+3+5+7+9+11+13+			
	15+17+19+21+23	144	288	276
4	1+3+5+7	16	32	28

Number of Odds	Sum	T
1	1	1
2	1 + 3	4
3	1 + 3 + 5	9
4	1 + 3 + 5 + 7	16
5		

started off by looking at the Stage Six and Stage Twelve models. We saw that each big triangle has rows of cubes that are odd numbers. Like for Stage Six, the rows have one cube, three cubes, five cubes, seven cubes, nine cubes, and eleven cubes. Stage Twelve was the same except it kept going to twelve rows—all the way to twenty-three cubes on the bottom row. Then we started a table to see whether we could find patterns. It looks like we need to find out what happens when we add up odd numbers, so we are working on that now."

Susanna added, "Also, we noticed when we built a Stage Four model and looked at one of the triangles, we saw it was four rows made of the first four odd numbers, so we *know* we want to add odd numbers. And I think the answers for each triangle are all going to be square numbers if our table keeps going this way."

Maria looked down at her own work for adding consecutive odd numbers and exclaimed, "Susanna, I think you're right! Four, nine, and sixteen are squares, and, oh yeah, one is, too. I'm not sure I would have noticed that, but I think it will help us."

I reminded the group that they should check any rule they found for more than the three stages they had examined so far, then left the group, confident that they would find an explicit rule for the pattern. This interchange reminded me of one of the main reasons I like my students to work in small groups. Having students work in groups fosters collaboration among students, and students soon learn the value of teamwork. When I first started grouping students in mathematics, I was fearful that they would simply depend on the student they perceived as the best mathematics student in the group to do all the thinking. However, I have found that group work fairly quickly produces appreciation for combining different ideas and perspectives to solve problems. Since collaboration is an integral part of to-day's workplace, I want my students to value its benefits as well as to have practice doing it.

When I later returned to Dan's group, I requested a progress report. Since I had not heard from Ron, I asked him to update us. "All done," he proudly declared. "It turned out that the rule for adding odd numbers is really simple, just like Susanna thought. If you have six odd numbers in a row and add them, you get six times six, or six squared. If you have twelve odd numbers and add them, you get twelve times twelve, or twelve squared. So if you have n odd numbers in a row and you add them, you have n times n, or n squared. That was really the biggest thing we had to find."

When asked to explain the rule for the number of cubes in a model or the number of units in the condo, Dan talked as he pointed to their group solution (see Figure 9–8).

FIGURE 9-8 Dan's group's solution

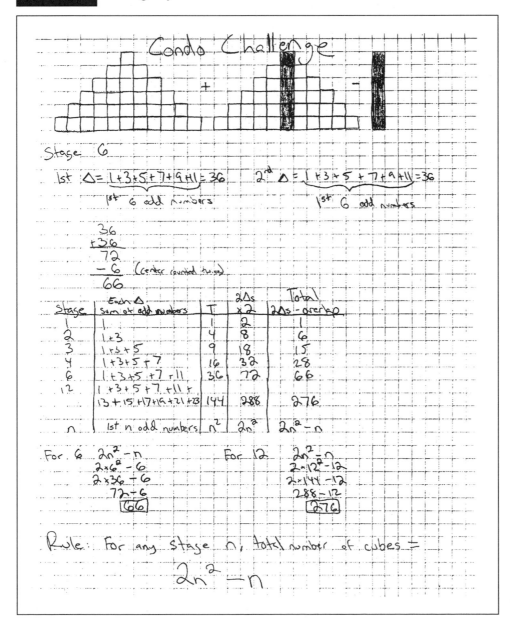

"Our rule for the total number of cubes is two *n* squared minus *n*. When you add all the cubes in one large triangle, you get the stage number squared. Since there are two large triangles, that gives you *n* squared plus *n* squared, or two *n* squared. But two *n* squared includes the center column, which is the stage number, *twice*, so you have to do two *n* squared minus *n* to get the correct number of cubes needed."

"And how does that connect to the condos problem?" I asked.

Susanna answered this way: "The builders of Clearview Condos could know how many units they needed to build a building of any height by using our rule. For example, if the building were going to be ten floors high, they would need two times ten squared minus ten, or one hundred ninety, units."

"Wait. How'd you get that?" Ron asked. Figure 9–9 shows what Susanna wrote as she reexplained the problem.

Ron nodded, but I asked him, "So show us how many units it would take to build a condo eight units high." He went through the steps to evaluate $2n^2 - n$ when $n = 8$. I told the group that I looked forward to their presentation to the rest of the class and left them to practice since they knew I might call on any one of them to do the explanation.

I find that many middle school students initially have trouble using a rule that contains variables even when they have derived the rule themselves. Somehow seeing the "naked variable expressions" seems to make them temporarily lose all meaning for the rule and how to use it. Grounding the rule in a real-world context and using the process of step-by-step substitution with explanations seems to help bridge the gap between the real-world meaning of the rule and the abstraction of the rule using symbols. It has been my experience that some students require a substantial amount of practice before they are comfortable evaluating a variable expression or a function rule. However, continually relating the rule to a model or context and evaluating each rule for several values of the variable eventually builds such students' confidence and skill levels.

A fourth group interpreted the model in a different way. As Colin explained it, "We noticed that some of the wings on the model looked like steps going up and some looked like steps going down, so two of them could be put together to make a rectangle." He demonstrated, using a Stage 6 model (see Figure 9–10).

FIGURE 9–9 Susanna's explanation

Notation	Comment
$T = 2n^2 - n$	In our rule, the total number of cubes or condo units needed is two times *n* squared minus *n* (*n* is the stage number or height).
$T = 2 \times 10^2 - 10$	Use **ten** for *n*.
$T = 2 \times \mathbf{100} - 10$	Ten squared equals **one hundred**.
$T = \mathbf{200} - 10$	Two times one hundred equals **two hundred**.
$T = \mathbf{190}$	And two hundred minus ten equals **one hundred ninety**.

FIGURE 9–10   Colin's group's Stage 6 model

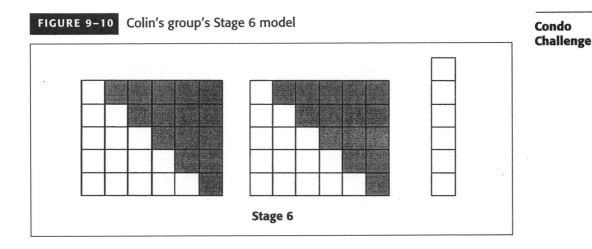

Stage 6

"We used the other two wings to make another rectangle. We still needed to include the center post. So now we're trying to find a way to make a rule by looking at each stage as two rectangles and the center, but we're having trouble."

When asked to explain their thinking, Mark showed me his work so far (see Figure 9–11). Pointing to his sheet of work, Mark stated, "We started with Stage Six. Each rectangle was six units wide, which we could call *n* units since that was the same as the stage number, and the rectangle was five

FIGURE 9–11   Mark's work

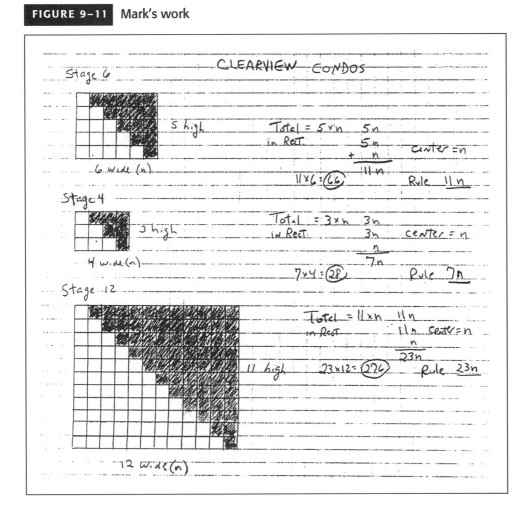

units high. That gave us five rows of *n* units or five *n* units for the number of blocks in the rectangle. The other rectangle also had five *n* units and the center column had *n* units since it was six blocks high.

"Adding it all together, we found that Stage Six contained eleven *n* blocks, or eleven times six, which is sixty-six blocks. This is what we counted, so that seems right.

"We tried this idea for Stage Four and Stage Twelve. The rule we got for Stage Four, as you can see, is seven *n*, or seven times four equals twenty-eight blocks. That is the right number of blocks. And for Stage Twelve, we got twenty-three *n*, which gives you twenty-three times twelve, or two hundred seventy-six, blocks—again, the right answer if you count the blocks."

"So what is the problem?" I asked.

Latisha frowned as she said, "Well, the rule is not the same for every stage. It's eleven *n* for Stage Six, seven *n* for Stage Four, and twenty-three *n* for Stage Twelve. We feel like we are close, because the rules all work, but we aren't quite there."

"We're going to organize the results to see if we can find some pattern that will help us," Mark said.

When I returned to the group, they had made the table shown in Figure 9–12. "We made a table and can see some patterns in it," Dimitri said, pointing to his table. "For example, each time the stage number increases, the number of *n*'s gets two larger. See, the rule for Stage Two is three *n*, for Stage Three is five *n*, for Stage Four is seven *n*, and so on.

"Also, when we broke the rule down into the numbers you would actually use [pointing to the "Pattern" column], the number you are multiplying times *n* gets one larger. For example, for Stage Two, the rule three *n* tells you to multiply three by two, but you could think of it as (*n* plus one) times *n* since three is one bigger than two, the stage number.

"When you move to Stage Three, the rule five *n* could be written (*n* plus two) times *n*. So what you add to *n* in that part of the rule gets bigger by one for each stage. But we still can't get an explicit rule!"

"What was your goal in the 'Pattern' column of your table?" I asked.

FIGURE 9–12 Dimitri's table

Table for Clearview Condos

Stage	Rule	Pattern	Total
2	3*n*	3×2 $(n+1)(n)$	6
3	5*n*	5×3 $(n+2)(n)$	15
4	7*n*	7×4 $(n+3)(n)$	28
6	11*n*	11×6 $(n+5)(n)$	66
12	23*n*	23×12 $(n+11)(n)$	276

"To make each part of the rule use the stage number, n, to tell about the number," Mark answered. "That way, you can get bigger and bigger answers for doing the same thing, and that's what we need."

While Mark did not word his observation in a very sophisticated way, he was on the right track. The fact that the total number of blocks increased rapidly from one stage to the next indicated that including variables whenever possible instead of numbers in their rule would be particularly desirable, since the value of expressions like $3n$ gets larger faster as the value of n increases. As teachers, we must encourage middle school students to express such ideas, even when they are not worded very clearly, because often other students understand the implications and can build upon them themselves. Furthermore, I have observed that often the student who is expressing the ideas, no matter how incompletely, often clarifies his or her own thinking and can then go to the next step.

"Now that you have made additional observations," I asked, "would it be useful to go back to your first drawings and try to do the same thing? Replace the numbers you found in each drawing with expressions that include variables."

It is a tough call for me to know when to give a hint to a student or group of students and how explicit to make such a hint. In this case, it seemed to me that the students were thinking in some appropriate and relevant ways, but that they were wasting a lot of time applying those ideas in a context that was not likely to have useful results. The reality of the time constraints of short class periods compels teachers to make some choices we know are not optimal. This was one of those occasions.

Meanwhile, the students in this group eagerly began to revisit their first drawings (refer back to Figure 9–11). I listened as the following sequence of comments occurred:

Mark: OK, for Stage Six, the rectangle is six blocks wide and five high.

Dimitri: So we can use "n minus one" for five, right?

Latisha: That makes sense. Oh, look! For Stage Four, the rectangle is four blocks wide and three high and the three can be written "n minus one," too, since three is one less than the stage number!

Colin: And the height of eleven for Stage Twelve can also be n minus one. We got it!!

Mark: Not quite. So what does that make our rule?

Dimitri (after a pause): I think each rectangle is n times (n minus one) blocks!

Mark: Oh yeah! So everybody write down the rule.

When a few moments had passed, Mark asked if everyone had a rule. When the other students nodded, he said, "I got 'Total equals two times [n times (n minus one)] plus n."

All except Colin nodded. "Wait a minute. Wait a minute. You're right. I forgot to add the last part, the n, but we need it for the center." The students gave each other high fives and set out to organize their group presentation (see Figure 9–13).

Annie's group found a solution that I had not seen before. Unlike any other group, they started by combining the four wings and the center of a Stage 6 model into a single triangular shape (see Figure 9–14).

When I asked the group why they had chosen to arrange the cubes into that particular shape, Sara replied, "We wanted to put all the blocks together so we could work with one pattern instead of five (the four wings and the center)."

Annie added, "After forming the triangular shape for Stage Six, we noticed that it contained eleven columns, starting with one block and going up by one each time, to eleven blocks." Of course, this way of viewing the array presented the group with essentially the same challenge as the other groups who were trying to find a formula for adding the first *n* counting numbers. The difference was that this group *was* able to find an explicit formula.

FIGURE 9–13 Mark's group's solution

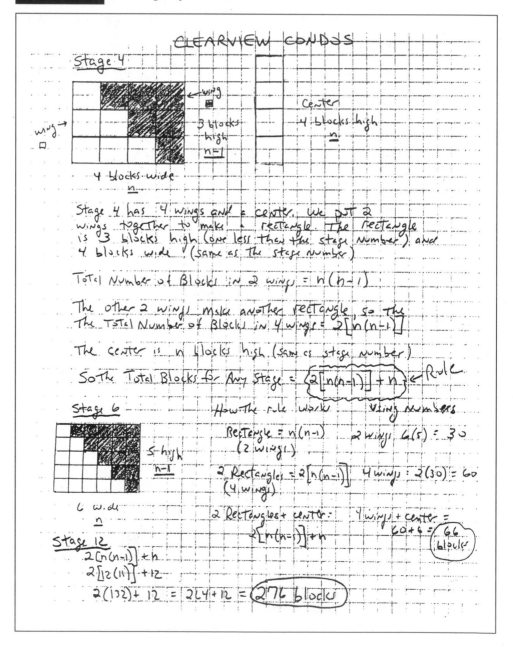

FIGURE 9-14 Annie's group's solution

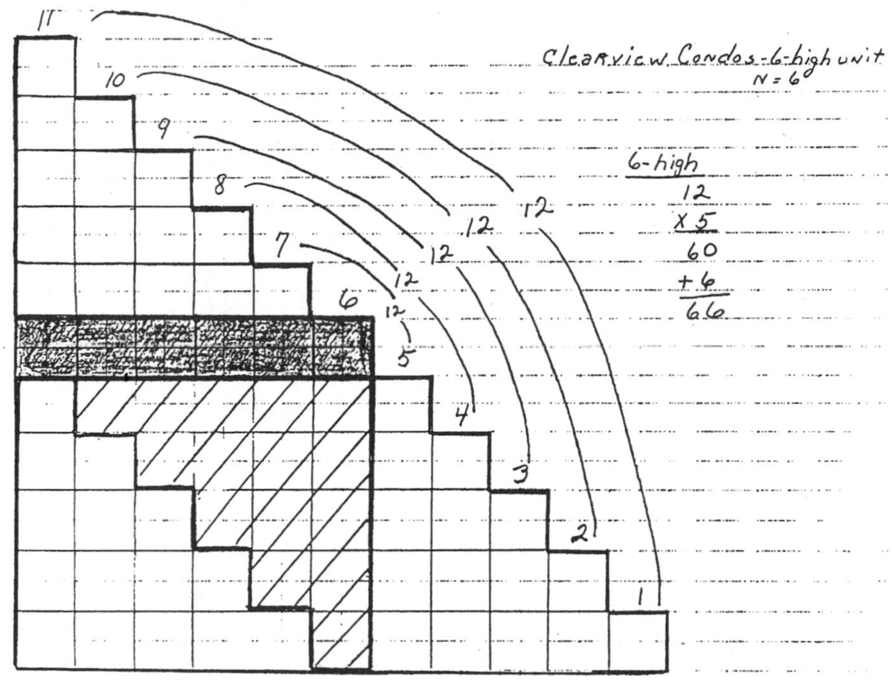

Condo Challenge   **203**

Clearview Condos - 6-high unit
N = 6

6-high
12
× 5
60
+ 6
66

Explanation: We formed one large Triangle from the blocks. We added the columns in pairs (7+5, 5 pairs 8+4, 9+3, 10+2, and 11+1) We had one 6 left over. Since N=6 for this stage we got 5 × 2N or (N-1)2N for the pairs + N for the extra 6. $\frac{N-1}{5}$ $2×6=12$

Our rule is (N-1)2N+N or 2N²-2N+N or 2N²-N

For a 6-high unit, the model would use 2×6²-6 or 2×36-6 or 72-6 or 66 blocks

For a 12-high unit, the model would use 2N²-N or 2×12²-12 or 288-12 or 276 blocks

It works!

In trying to determine why this group was successful when the other two were not, I asked, "What did you notice next?"

Annie continued, "We looked for something that matched the height of the model because we knew that number [six] was _n_ for our rule. We found the column that was six blocks high. When we looked on each side of that column, they were one more and one less than six [seven and five] blocks high. The next two, moving outwards, were two more and two less than six [eight and four] blocks high. We all thought we had found a pattern that might help us, but it was Kimya who noticed that each pair added up to twelve, and that was like averaging them all out to be six each."

Kimya interjected, "What I thought about the twelve was that twelve equals two times six, and that was good because we could call it 'two n.' "

Tawny interrupted, "When we put it all together, we decided to explain it to this class this way: From our model that was six blocks high in the center, we formed one large triangle from all the blocks." Pointing to the drawing, she continued, "We added the columns in pairs (seven plus five, eight plus four, nine plus three, ten plus two, and eleven plus one) and had one column of six blocks left over. So we had five (which was n minus one) pairs times twelve blocks (which was two n), or [(n minus one) times (two n) for all the blocks in the pairs of columns, plus n for the extra column that was six blocks high]. We checked our rule, [(n minus one) times (two n) plus n], using n equals six, and the total of sixty-six blocks was correct. We tried the rule for several other heights and it always gives the right total because it makes sense from the way we arranged the blocks."

I asked, "So who would like to summarize your group's *strategy* for finding the rule?" I asked this question because I wanted a better feel for why this group was able to come up with an explicit rule for the sum of n counting numbers when the other groups could not—some strategy that could be verbalized to help the other students in this or similar situations.

After thinking a moment, Sara put it nicely: "I would say we were looking for patterns, and we were especially looking for ways to connect any patterns we found to the stage number. That way our rule would hopefully work for other stages, too." While Sara did not verbalize the strategy as a teacher might, her contribution was valuable. Struggling students need to hear strategies for finding explicit function rules expressed in several ways and in the context of several situations. I made a mental note to ask Sara to repeat the explanation of the strategy when this group reported to the whole class.

Helping students develop many appropriate ways of attacking problems is an important goal of my middle school mathematics classes, and my students continually help me in this endeavor. I have found that having students explain their mathematical ideas in their own words is often more helpful to other students than hearing me explain them. I believe it not only helps the students who are listening, but also clarifies the thinking of and builds confidence within the students who are asked to make such explanations.

Next, each of the student groups made a brief presentation to the rest of the class, explaining their thinking using the poster or transparency they had prepared for this purpose. Following established class procedure, each student in the group contributed to the presentation.

After each presentation, other students in the class were invited to ask questions or make comments. Most of the questions seemed aimed at clarifying some detail of the solution. I found it interesting that the only flurry of questions centered on the discovery by Steve's group that the total number of cubes for any stage could be easily determined if the total for the stage with one-half the height of the stage in question were known. The rest of the students asked the group to go through another example of how their "shortcut" worked and comments like "cool" and "neat" were offered by several classmates after the explanation.

The comments about the solutions offered by other groups were quite supportive. After each presentation, students often expressed their sentiments by communicating in various ways, "I would have never thought to do it that way!"

Members of Valerie's and Steve's groups were especially open with their admiration for the method Annie's group used to add consecutive integers. As Leroy pointed out, "Our group and Steve's can use that method to find the total number of cubes for each wing," and they later did so.

It was gratifying to see the students appreciate the mathematical thinking of their classmates. I believe that when a class of students becomes a community of learners, everyone gains more in a comfortable environment. I see students in such a class as being willing to take risks, open to the ideas of other students, and eager to find connections between their own work and that of their classmates.

One final example of finding connections was illustrated by the postscript Steve provided for this lesson. The next day he asked to share something with the class (see Figure 9–15). "The way Annie's group rearranged the cubes to solve their problem really shows why the rule our group found works. We worked with numbers, but they did the same thing using the cubes. As you can see, we can put all the cubes of a Stage Four model together and it gives us the wing of a Stage Eight model. You can actually see how our rule works; I think it is easier to understand and believe that it always works when you look at the cubes as well as the numbers. This would work for any stages where one is half as tall as the other, as you can now *see*."

I felt Steve's contribution was a fitting way to end a lesson that emphasized the value of viewing problems *visually* in several different ways. I felt that my students gained an increased awareness of and appreciation for multiple approaches to solving problems. I hope they are more aware of the connections between numerical and visual or geometric patterns and solutions. Their findings certainly emphasize that many forms of a function rule can be correct and valid. These understandings should help these students develop algebraic thinking and become better problem solvers.

FIGURE 9–15   Steve's wing of Stage 8

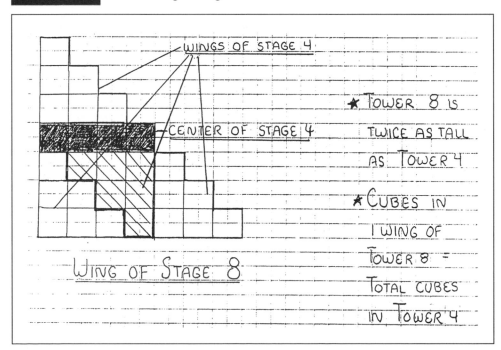

This problem is appropriate for a lesson similar to *Condo Challenge*.

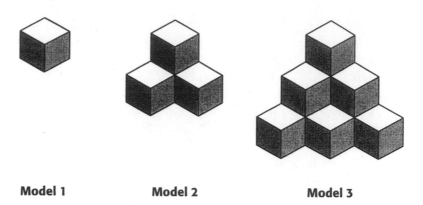

Model 1   **Model 2**   **Model 3**

Corner Condos

The builders of Corner Condos have a project. They are not sure yet how tall they want the building to be.

1. How many cubes are needed to build a 6-high model of Corner Condos?
2. How many cubes are needed to build a 12-high model like this?
3. Explain how you got your answer for question #2.

How many cubes are needed to build a model of any height? Explain your thinking and make a rule, using a variable if possible.

How could your findings help the builders of Corner Condos?

Iterative Rule: Add the next odd number to the total from the previous stage.

Explicit Rules: Rules will vary according to the visual interpretation of the models by each group of students, as shown below.

Stage	Iterative Rule	Explicit Rule Version #1	Explicit Rule Version #2	Total Cubes
1	1	1	1	1
2	1 + 3	2(1 + 2) − 2	1 + 3	4
3	1 + 3 + 5	2(1 + 2 + 3) − 3	3 + 6	9
Verbal Description	For each new stage, add the next odd number to get the new total	Total = 2 (total cubes in each side, or sum of n counting numbers) − n or cubes counted twice	Total = sum of 2 triangular numbers (the nth and $(n − 1)$th triangular numbers)	
Rule in Symbols	$f(n) = f_{(n-1)} +$ next odd number (after the one added to find previous stage)	$2\left[\dfrac{n(n+1)}{2}\right] - n$	$\dfrac{n(n+1)}{2} + \dfrac{(n-1)n}{2}$	n^2

Multilink cubes should be used by students to show the visual interpretations that underlie their explicit rules. In this way, all students have the opportunity to expand their ways of visualizing patterns.

Sums of Consecutive Cubes

Consecutive Cubes

The cubes in the following pattern have side lengths of 1, 2, and 3. If the pattern is continued, what will be the sum of the volumes of the first 10 cubes? 100 cubes? *n* cubes?

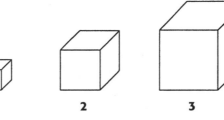

side lengths   **1**   **2**   **3**

Values for Consecutive Cubes

Number of Cubes	Sums of Volumes	Total of Sums
1	1	1 (1^2)
2	1 + 8	9 (3^2)
3	1 + 8 + 27	36 (6^2)
10		3,025 (55^2)
100		25,502,500 ($5,050^2$)
n		(nth triangular number)^2 $$\left[\frac{n(n+1)}{2}\right]^2$$

Notice that students must recognize the values in the last column as the squares of the triangular numbers and must know or derive the formula for triangular numbers to express an explicit rule for this problem using a variable.

The similar and extension problems offered for the lesson *Go Figure!* in this book also involve figurate numbers.

Following are the rules for the *Condo Challenge* lesson found by this class:

Iterative Rule

$4 \times$ [(number of cubes in the wing from one stage before) + (number of stage before)] + (stage number)

Explicit Rules

$4 \times$ [cubes in one wing—e.g., for Stage 6, (5 + 4 + 3 + 2 + 1)] + stage number

$2n^2 - n$ for any stage *n*

$2[n(n - 1)] + n$ for any stage n
$2n(n - 1) + n$ for any stage n

Of course, other forms of the rule are possible as well.

A nice follow-up activity for *Condo Challenge* is to have the students create a spreadsheet to display the various forms of the rule for this pattern that were found in their class, and the values each rule generates. This activity will reinforce for students that there can be equivalent forms for a rule and that all such forms produce the same results. The spreadsheet can also be used to view values for large stage numbers.

Sample column headings and formulas for such a spreadsheet are shown in Figure 9–16. Each set corresponds to one of the rules derived during the lesson.

FIGURE 9–16 Condo Challenge: Sample spreadsheet headings and formulas

	A	B	C	D
1	Step or Stage = n	$2*n\wedge2$	n	Total Using $2n\wedge2 - n$
2	1	2	1	1

	A	B	C	D
1	Step or Stage = n	$2*n\wedge2$	n	Total Using $2n\wedge2 - n$
2	1	=PRODUCT(A2,A2,2)	=A2	=SUM(B2,C2)

	A	E	F	G
1	Step or Stage = n	$n - 1$	Product Subtotal $2*[n(n - 1)]$	Total Using $2*[n(n - 1)] + n$
2	1	0	0	1

	A	E	F	G
1	Step or Stage = n	$n - 1$	Product Subtotal $2*[n(n - 1)]$	Total Using $2*[n(n - 1)] + n$
2	1	=(A2) – 1	=PRODUCT(2,A2,E2)	=SUM(A2,F2)

	A	H	I	J
1	Step or Stage = n	$2n$	Subtotal of $2n*(n - 1)$	Total Using $2n(n - 1) + n$
2	1	2	0	1

	A	H	I	J
1	Step or Stage = n	$2n$	Subtotal of $2n*(n - 1)$	Total Using $2n(n - 1) + n$
2	1	=PRODUCT(2,A2)	=PRODUCT(H2,E2)	=SUM(I2,A2)

CHAPTER 10

The Window Problem

OVERVIEW

In this lesson students are given a nonroutine problem to solve. They use manipulatives to help them generate data related to the problem, enter the data in a table, and construct appropriate graphs. They then try to find function rules to fit the data sets and explain how their conclusions fit with the data and the context of the problem. They compare the explicit function rules as examples of constant, linear, and quadratic functions. Finally, the students analyze, discuss, and write about the various representations of the data. By comparing tables, graphs, and function rules and connecting them to an investigation within a meaningful context, students should begin to internalize the meaning of such concepts as function (constant, linear, and quadratic), rate of change, and slope. Overall, the lesson provides students with initial exposure to different kinds of functions as well as experience using algebraic thinking to describe and predict phenomena.

BACKGROUND

Prior to this lesson, the students in this sixth-grade class had some practice extending visual and numerical patterns and finding iterative and explicit rules for those simple patterns. However, their work with patterns had not included exposure to the concepts of constants and variables. Thus, they had studied functions as generalized rules for patterns but had not examined functions as constant, linear, or quadratic. They also had some experience graphing on the coordinate plane but the concepts of slope, intercepts, and graphs of functions had not been linked to patterns.

PREREQUISITE CONCEPTS OR SKILLS

- Extending visual and numerical patterns
- Finding rules for simple patterns
- Recognizing square numbers
- Graphing coordinates in Quadrant I

VOCABULARY

axis, axes, constant, constant function, explicit rule, function, function rule, iterative rule, intercept, linear function, multiple representations, quadratic function, slope, stage number, variable

TIME

This lesson was completed in two sixty-minute classes. In addition, the students created graphs for homework after the first day of the lesson. If your classes are shorter, I suggest that you aim to get as far as possible on the first day and be sure to save time for students to discuss and set up their graphs (label and scale the axes) before class ends. It may be that you need to save the discussion and graph for the center panes until the second day. If so, the students will most likely need to do their written reflections as homework after the second day of the lesson.

MATERIALS

- *The Window Problem* activity sheets, 1 per student (see Blackline Masters)

- Colored squares in three colors (tiles or paper), up to 36 total per student

- Transparent overhead squares in three colors (16 each of two colors, 4 of a third color)

- 1 sheet of grid paper per student

The Lesson

Gathering and Analyzing Data; Constructing Tables and Graphs

Students were presented with the following problem:

The Window Problem

Peerless Window Company puts together square windows from three kinds of units:

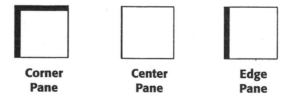

| **Corner Pane** | **Center Pane** | **Edge Pane** |

The production manager at Peerless needs to decide how many of each type of unit to make so the company can avoid wasting units. Complete the labeled rows in the following table. You may complete extra rows if you wish. Look for patterns and find a rule for each kind of pane for any size square window.

Window Size	Number of Corner-Pane Units	Number of Center-Pane Units	Number of Edge-Pane Units	The Window Problem 211
2 × 2				
3 × 3				
4 × 4				
5 × 5				
6 × 6				
n × n				

I encouraged the students to use squares of various colors and grid paper to build a model and/or draw a picture for each window size. I pointed out that these models or drawings could be used to help generate data to complete the table. The class worked together with one volunteer student at the overhead to construct models and make drawings for two stages. I reminded the students to keep in mind that the thick edges of the panes shown on their problem sheet represented reinforcement that was needed around the outside edges of each window.

I began by asking the students to build a model and draw an example of such a window two units wide and two units high. After giving the students a few moments to complete this task, I asked for a volunteer to construct a model on the overhead projector, using transparent colored squares. There were squares of three colors at the overhead: blue, pink, and clear. I instructed Megan to choose a color for each type of pane, construct a model using squares of the appropriate color, and make a drawing of the window with thick edges around the outside.

I asked the students to build a model and make a drawing for windows of two different sizes before having them work independently to make certain every student clearly understood when it was appropriate to use each of the three kinds of panes. I felt some students needed one or both of these aids to find correct answers to enter into the table. I knew that having the correct data in the table was essential for students to find patterns that would lead them to derive the appropriate function rules, and I didn't want students to be lost when the class began to discuss the patterns the students found in the table.

Megan used four blue squares (designated by **b** in Figure 10–1) to build her model. She also drew a diagram.

I asked Megan to explain her work. She said, "To make a window that is two units wide and two units high, you would have to use four panes. All of them would need two thick sides because they are on the outside edges of the window and each one is a corner."

I asked whether the rest of the class agreed that Megan's model and drawing were correct. They nodded. Circulating around the classroom, I

FIGURE 10-1 Megan's diagram of a two-by-two window

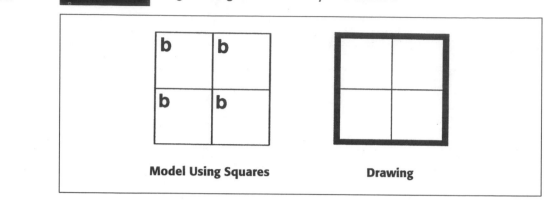

Model Using Squares   **Drawing**

could see that most of the students had elected to draw diagrams on their sheets of grid paper similar to Megan's and a few had used the squares to build a model.

"So what information should you enter in the table?" I asked.

Hands shot up around the room. I called on Mike, who answered, "On the first row in the table (the row for two-by-two windows), you fill in four for the number of corner panes and zero for the other two kinds of panes."

Often middle school students remark that they are reluctant to record data in a table, especially for the first few stages, because they believe the initial information is so obvious that this step should not be necessary. I have found it advantageous to respond to their remarks in order not to lose the interest of some students. I always agree that these are easy stages but point out that we need this data to help see how patterns develop. I also stress that we need to look at several stages of any pattern to develop confidence before hypothesizing generalizations.

When all the students agreed that Mike was correct, I asked whether there were any questions. There were none, so I suggested that the whole class try one more size window together. "Everyone build a model and make a drawing for a window five units wide and five units high," I announced, "to make sure we all understand this problem in exactly the same way."

Students went to work right away. Again I circulated among the students to see that they were doing the work correctly. Soon they had completed the task. I called on George to do the work at the overhead. He drew the diagram and constructed the model shown in Figure 10–2, using blue squares (designated by **b** in the illustration) to represent corner panes, pink squares (designated by **p**) for edge panes, and clear squares (designated by **c**) for center panes.

I asked the other students whether they agreed with George's model and drawing and they indicated that they did. Then I asked that each student use the model and/or drawing to determine the information about the kinds of panes needed for a five-by-five window and complete the appropriate row in the table. After a few moments I asked for volunteers and called on Angela to share what she had recorded.

"I counted four corner panes, nine center panes, and twelve edge panes," she reported.

"Did everyone get those same numbers?" I asked.

"I didn't," Dixon spoke up. "I got twenty edge panes."

I asked Dixon to come up to the overhead and explain his thinking.

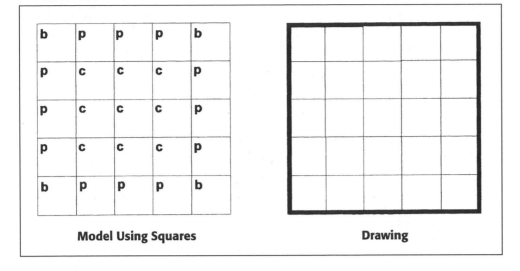

Model Using Squares   **Drawing**

Pointing to one side of the model of squares on the overhead, he said, "There are five squares along each of the four sides and five times four equals twenty, so there are twenty edge panes."

"Would anyone like to agree or disagree with Dixon and explain why?" I asked.

George, who was still standing beside the overhead, pointed to the diagram and said, "You're right, Dixon, that there are five squares along each edge. But two of them are corner panes each time," pointing out the two corners on the left side of the square. "So there are really only three edge panes for each side of the square," he added, pointing to each of the appropriate squares along the same side of the square, "or twelve in all."

Dixon nodded. "I see what you mean. I counted the corner squares as edge squares, too. I should have realized something was wrong because I have too many squares."

"What do you mean when you say, 'I have too many squares,' Dixon?" I asked.

"For a five-by-five window, you need five times five, or twenty-five, panes, but if I add up the numbers I wrote for corner, center, and edge panes, I get thirty-three panes. That can't be right," Dixon explained.

I was pleased that Dixon had recognized his mistake and the reason for it. I believe students are much less likely to repeat an error when they figure out the error in their thinking or procedure for themselves rather than when I simply tell them. It also helps the student regain any loss of confidence caused by such an error, especially when the student is working or talking to the whole class. I don't want to make it more difficult for a student who might be hesitant to speak up in the first place. In my classes I try to establish an attitude among the students that everyone makes errors and that these should be viewed as opportunities for learning rather than mistakes that indicate some inadequacy in the student. My efforts in this direction are a part of trying to establish an atmosphere that is conducive to maximizing opportunities for learning for every student. I watch for opportunities to reinforce comments and behaviors that support such an atmosphere.

Consequently, I told the class, "Dixon just did something very important. He listened to George's thinking and then checked it for himself using a different line of reasoning. Who can explain again how Dixon verified that George was correct?"

Emily volunteered and offered, "Dixon realized that, for each window, the number of corner panes, center panes, and edge panes must add up to the total number of panes you need to make a window that size."

"Exactly, Emily," I replied. "And because we know it is always a good idea to verify answers by using a different technique than the one you first used, I think you should add a column to the table on your problem sheet. What do you think?"

With only a couple of small groans, the students added another column to their tables. I have found that the number of protests in such a situation is smaller if I acknowledge the students who provided the impetus for adding it. In this case, it provided the chance to add a self-checking component—a behavior I like to encourage whenever possible.

"What do you think the column should be labeled?" I asked.

"I just labeled mine *Dixon's Total*," Lawson offered.

"I called it *Total Panes by Dixon*," Jessica said.

Notice that the activity sheet in the Blackline Masters section of this book includes this additional column in order for the form to be most useful for the reader, although it was not present on the original version that the students in this class received.

I assured the students that either title was acceptable. "Now, how will you calculate the values you enter in the new column in your table and how will you use that information?" I asked.

Melinda raised her hand and offered, "You can just multiply the window size, like for a five-by-five window you do five times five and get twenty-five total panes needed. You have to make sure that number is the same total you get when you add up the numbers you put for the three kinds of panes."

"Does that make sense to everyone?" I asked. Everyone nodded. I instructed the students to work with other window sizes to complete the table. I reminded them that they could make diagrams or build models to help. I also asked the students to record any patterns or other observations they noticed as they worked to complete the table.

The students knew they were free to work with other students at this point if they wished. Most worked in pairs. Working together is the norm in my classes, so much so that I announce only when I want the students to work independently. This practice is based on my firm belief that collaboration is natural and that students usually learn more through this method than by working alone. However, encouraging collaborative learning is combined with the clear expectation that each student is responsible for understanding the work that he or she produces. I didn't start out teaching this way, but am now convinced that our students benefit greatly from being part of a community of learners.

The students worked diligently to complete their tables. While they worked, I circulated among the students and stopped occasionally to ask a question, make a comment, or listen to a student or group. Besides monitoring to see that students were doing their work and not completely off-track with their results, I used this time as an opportunity to converse briefly with individual students in order to hear them explain their thinking. I did this for several reasons. First, whenever possible, I try to informally assess the kind of thinking my students are doing. This helps me ascertain what the students are observing, whether they are thinking soundly, and whether they are progressing toward the objectives or goals I have set for the lesson, the month, or the year.

For example, while circulating during this lesson, I noticed that Carolyn and Kim had completed their table early and were looking for patterns in their data while other students finished up. "Have you girls found any interesting patterns in your table?" I asked.

"Yes," Kim answered. "We are looking at the pattern for the number of edge panes right now. We found that the number of edge panes grows by four each time the window size increases, but we can't find an explicit rule for the number of edge panes for *any* size window yet."

"What have you tried?" I asked.

"Well, we have been looking at the numbers of edge panes and trying to relate them in some way to the window size but we aren't getting anywhere," Carolyn offered.

Seeing a sheet of drawings that the girls had created for several window sizes, I pointed to it and said, "Go back to your drawings. Remember that you want the rule you come up with to make sense with what you find actually happening with the windows as they grow in size. So go back to your drawings and focus on what happens with the edge panes each time the window size grows." (See Figure 10–3.)

Conversations like this between the teacher and an individual or small group also give students opportunities to express their mathematical thinking verbally. Some students are too shy to speak up in front of the class. For them, a quick private "rehearsal" is invaluable in boosting their confidence to contribute to a subsequent whole-class discussion, especially if they are asked the same question they have already verbalized to the teacher and know their answer to be correct. During this lesson, I noticed that OJ had filled in the column for the number of corner panes with 4s although he had completed only a few rows in the table. I asked him how he knew to do this, and he replied, "Well, all the windows are squares, and every square has four corners, so you will always use four corner panes for each window no matter how big or small it is." I told OJ that I wanted him to share his observation with the class when we discussed patterns in the table later during the lesson.

"You not only noticed the pattern, OJ, but you also can explain *why* that pattern occurs. That is exactly the kind of thinking you should be doing." OJ grinned. He did not yet have a lot of confidence in his mathematical ability and was not usually an enthusiastic volunteer in a whole-class setting. On this day I knew he would participate and contribute to the understanding of other students as well.

FIGURE 10–3 Kim and Carolyn's initial drawing

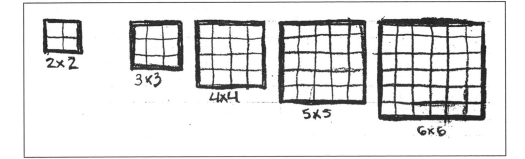

At the other end of the spectrum, some students feel the need to think aloud when they are formulating a hypothesis or new understanding. These miniconferences often help such students clarify their thinking.

Occasionally, a student is thinking at a level well beyond that of his or her classmates and such conversations can be private or serve as a time in which to help the student decide what is appropriate to share with the class. In the broadest sense, I consider times like these to be opportunities to enrich a mathematical experience for each of my students at one time or another and for me to gather information that can make me a better teacher.

When all the students had completed their tables, I let volunteers enter the data into a transparency version of the table. I added the column *Total # of Panes* (see Figure 10–4).

First, I asked students to share and explain any patterns they noticed with a partner. I did this to give every student the opportunity to explain his or her thinking to at least one other student. I then asked who would like to share one pattern he or she had found in the table or one observation he or she had made while investigating the problem. After each contribution, every student who made that same discovery was asked to raise his or her hand. Also, students could make additional comments or ask questions after an idea was presented.

Following are some of the patterns found by every pair of students in the class:

- The total number of panes for any size window is the sum of the three kinds of panes listed in the table. (Jessica noted that this means there aren't any other kind of panes needed, such as a pane with three reinforced sides. Ben commented that multiplying the dimensions of the

FIGURE 10–4 Class table (Melinda's version)

Total # of panes	Window Size	Number of Corner Pane Units	Number of Center Pane Units	Number of Edge Pane Units
4	2 x 2	4	0	0
9	3 x 3	4	1	4
16	4 x 4	4	4	8
25	5 x 5	4	9	12
36	6 x 6	4	16	16
49	7 x 7	4	25	20
64	8 x 8	4	36	24
81	9 x 9	4	49	28
100	10 x 10	4	64	32
	n x n			

window gives you this same total, since the number of panes across times the number of panes up and down is another way to find the total number of panes for any window.)

- The number of corner panes is always four. (OJ pointed out that this is logical, since all windows are square and squares always have four corners.)

- The number of edge panes increases by four for each window size. (Jessica pointed out that one edge pane was added along each of the four sides of the window each time you go from one size to the next larger size window.)

- The number of center panes increases by more each time. That is, the amount of increase in the number of center panes gets larger each time as you change from one size to the next larger size window. (Several pairs of students noted that the increases corresponded with the odd numbers, i.e., there were increases of 1, 3, 5, 7, 9 . . . for each successive increase in side length.)

Following are some of the patterns found by one or more pairs of students in the class:

- The center panes always form a square. (After this observation was presented, the rest of the students professed that they, too, had noticed this phenomenon but did not consider it a pattern. This gave me the opportunity to remind the students that not all patterns are numerical. I also commented that, in fact, this observation should be helpful to the students as they began to search for and make sense out of the function rules for each kind of pane.)

- The numbers in the table for the total panes are the same numbers as those for the number of center-pane units, except they appear two window sizes earlier. (**Note:** When this observation was presented I could not resist the opportunity to point out that it was unlikely to be discovered without the benefit of information organized in a table!)

- The square of center panes for any window size is the same size and shape as the total window with side lengths two smaller than it. For example, the center panes for a 5-by-5 window form a 3-by-3 square. (Again, this is a geometric pattern that is important to notice in order to understand why a numerical rule works.)

- For any window size, the total squares for the center panes equals the total squares for the entire window minus the total of all the edge panes for the next level. (Rinaldo proudly offered the symbolic version of his rule as $(n - 2)^2 = n^2 - [4 ((n + 1) - 2)]$. The other students were clearly impressed—several "oohed" and "aahed" and others copied the equation on their papers—but none expressed interest in finding out more about it. I was in a slight quandary: I wanted to send a clear message that I valued Rinaldo's contribution, but at the same time, I recognized that an immediate, detailed examination of his rule would cause a protracted distraction from the focus of the lesson. I opted to ask Rinaldo to create a transparency for the next day that used substitution to illustrate how his rule worked for a particular window size, along with an explanation of why his rule made sense.)

During this discussion, I could have chosen to ask the students to focus exclusively on patterns that they felt would lead directly to function rules. There were two reasons I thought it beneficial to spend as much time as needed for the students to share *any* patterns and observations they gleaned while completing the table. First, such a discussion obviously involves students' verbalizing mathematical ideas. I believe this process not only promotes the acquisition and retention of concepts but also often leads to deeper understanding by learners. In addition, I have found that over time, students naturally adopt strategies or ways of thinking from their peers through such sharing. Also, in this particular lesson, I felt that some of the visual and geometric patterns—patterns that could help all the students better understand the rules they would derive during the lesson—would probably go unnoticed by many of the students without such sharing.

When the students had completed the discussion of patterns and observations, I asked them to focus on sharing and writing down ideas for rules that might be used to find the number of each kind of pane needed for any size window. I gave them a few minutes to work with a partner and then asked for volunteers.

When I launched the discussion, I first asked the students to focus on the number of edge panes. I did this because I knew that most likely the students would offer two forms of the rule, an iterative and, hopefully, an explicit version. Also, I wanted to establish some important vocabulary before dealing with the corner panes. Royce volunteered, "The number of edge panes is always four more than the number needed for the size before."

I asked Royce to state his observation as a rule and he then said, "Total number of edge panes equals the number of edge panes for the size before plus four."

"Will this rule work for every size window or every stage for edge panes?" I asked. The students agreed that it would. "What do we call this kind of rule and why?" I asked.

Ky answered, "Royce's rule is an iterative rule because it tells you how to get the answer for any step using the answer from the step before it."

"Exactly. So can someone use Royce's rule to find the number of edge panes for a seven-by-seven window?" I asked.

Carolyn quickly offered, "A seven-by-seven window, according to Royce's rule, has twenty edge panes because you add four to sixteen, which is the number of edge panes for a six-by-six window. Total equals sixteen (from the step before) plus four."

When everyone indicated agreement, I asked, "Who can explain why that rule makes sense in this problem?" The students seemed to be struggling with this question, so I reworded it, "How does the rule fit with what happens with the edge panes as the window gets one size larger? Look at your models and drawings."

Chan proclaimed, "Every time the window gets one size bigger, each edge of the window gets one edge pane longer. Since there are four edges on a window, the total number of edge panes grows by four."

I asked, "Can someone word that another way?"

"I think Chan is saying that when the window goes up by one stage, like from a six-by-six to a seven-by-seven, you always need to add one new edge pane on each side of the window, so the total number of edge panes increases by four for each new size," Megan offered.

I often ask students to reword an answer one student has offered in order to get every student to think about the idea in his or her own way.

Through this process, each student who explains or rethinks the idea can construct her or his own meaning—a meaning that is far more likely to persist than if a student just memorized the way someone else expressed the same idea. This technique also gives students another chance to catch on if they didn't understand the first student's version.

At this point in the lesson I felt it was time to remind students of the value of an explicit rule to predict values.

"Let's do one more example using Royce's rule," I said. "Who can use the rule to tell us the number of edge panes needed for a hundred-by-hundred window?"

Royce quickly spoke up. "The rule will work for a hundred-by-hundred window, but you can't do it quickly because you have to know how many edge panes there are in a ninety-nine-by-ninety-nine window. It would be better to use an explicit rule for that problem."

"Does everyone understand what Royce is saying? And who can remind us what an *explicit rule* is?"

Emily said, "An explicit rule is one that uses the stage number to get the answer so you don't have to know the answer for the stage before it to do the work."

When there were no questions about Emily's explanation, I asked whether anyone had found an explicit rule for the number of edge panes needed for any size window.

Kim and Carolyn waved their hands in the air. Since I knew they were struggling with this rule earlier, I asked them to share their work and their thinking with the class (see Figure 10–5).

Carolyn copied their drawings for 3-by-3, 4-by-4, and 5-by-5 windows on the overhead. "Our rule is 'Number of edge panes equals four times (length of a side minus two).' We knew from the numbers in our table that the number of edge panes increases by four for each new size, but we had to go back to our drawings to find the explicit rule. When we labeled the edge panes for each stage [pointing to their drawing], then it was easy. First, look

FIGURE 10–5 Kim and Carolyn's revised drawing

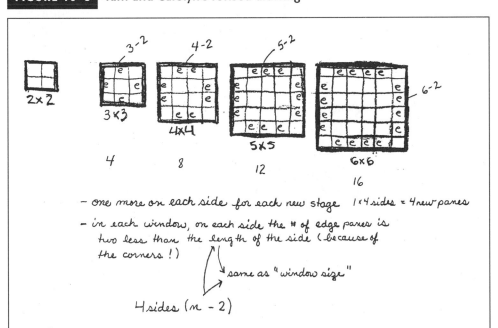

along one edge in each window as they get larger. Even though the number of edge panes grows each time, there are always two panes along each edge that are not edge panes. When you think about it, that makes sense because every edge has a corner at each end. So the number of edge panes along one side of any window is the length of the edge minus two." She wrote *(n – 2)* on the overhead transparency. "Since there are four edges, the total number of edge panes for any window is four times the stage number minus two." She grinned as she added to the expression on the transparency so that it read *Total = 4(n – 2)*.

"Does everyone understand Kim and Carolyn's rule?" I asked.

Lawson commented, "When I look at the drawings, that rule makes sense because of what Carolyn said, but I'm not quite sure what the *n* in the rule stands for."

Kim answered, as shown in Figure 10–6. (The writing she did on the board is labeled "Notation" and her spoken words are labeled "Comment.")

"Does that answer your question, Lawson?" I asked.

"Not really," he replied. "Kim said *n* stands for the stage number, but I thought it was the length of each side of the window."

"Aha," I said, "I see how that could be confusing. Kim or Carolyn, can you help Lawson?"

Kim answered, "Actually, Lawson, you can think of it either way. Look—the stage number is the same as the length of one side of the window. For a Stage Five window, it is five-by-five, *and* the length of each side of the window is five. For a Stage Four window, it is four-by-four, and the length of each side of the window is four. We said 'stage number' in our rule, but we could have used 'length of one side of the window' instead."

Lawson asked, "So I *could* write the rule 'Total edge panes for any stage equals four times (length of a side minus two)'?"

"Yes," I answered. "So what answer would you get for a ten-by-ten window?" I asked.

Lawson said, thinking aloud, "Four times (ten minus two), four times eight, so thirty-two edge panes."

Kim pointed out, "Your way of thinking about the rule works because the stage number is always the same as the length of the side of a window."

Lawson nodded, indicating that he was satisfied, but I felt an additional comment was needed. "Remember, class, an explicit rule will almost always include a variable, a part of the rule that changes for each stage of the pattern

FIGURE 10–6 Kim's explanation

Notation	Comment
Total = 4(n – 2)	Our rule is "Total number of edge panes = 4 times (length of a side – 2)" or "Total = 4(n – 2)". We used n to stand for the stage number or size of the window.
$T = 4(5 – 2)$	Like, for a five-by-five window, you would start with five, the stage number, and subtract two (the corner panes).
$T = 4(3)$	Then you would multiply four (the number of sides) times three (number of edge panes on each side), which equals twelve.
$T = 12$	There are twelve edge panes in a five-by-five window.

or function. When you are using an explicit rule for a particular stage, you substitute the stage number for that variable. But it is also important to realize that as the stage number changes, something about the pattern itself changes or varies—in this case, the side length of the window. And that change is both why there is a new stage and why the rule works for any stage."

Lawson's comments may have revealed that he was actually struggling with a very common conceptual hurdle, grasping the concept of a variable. Like many students, Lawson seemed to have trouble recognizing that the stage number for the figures can represent a value that changes. He indicated that he understood there was a quantity (the number of edge panes along the side of a window) that was different from one stage to the next, but he did not yet grasp how using the term *stage number* in a rule could represent change. Once he grasped that the number of edge panes on each side of the window and the stage number changed in the same way, I felt he was making progress toward understanding the critical algebraic ideas of change and variables.

"Did anyone have a different way to express the rule for the total number of edge panes for any size window?" I asked.

"We did," George answered. "Angela and I wrote the rule 'Total edge panes equals four *n* minus eight' when *n* stands for stage number or length of each side of a window. Actually, we were thinking about the same as Carolyn and Kim, but we kind of looked at the edge panes all at once instead of just the ones along one edge. If you multiply four times the stage number or length of each side, you get the total number of edge panes, but you have to subtract eight to get the correct answer for the total number of edge panes for that size window."

"Why did you subtract eight from the total panes along the edges?" Ky asked.

"Because of the corners," George said.

"But there are just four corners," Ky protested.

"You're right," Angela answered, "and that confused us a little at first. But we forgot the corner panes like Dixon did earlier—except worse! Look . . ." And she pointed to Carolyn's sketch at the overhead for a 5-by-5 window. "For a five-by-five window, our rule says to multiply the side length by four. But that means we counted each corner pane twice in that total. See, for example, we counted this corner [pointing at the upper left corner pane] when we counted the panes along the top of the window and also when we counted the panes on the left side of the window. In other words, we included each corner pane *twice* when we multiplied four times the edge length, so we needed to subtract eight to get the correct number of edge panes."

"I see," Ky declared.

Once again this interchange reminded me of the power of drawings or models in helping students understand the thinking of others. I was also glad George and Angela presented the rule as $4n - 8$ because it helped me emphasize another important target concept of the lesson. "Let's look at this rule a little more," I said. "In the rule 'Total equals four *n* minus eight,' there are two parts, a *variable* part and a *constant* part. Who can tell me the variable part in the function rule and why it is called that?" I asked.

Melinda offered, "*Four n* is the variable part. That is because the value of *four n* changes or varies for each stage of the function. For Stage Three, four *n* equals twelve (four times three), for Stage Four, four *n* equals sixteen (four times four), and so on."

"Now who can tell me the constant part in the function rule and why it is called that?" I asked.

"I think the eight is the constant part because it stays the same for each stage. You always have to subtract eight to get rid of the corner panes in your total," Chan stated.

"Yes," I affirmed. "In mathematics when a number stays the same for every stage of a situation, that number or value is called a *constant*. The value of a constant always stays the same, whereas the value of a variable expression changes. Is that clear to everyone?" The students nodded.

I felt it was important to have this brief discussion for two reasons. First, I wanted to strengthen the students' understanding of constant and variable in this context. Second, I wanted to lay some foundation for the terms *constant function, linear function,* and *quadratic function,* upcoming in the lesson. However, I did not want to simply use these terms or give definitions for them before the students encountered the upcoming ideas and examples.

When no other forms of the rule for total edge panes were offered by the students, I asked for any explicit rules for the total number of corner panes.

Jessica volunteered and expressed the rule for the number of corner panes as "The number of corner panes is always four no matter how big or small the window is."

All the other students raised their hands to indicate that they agreed with Jessica. I then requested, "Will someone write the explicit rule for the number of corner panes for any window size at the overhead?"

Several students raised their hands. Maria wrote *Total Corner Panes = 4.*

"Does this rule work for every stage or every size window?" I asked. The students agreed that it would. "Do you have any observations or questions about this rule?" I asked.

"There is no variable expression in the rule," Jim remarked.

Upon hearing this observation, most of the students looked surprised and then a little confused. But OJ came to the rescue. "You don't need to use a variable because nothing changes from one window size to the next or one stage to the next. The number of corner squares is always four because every square, no matter how big or small, has four corners."

I decided to introduce the term *constant function* at this point in the lesson to give students the opportunity to see the connection between the two ideas. I knew that the graph they would soon produce would reinforce this concept as well.

I added, "When a function rule contains only one value that stays the same and does not change from stage to stage, the pattern it reflects is called a *constant function*. The pattern for corner panes in this problem is an example of a constant function and the rule contains only a constant expression. Is that clear?"

The students seemed comfortable with this idea so I asked for an iterative rule for the total number of center panes for any stage in the window problem. Most members of the class raised their hands. Kevin volunteered, "The number of center panes grows by odd numbers. The increases from one window size to the next are one, then three, then five, and so on. So the rule is 'Total number of center panes equals previous number of panes plus the next odd number.' For example, to get the total number of center panes for a six-by-six window, you have to add seven to the total for a five-by-five window. Since there are nine center panes in a five-by-five, there are nine plus seven, or sixteen, center panes in a six-by-six window. This rule doesn't work as easily as most of the iterative rules we have used before because you either have to make a complete table or figure out some way to know which odd number to add to the previous total. Like for my example, to get the number of center panes for a six-by-six window, you needed to know that there are nine center panes in a five-by-five window *and* you have to know that you added the odd number five to get the answer for the five-by-five window."

Several students were nodding their heads in agreement with Kevin's concern.

"First of all, can someone use Kevin's rule to find the number of center panes for a seven-by-seven window?" I asked.

"I can," Jessica offered. "Since there were sixteen center panes for a six-by-six window and since we know you added seven to get that total, you would take the previous total, sixteen, and add nine, the next odd number, to get a total of twenty-five center panes for a seven-by-seven window."

"Does everyone agree?" I asked. When everyone nodded, I added, "So can anyone tell us a way to know which odd number you would need to add to the previous total to get the answer for any stage?"

No one volunteered immediately so I made a quick decision. "I'd like you to think about that question tonight. We'll revisit this question before we leave this problem, but you have found an iterative rule that works here, so let's go on now to the explicit rule for finding the number of center panes for any size window."

I made this decision because I felt it was more important to go on to the final explicit rule for this problem before class ended so that the students would have all the information they needed to construct appropriate graphs. All too often we teachers have to make instructional decisions midlesson or even midsentence, but at each such decision point I try to keep in mind the content objectives of the lesson and balance those objectives with all the factors that maximize student learning. Often, departing from the lesson plan results in learning that is actually critical to the success of a lesson—even if such a departure means extending the lesson far beyond the time frame I originally planned. Sometimes such detours result in extended investigations sparked by student interest—investigations that may have far more impact than one lesson could ever have. But sometimes taking time out at an important juncture in a lesson to pursue a mathematical question, no matter how interesting, can cause students to lose sight of the big conceptual picture they are putting together. It is those detours I have to try to recognize and prevent or postpone. At this point in this lesson, I decided "So much for the $(n-2)$th odd number: it can be dealt with later!"

Only Rinaldo raised his hand to offer an explicit rule for finding the total number of center panes for any size window. Luckily, Rinaldo understood the importance I place on having students construct their own learning whenever possible, so he pleasantly obliged when I asked him not to tell the rule but instead to make an observation he thought would help his classmates derive the rule themselves. After pondering for a few moments, Rinaldo offered, "Look back at the drawings for several stages of the pattern. Concentrate on any patterns you *see* for the center panes."

Having benefited from Rinaldo's shared observations in the past, the other students looked back at their drawings. But no one offered a comment.

"You had some important observations that you shared earlier about the center panes," I reminded them. "Recall patterns you shared before about the center panes and everyone think about how they might help you find a rule."

"Well," Emily said, "we noticed that the center panes always form a square."

"And what does that suggest about a rule for the number of center panes?" I asked.

"That the rule has something to do with a square?" Ben offered timidly.

"Yes. Was there anything else you noticed earlier?" I asked.

"Oh yeah, oh yeah," Kim chimed in. "We noticed that the square of center panes for any window size is the same size and shape as the total window with side lengths two smaller than it."

"I don't remember what that means," Yoko commented.

Rinaldo quickly went to the overhead and sketched a 5-by-5 window, shading the center panes, as shown here:

He instructed, "Look at this five-by-five window. The nine center panes form a square like Ben said, and that square has the same number of panes as an entire three-by-three window—the window with sides two shorter than it."

"I see what you are saying with the drawings," Ky said, "but I still can't get a rule."

"Ky," I said, "tell us in words what you see happening in the drawings."

"For any window (like a five-by-five), the center panes are a square with sides that are two units smaller (like a three-by-three square of center panes for the five-by-five window)."

I wrote Ky's words on the overhead, adding the indicated parentheses. "Now who can help write a rule from what Ky said?" I asked.

Several students raised their hands. Royce offered, "Total number of center panes equals two less than the length of one side—and you have to square or multiply that part times itself."

I asked Royce to show his rule on the overhead and he wrote the following: *Total Center Panes = (side length − 2)²*.

Lawson raised his hand and said, smiling, "I think you could write the rule 'Total center panes equals (stage number minus two) squared.'"

"Yes," Emily added, "or 'Total center panes equals (*n* minus two) squared,' if *n* stands for side length or stage number!"

It was nice to have three different ways of expressing the rule presented quickly in succession so that students could connect them as equivalent.

"Can anyone explain how that rule makes sense when you think about the center panes in square windows in this problem?" I asked.

Jim went up to the overhead, pointed to Rinaldo's sketch, and explained, "The center panes are always a square of panes that has a layer of edge and corner panes around the outside. So for any window you can just take off that outer layer and you are left with a square that is two panes shorter on each side than the window you started with."

I acknowledged Jim's idea and asked everyone to try the rule for a 10-by-10 window. All students gave the thumbs-up signal when Maria indicated she got sixty-four center panes.

Now that the students had examined the data in a table and had symbolic rules to fit that data, I felt they were ready to create the representation of the data in a graph. Therefore, I asked the students to work with a partner to construct three graphs on the same sheet of paper: graphs for the number of edge, center, and corner panes for windows of sizes 2-by-2 through 8-by-8.

The whole class had a brief discussion before starting to work. When asked to suggest appropriate labels for the axes, Yoko suggested the *x*-axis be labeled *Side Length* or *Window Size* and the *y*-axis *Number of Panes*. Emily suggested that one square could be used for one unit along both axes, and Mike pointed out that three different marks should be used to designate the corner, edge, and center panes. Then the students set to work.

I verified that each pair of students was adhering to the guidelines the class had outlined for creating the graphs before class time ran out. I asked the students to complete the graphs for homework and to consider the following two questions, which the class would address the next day:

1. How would you describe the graph for each kind of pane to someone over the phone?

2. Thinking about *The Window Problem*, why does each graph look like it does? (How does the shape of the graph make sense when you think about what happens to the number of each kind of pane as the windows get larger?)

Comparing Graphs and Multiple Representations

The students arrived in class the next day with their completed graphs. They exchanged papers with a partner and checked each other's graphs for accuracy. Except for a few misplaced coordinates (quickly fixed), the graphs were deemed correct, so we began a discussion about the graphs.

I told the students they should first discuss just the appearance of the three graphs. When asked to describe the graph for corner panes, Chan said, "It is just a straight line across." (See Figure 10–7 on page 226.)

Ky added, "It is a line of unconnected dots up four units from the *x*-axis."

Rinaldo pointed out that each point could be thought of as (n, 4) if n is the side length of the window and 4 is the number of corner panes.

I asked two questions about the graph of corner panes. "How does the graph show how the number of corner panes changes as the size of the window increases?" Many hands were raised and Kevin reported that the "straight line across" shows that the number of corner panes does not change at all as the window sizes grow. I then asked, "And what does the explicit rule for this function look like, using the variables *x* and *y*, as used on the graph?"

FIGURE 10–7   Chan's graph

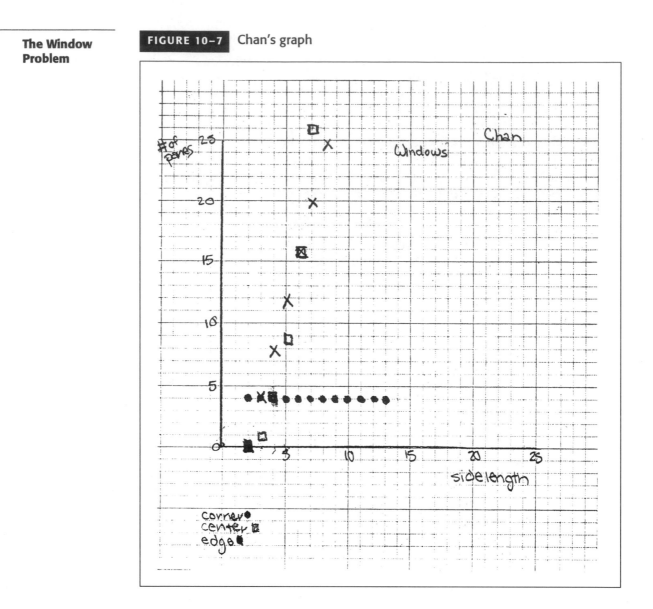

Emily replied, "It doesn't have an *x* variable or a variable expression with *x* in it, just a plain number or constant."

Jim added, "I think the rule is *y* (or the number of corner panes) equals four [*y* = 4]. You don't need an *x* in the rule because nothing changes as the windows grow."

I agreed and reminded the students that such a function is called a *constant function*.

I was pleased that the students in this class seemed to find it so easy to interpret the graph and grasp the concept of a constant function. I believe this happened in part because the students spent a lot of time doing investigations and discussions to lay the groundwork for this understanding during the first part of the lesson, and also because the students were interpreting the concept of a constant function within a now-familiar context. They could clearly see why there was no variable part to the function: every square had exactly four corners.

The discussion moved to the graph of the edge panes. When asked to describe that graph, Kim said, "The graph is a diagonal line of dots that goes up and to the right."

Royce added, "Each coordinate is over one space to the right and up four spaces from the one before it."

I asked more questions. "How does the number of edge panes change as the size of the window increases?" Again many hands were raised. Carolyn stated that each time the length of the edge of the window increases by one, the number of edge panes increases by four. I followed up with "And how is the explicit rule for such a function different than that of a constant function?"

OJ replied, "It has an x variable part."

I wanted to introduce another concept through the appearance of the graph for edge panes. "Carolyn said *each* time the window size grows by one, the number of edge panes grows by four. What does that mean about the growing pattern of this function?"

Melinda stated, "The pattern increases by the same amount every time."

I asked whether everyone agreed with Melinda's statement. They did. I then explained that when there is a *constant rate of growth*, as with the edge panes, the function is called a *linear function*. I asked whether someone could venture a hypothesis about why such functions were called linear functions. Lawson answered, "I guess the graph would always make a line."

"Yes," I affirmed, "the graph of a linear function is always a line. Can anybody explain why that makes sense?"

Kim volunteered, as she pointed to her graph, "If the changes in the variables are always the same, like plus four for the y whenever it is plus one for the x, then the coordinates on the graph will make a line."

I knew that a lot more exploration and discussion would be needed before most of the students would develop a clear understanding of linear functions. But I wanted to keep the focus of this part of the lesson on the comparison of the three types of functions and their graphs related to the context of *The Window Problem*, so I steered the discussion to the graph for the center panes.

First, I asked for descriptions of the graph for the center panes. Jessica volunteered that the graph is not a straight line.

Yoko added that it looks sort of like a steep line that increases more every time. When asked to clarify "every time," she stated, "Each time you move one dot to the right, you go up more on the graph than you did between the last two dots."

Jim clarified Yoko's comment by adding "The distance between coordinates always increases. It always goes up by two more than the previous increase."

When the class agreed that the statements given by the three students generally described the graph quite well, I asked, "So do you think this graph is either a constant or a linear function?"

Emily stated emphatically, "It can't be. It's not a constant function because it has variable parts. And it can't be a linear function because it doesn't change the same amount for each stage."

I acknowledged Emily's logic and explained that this kind of function—one for which the rate of change is not constant—is sometimes called a *quadratic function*.

OJ surprised me with his next question. "Does the name *quadratic function* have anything to do with the rule having an exponent in it?" he asked.

"Great question, OJ," I answered. "As a matter of fact, it does. Whenever the explicit function rule for a situation can be written to include a variable expression with an exponent of two, that function is a quadratic function. The rule for the center panes, y equals (n minus two) squared [$y = (n - 2)^2$], as you know, means that you are squaring a quantity. As that quantity gets larger, the rate of change increases; for example, there is more difference between five squared and six squared than there is between four squared and five squared. As you have noticed, that makes the coordinates on the graph farther and farther apart."

It was not my intention to include the ideas brought out by OJ's question in this lesson. However, I encourage thoughtful questions in my classes to foster the enrichment they can add to a lesson, exactly as happened in this case. I find that once students in a class have taken ownership for their learning, serendipitous learning is often sparked by such questions.

In the next part of the lesson I wanted the students to concentrate on connecting the appearance of the graphs to their meaning in relation to the problem. I reminded the students that they were asked to consider the following questions after constructing their graphs the night before: Thinking about *The Window Problem*, why does each graph look like it does? How does the shape of the graph make sense when you think about what happens with each kind of pane as the windows get larger?

I started with the graph for the corner panes. Quickly and confidently the students agreed with Carolyn when she said, "It makes sense that the graph for the total number of corner panes is a horizontal straight line. The line shows that the number of corner panes is four no matter how large the window is because every square, regardless of its side length, has four corners."

When asked to relate the graph for edge panes to *The Window Problem*, Ky explained, "Whenever the window grows in size, each edge gets one more pane, so there are four more edge panes in all for each new window size. The graph shows this because each time you move one along the x-axis (the window size), you move up four along the y-axis (the number of panes). That's just logical!"

Finally, I asked the students to explain how the graph for center panes makes sense when thinking about *The Window Problem*. George expressed his thoughts this way: "The center panes for any size window make a square shape. That means the number of square panes is always a square number. The graph shows this because as the windows get bigger, the coordinates go up more each time, since square numbers go one, four, nine, sixteen, and so on, with the number of panes you gain getting bigger each time. This fast way the number of center panes grows means the coordinates don't make a straight line and the coordinates get farther and farther apart along the y-axis."

As often happens, I felt George gave a wonderful explanation. While the language he used might not have been as precise as that I might have chosen, the students certainly seemed to follow his thinking. George expressed the essence of the relevant mathematical ideas in a way that the students seemed to understand. I believe this is one of the main benefits of having students share their thinking instead of teachers providing all explanations.

As a wrap-up, I asked the students to give a reason why the lesson might be important. Two main sentiments were expressed. The first response was quite practical and directly linked to the problem. As George expressed it, "The Peerless Window Company could figure out how many of each kind of pane to make. Just from looking at our tables, they could see that they need a lot more center panes than any other kind. But with a little work, they could know what their customers like to order and use the rules to make a big batch of panes without having to worry that they'd have a whole bunch of one kind left over."

The second group of responses addressed the question in a more general sense. Emily summed it up when she stated, "In a lot of situations, finding patterns can lead to working out rules. Using those rules, you can find the answer for any stage of a pattern. You can also make predictions for large stages or situations that don't even exist."

I was pleased that the students saw both the contextual application and the broader mathematical implications of what they did in this lesson.

The content of the lesson had been covered to my satisfaction. There was much student discussion. Now I wanted each student to process the lesson as a whole for him- or herself. I asked students to reflect upon each of four questions and then answer them in writing. Following are the questions and a sampling of the responses (such as Figure 10–8, below). I had students share their answers the next day in class.

FIGURE 10–8   Student answers for question #1

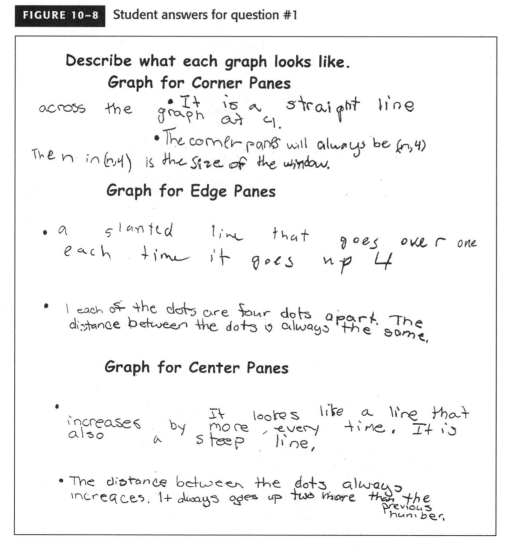

Describe what each graph looks like.
Graph for Corner Panes

across the •It is a straight line
graph at 4.

•The corner pans will always be (n,4)
The n in (n,4) is the size of the window.

Graph for Edge Panes

• a slanted line that goes over one
each time it goes up 4

• l each of the dots are four dots apart. The
distance between the dots is always the same.

Graph for Center Panes

• It lookes like a line that
increases by more every time. It is
also a by steep line.

• The distance between the dots always
increaces. It always goes up two more than the
previous
number.

1. Describe what each graph looks like. (See Figure 10–8.)

2. Explain why each graph looks like it does. How does the shape of the graph make sense when you think about the data you found about the windows? (See Figure 10–9.)

3. Explain how your table and graph are alike and how they are different. (See Figure 10–10.)

4. Would you rather use the table, the graph, or the rule to find the number of each kind of panes needed to make a window of a certain size? Why? (See Figure 10–11.)

I was pleased with both the quantity and the quality of the answers written by the students. Those answers satisfied me that the students in this class showed growth in their algebraic thinking during this initial exposure to the concepts of constant, linear, and quadratic functions. Their writing also indicated that they were able to understand the connections among the multiple representations (tables, graphs, and function rules) used in this investigation and relate the numbers and symbols in them to *The Window Problem*. I believe such experiences will help these students begin to internalize the meaning of important algebraic concepts such as function, rate of change, and slope as well as appreciate the power of mathematics to describe and predict phenomena.

FIGURE 10–9   Student answers for question #2

Explain why each graph looks like it does. How does the shape of the graph make sense when you think about the data you found about the windows?

Graph for Corner Panes

• You should have a straight line because every square window pane will have 4 corner panes, because there are 4 corners in a square.

• Because there are always four corner panes on a square. Only the side length of the window changes

Graph for Edge Panes

• You go up 4 and over 1 because for every next step you add one edge to the side and you go over 1 because the side length always changes one.

• 4(N-2) is the edge rule because first you take off the 2 corners from each side, which leaves you with one side's edge x4 because there are 4 edges

Graph for Center Panes

• It looks like that because if you take off the sides, it is always the same as the window square below it.

• Center panes match total for 2 steps before (You take away the edges to get a smaller square, which equals the square from 2 steps back)

FIGURE 10–10 Student answers for question #3

Explain how your table and graph are alike and how they are different.

- They are alike because they show the same info and they both have the same patterns. They are different because they show info in different ways. They also don't both use numbers to show info.
- They're alike because both go in the same patterns. They're different because the graph's a visual plot and the table's numeric data.
- They both show the information, but only the graph shows the patterns and them in relationship to each other.
- They express the same thing in different ways. They are different because the table is easier to read.
- Just looking at the rule, it is hard to tell what is happening all along.

FIGURE 10–11 Student answers for question #4

Would you rather use the table, the graph, or the rule to find the number of each kind of panes needed to make a window of a certain size? Why?

- I like the table better because it easier to understand the rules and what comes next in the pattern.
- I would want to use the graph paper because it is fun to see it as a picture and it makes it easier and more organized and I am a visual learner.
- I think the graph ± the table would help teach someone quickly. I think this because they help each other teach and you understand it.
- I'd use the rule to find the number of each panes because it is always correct and quick.
- I would like to use the rule because with the rule you can do the inlimitable.
- I like the rule because you can go as far as you want.

The following problem is appropriate for a lesson that ties to *The Window Problem* lesson.

Peerless Window Company is now making triangular-shaped windows from three kinds of units:

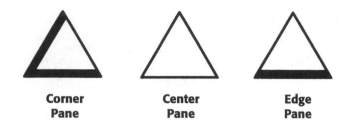

| Corner Pane | Center Pane | Edge Pane |

Again, the people in the company need to decide how many of each kind of unit to make so they can avoid wasting units.

1. Complete a table with the following columns. Add needed rows.

Window Size (Edge Length)	Number of Corner Pane Units	Number of Center Pane Units	Number of Edge Pane Units	Total Number of Panes Needed
2				
3				
n				

2. Look for patterns and find a rule for any size triangular window.

3. Do the following:

   - In words, write the rule you found for the number of each kind of unit needed for any triangular window.
   - Use your rules to find the number of each kind of unit needed for a window with edge length 100.
   - Graph each rule for windows with edge lengths 2 to 8 units on a side (all on one grid).
   - Looking at your grid, describe each graph in words.
   - Thinking about this problem, explain why each graph looks like it does. (How does the shape of the graph make sense when you think about the data you found about the windows?)
   - Explain how your table and graph are alike and how they are different.
   - Would you rather use the table, graph, or rules to find the number of each kind of pane needed to make a window with a certain edge length? Why?

Appropriate explicit function rules for the *Triangular Windows* problem are as follows:

Total panes with 2 reinforced sides = 3

Total panes with 1 reinforced side = $3(n - 2)$

Total panes with no reinforced sides = $(n - 2)^2 + (n - 1)$ when n = stage number

          ↓   ↓

      sum of $(n - 2)$ panes with no
      odd numbers   reinforced sides
                  on bottom row

Of course, students may offer other forms of these rules.

Painted Cube | Extension Problem

A 10-by-10-by-10 cube (made of 1-by-1-by-1 cubes) is dropped into a bucket of paint. What is the number of small cubes with paint on three faces, two faces, one face, and zero faces? Investigate cubes with different dimensions. Find patterns and rules for how many cubes would have paint on three faces, two faces, one face, and zero faces.

Note: This problem includes a cubic function as well as quadratic, linear, and constant functions.

Appropriate function rules for the *Painted Cube* problem are as follows:

Total cubes with 3 faces painted = 8

Total cubes with 2 faces painted = $12(n - 2)$

Total cubes with 1 face painted = $6(n - 2)^2$

Total cubes with 0 faces painted = $(n - 2)^3$ when n = side length of cube

As with *The Window Problem*, students should create various representations of the data and compare them for each function rule. Also, emphasis should be placed on contrasting the rates of change for the different kinds of functions:

- *constant:* no change from one stage to the next
- *linear:* constant rate of change from one stage to the next
- *quadratic:* increasing rate of change from one stage to the next
- *cubic:* even greater increases in the rate of change from one stage to the next

Other activities appropriate for use after *The Window Problem* lesson can be found in *Navigating Through Algebra in Grades 6–8* (Friel et al. 2001). They are "Jason's Savings Plans," "Perimeters and Areas of Squares," and "Areas of Garden Plots" (52–55), all of which involve comparing linear functions to other types of functions.

If graphing calculators are available, the rules for corner, center, and edge panes can be entered in the y = menu and the tables and graphs can be viewed. The tables and graphs can be compared and can show data for large numbers that would be awkward to calculate or graph by hand.

Also, scatter plots can be created using actual values from student-generated lists, and a discussion about whether points should be connected in the plots can be initiated.

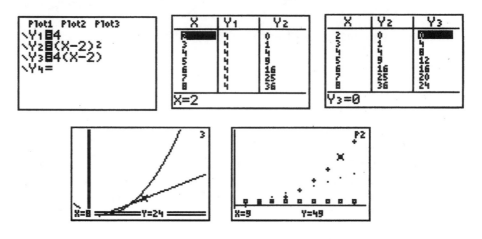

Viewing the graphs with different window settings is a nice addition to this technology connection.

Blackline Masters

Grids for Coordinate Graphing

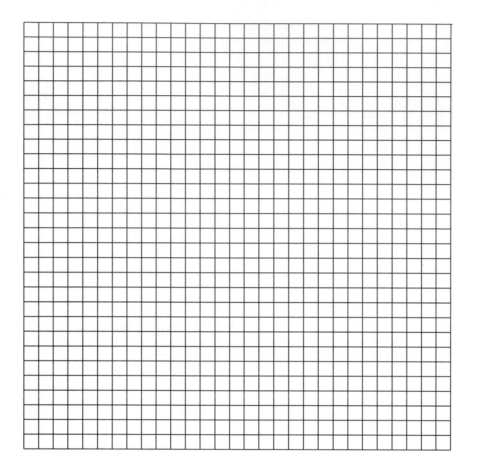

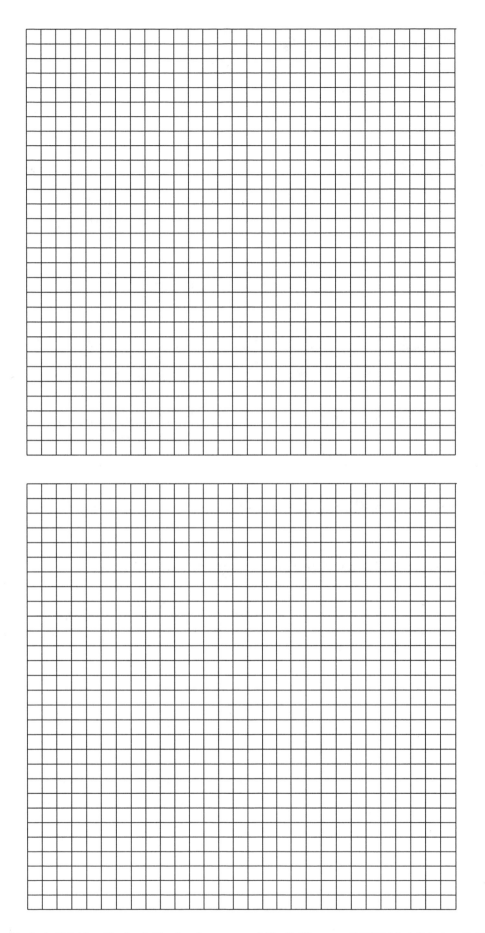

From *Lessons for Algebraic Thinking, Grades 6–8* by Ann Lawrence and Charlie Hennessy. © 2002 Math Solutions Publications.

Personalized Patterns

Part One

Exploring the H Pattern

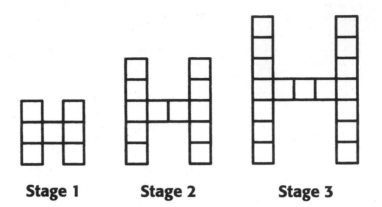

Stage 1   **Stage 2**   **Stage 3**

Given Stages 1, 2, and 3 of the H Pattern, do the following:

- Draw Stage 4 and Stage 5 of the H Pattern.

- Find a pattern to predict the number of squares needed for higher stages of the H Pattern.

- Give a rule that will work for any stage of the H Pattern.

From *Lessons for Algebraic Thinking, Grades 6–8* by Ann Lawrence and Charlie Hennessy. © 2002 Math Solutions Publications.

Personalized Patterns

Part Two

Creating Your Own Personalized Pattern

Create a personalized pattern for one of your own initials, similar to the H Pattern.

- Choose one of the initials in your name.

- Use squares to build a figure that looks like that letter.

- Make a rule to produce each new stage of your pattern.

- Build the first three stages of your pattern, using your rule.

Make an Answer Key for the following questions:

- Draw Stage 4 and Stage 5 of the pattern.

- Describe Stage n of the pattern in words.

- Make a drawing to show which parts of the pattern are variable and which parts are constant.

- Write an iterative and an explicit rule for any stage of the pattern.

Go Figure!

Juan is saving money to give both his mother and his grandmother a very nice box of candy for Mother's Day. The clerk at the candy shop tells Juan that the store packages candy in certain square, rectangular, or triangular boxes (see the figurate number investigations on your activity sheets). Juan has decided the following:

1. He will buy the same number of pieces of candy for his mother and his grandmother.

2. He can afford up to fifty pieces of candy each for his mother and his grandmother.

3. He wants the two boxes to be different shapes.

After completing the investigations about square, rectangular, and triangular numbers, write a paragraph to recommend to Juan the shapes and sizes of boxes you think he should buy. Be sure you explain your mathematical thinking.

Figurate Numbers Less than 50

Square Numbers	Rectangular Numbers	Triangular Numbers

Your Recommendation to Juan (Write on the back of this sheet or on a separate piece of paper.):

From *Lessons for Algebraic Thinking, Grades 6–8* by Ann Lawrence and Charlie Hennessy. © 2002 Math Solutions Publications.

Go Figure!

Investigating Figurate Numbers #1: Square Numbers

---

1. The first three square numbers are shown below.

o · · o · · o · · ·
· · o · o · · o · · o
· · · · · · o · · o

  1   **2**   **3**

2. Draw the fourth and fifth square numbers in the space below.

3. Find a pattern and predict the number of dots needed to show the tenth square number and the one hundredth square number.

4. Give a rule that will work for any square number.

Go Figure!

Investigating Figurate Numbers #2: Rectangular Numbers

1. The first three rectangular numbers are shown below.

2. Draw the fourth and fifth rectangular numbers below.

3. Find a pattern and predict the number of dots needed to show the tenth rectangular number and the one hundredth rectangular number.

4. Give a rule that will work for any rectangular number.

Go Figure!
Investigating Figurate Numbers #3: Triangular Numbers

1. The first three triangular numbers are shown below.

```
 o          o  o        o  o  o
            o           o  o
                        o
 1          2           3
```

2. Draw the fourth and fifth triangular numbers below.

3. Find a pattern and predict the number of dots needed to show the tenth triangular number and the one hundredth triangular number.

4. Give a rule that will work for any triangular number.

Who Finishes When?

Alice's walking rate is 2.5 meters per second. Her younger brother, Mack, walks 1 meter per second. Because Alice's rate is faster than Mack's, Alice gives Mack a 45-meter head start in a 100-meter race. What happens in the race?

Explain your strategy for solving this problem and give evidence to support your answer.

Stretching Slinkies

Version 1

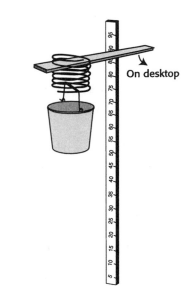

On desktop

1. Setup

Set up your experiment as shown in the illustration on the right. Place the ruler on the desk and make sure it stays flat when you are measuring.

2. Gathering Data

- Measure the distance from the bottom of your cup to the floor (nearest half-inch).

- Put one coin in the cup at a time (1–10). Measure and record the distance from the bottom of your cup to the floor (nearest half-inch) for each number of coins.

- Repeat for your other type of coin.

Number of Coins	Distance from floor	
	Coin 1	Coin 2
0		
1		
2		
3		
4		
5		
6		
7		
8		
9		
10		

Stretching Slinkies
Version 1, continued

3. Graphing

Make a graph for both your sets of data on graph paper. Remember to scale and label your axes.

4. Analyzing the Data

Answer the following questions on loose-leaf paper:

- Find a rule for each set of data. Explain the rule in words and how it relates to the experiment you did.

- Predict the distance from the bottom of your cup to the floor for twenty coins of each type. Explain your thinking.

- Predict the number of coins needed to make this statement true: The distance from the bottom of your cup to the floor = exactly 2 cm. Explain your thinking.

- Do the sets of data in your table represent functions? Explain your thinking.

- Compare the rules you found for the two kinds of coins (similarities and differences).

- Compare your graphs for the two kinds of coins (similarities and differences).

- How are your graphs different from the graphs of people who measured the distance from the top of the Slinky to the bottom of the cup? Why?

- Write a paragraph about what you learned (or how this experiment reinforced what you already knew) about functions.

From *Lessons for Algebraic Thinking, Grades 6–8* by Ann Lawrence and Charlie Hennessy. © 2002 Math Solutions Publications.

Stretching Slinkies

Version 2

1. Setup

Set up your experiment as shown in the illustration on the right. Place the ruler on the desk and make sure it stays flat when you are measuring.

On desktop

2. Gathering Data

■ Measure the distance from the top of the Slinky to the bottom of your cup (to the nearest half-inch).

■ Put one coin in the cup at a time (1–10). Measure and record the distance from the top of the Slinky to the bottom of your cup (to the nearest half-inch) for each number of coins.

■ Repeat for your other type of coin.

Number of Coins	Distance from top of the Slinky to the bottom of the cup	
	Coin 1	*Coin 2*
0		
1		
2		
3		
4		
5		
6		
7		
8		
9		
10		

Stretching Slinkies
Version 2, continued

3. Graphing

Make a graph for both your sets of data on graph paper. Remember to scale and label your axes.

4. Analyzing the Data

Answer the following questions on loose-leaf paper:

- Find a rule for each set of data. Explain the rule in words and how it relates to the experiment you did.

- Predict the distance from the top of the Slinky to the bottom of your cup for twenty coins of each type. Explain your thinking.

- Predict the number of coins needed to make this statement true: The distance from the top of the Slinky to the bottom of your cup = exactly 24 inches. Explain your thinking.

- Do the sets of data in your table represent functions? Explain your thinking.

- Compare the rules you found for the two kinds of coins (similarities and differences).

- Compare your graphs for the two kinds of coins (similarities and differences).

- How are your graphs different from the graphs of people who measured the distance from the bottom of the cup to the floor? Why?

- Write a paragraph about what you learned (or how this experiment reinforced what you already knew) about functions.

From *Lessons for Algebraic Thinking, Grades 6–8* by Ann Lawrence and Charlie Hennessy. © 2002 Math Solutions Publications.

Condo Challenge

Building planners are designing a new condominium. They are not sure yet how tall they want the building to be.

1. How many cubes are needed to build this 6-high model of Clearview Condos?

2. How many cubes would be needed to build a 12-high model?

3. Explain how you got your answer for Question #2.

4. How many cubes would be needed to build a model of any height? Explain your thinking and make a rule, using a variable if possible.

5. How could your findings help the builders of Clearview Condos?

The Window Problem

Peerless Window Company puts together square windows from three kinds of units:

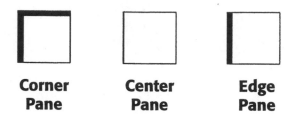

Corner Pane   **Center Pane**   **Edge Pane**

The production manager at Peerless needs to decide how many of each type of unit to make so the company can avoid wasting units. Complete the labeled rows in the following table. You may complete extra rows if you wish. Look for patterns and find a rule for each kind of pane for any size square window.

Window Size	Number of Corner-Pane Units	Number of Center-Pane Units	Number of Edge-Pane Units	Total Number of Panes
2 × 2				
3 × 3				
4 × 4				
5 × 5				
6 × 6				
n × n				

From *Lessons for Algebraic Thinking, Grades 6–8* by Ann Lawrence and Charlie Hennessy. © 2002 Math Solutions Publications.

Glossary

We have included in this glossary mathematical terms, phrases, and expressions that appear in the book and that we think are mathematically important and likely to be new to your students. We tried to write definitions that are both mathematically accurate and useful to students who are struggling to make sense of these ideas. We chose language that is accessible to middle school learners, and have provided examples and illustrations when we felt they were needed.

We hope that you use the definitions in this glossary as guidelines and give your students as many opportunities as possible to express ideas in their own words and listen to how their classmates express those ideas. We don't expect our students to use the language that we choose and we don't require them to learn our definitions. A reasonable goal is that students recognize the terms, phrases, and expressions and can use them in the context of the learning activities they experience. Keep in mind that students will have further opportunities to formalize their thinking as they continue to develop their understanding of algebra through subsequent experiences.

axis (*plural: axes*)   a reference line on a graph used for locating points. On a coordinate graph, the horizontal reference line is often called the x-axis and the vertical reference line is often called the y-axis.

Cartesian coordinates   see *coordinates*. Named after Rene Descartes, a French mathematician (1596–1650) who worked on linking algebra and geometry, making it possible to visually represent any equation as a set of points on a graph.

Cartesian plane   see *coordinate plane*

coefficient   the numerical factor of a term; for example, $4x$ means "4 times x" and 4 is the coefficient of x. By convention, the coefficient precedes the variable and no multiplication sign is needed.

constant   a quantity whose value does not change. In a function rule, the constant term doesn't have a variable and, therefore, stays the same for every stage.

constant function   a function for which every ordered pair has the same second number. The graph of a constant function is a horizontal line.

coordinate graph   a visual representation of a set of ordered pairs seen as points on a grid (called a *coordinate plane*); each point is graphed using the axes to locate the position indicated by an ordered pair of numbers.

coordinate grid   see *coordinate plane*

coordinate plane   a grid formed by intersecting horizontal and vertical number lines used for plotting points identified by ordered pairs; often referred to as *Cartesian plane* or *coordinate grid*.

coordinates   the numbers in an ordered pair used to locate a point on a coordinate plane; the first number in the pair is often called the x-*coordinate* and the second number, the y-*coordinate*.

dependent variable   in a function with two variables, the variable that represents the output values in each ordered pair; the values are determined by applying a rule to the input values; see also *independent variable*.

domain of a function   the set of the first numbers (the input values) in the ordered pairs that make up the function.

equivalent expressions   expressions that may not look alike but that produce the same results or solutions for every input. For example, $(x + 1) + 4$ and $x + 5$ are equivalent expressions because they produce the same result for every value of x.

equivalent rules or functions   rules or equations that may not look alike but that produce the same results for every input value; for example, $y = 2x$, $y = x + x$, and $2y = 4x$ are equivalent because they produce the same value of y for each value of x.

explicit rule   a rule that can be used to find the value of any term in a pattern or stage in a function without knowing the value of the previous term or stage. For example, the total number of corners, c, in the number of squares for any stage number, n, can be represented by the rule $c = 4n$.

Square Numbers

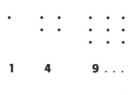

1   4   9 . . .

figurate numbers   special numbers associated with specific groups of geometric figures that can be represented using arrays of dots. For example, square numbers are 1, 4, 9, 16, . . . ; triangular numbers are 1, 3, 6, 10, ...

function   a relationship between two variables in which the value of one variable (often called the *output*) depends on the value of the other variable (often called the *input*); if the variable y is a function of the variable x, then there is exactly one y value for every x value.

Triangular Numbers

1   3   6 . . .

function rule   a description of a function that uses words and/or symbols to pair every input number with exactly one output number.

horizontal axis   the number line on a coordinate grid that goes left and right, usually called the x-*axis*.

independent variable   in a function with two variables, the variable that represents the input values in each ordered pair. The output values are determined by applying a rule to each input value. See also *dependent variable*.

intercept (y intercept)   when graphing a function, the point on the vertical axis (the y-axis); for example, the point (0, 4) is the y-intercept for the function $y = x + 4$. The input value of the ordered pair for the y-intercept is 0. The term is also used for the output value of a function when the input value is 0; for example, 4 is the y-intercept for the function $y = x + 4$.

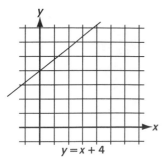

$y = x + 4$

iterative rule   a rule that can be used to find the value of any term or stage in a pattern by using the value of the previous term or stage. For example, an iterative rule might state, "Add 3 to the output value for the previous stage."

linear function   a function whose ordered pairs, when graphed on a coordinate plane, form a straight line.

multiple representations   different forms for presenting information about a set of data; for example, diagrams, words, tables, graphs, and symbols.

order of operations   the agreed-upon order to follow when performing mathematical operations: (1) simplify inside grouping symbols, (2) evaluate all powers, (3) do all multiplication and division from left to right, then (4) do all addition and subtraction from left to right.

ordered pair   a pair of numbers in a specific order; an ordered pair can be used to plot a point on a coordinate plane.

origin   the point where the horizontal and vertical axes intersect on a coordinate plane; the point on a coordinate plane located by the ordered pair (0, 0).

plot   to use an ordered pair to mark a point on a coordinate plane.

quadrant   one of the four regions of a coordinate plane formed by the two axes. The quadrants are numbered counterclockwise, starting with the upper right region. Points on the axes are not in any quadrant.

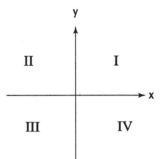

quadratic function   a function whose equation contains squared terms as the term(s) with the highest exponent; for example, $y = x^2 - 3$.

range of a function   the set of the second numbers (the output values) in the ordered pairs that make up the function.

scatter plot   a graph that shows the relationship between two sets of data as points on a coordinate grid.

slope   the steepness or slant of a line on a graph, measured by how much it rises or falls for each unit the line moves to the right. For the line represented by $y = x$, some points are (0, 0), (1, 1), (2, 2), (3, 3), and so on; as points move one unit to the right, they move one unit up; therefore, the slope is 1. For the line represented by $y = 2x$, some points are (0, 0), (1, 2), (2, 4), (3, 6), and so on; as points move one unit to the right, they move two units up; therefore, the slope is 2.

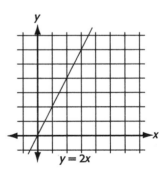

stage number   term, step, or figure number in a pattern; also, a member of the domain of a sequence or function.

T-chart   a table for recording ordered pairs of functions with two variables. For each row, the first column usually contains the stage or input number; the second column, the value or output number.

term   a member of a sequence of numbers arranged according to some pattern; a part of an algebraic expression that can be variable or constant; for example, $3x + 2y + 6$ has three terms $3x$, $2y$, and 6.

value of an expression   the number that results from substituting a number for each variable in an algebraic expression, then simplifying.

value of a function   for any ordered pair (x, y) of a function, y is its value.

variable   a letter, symbol, or other placeholder in a mathematical expression that can serve different purposes. It can represent an unknown value; for example, x

in $4x = 12$ represents the number 3. It can represent part of a function rule that changes from stage to stage; for example, in $y = x + 4$, y and x are variables while 4 is a constant. It can represent quantities in formulas; for example, the C and d in $C = \pi d$ are variables. It can be used to represent a general mathematical pattern; for example, in $a + b = b + a$, a and b are variables used to describe the commutative property of addition.

vertical axis   the number line on a coordinate plane that goes up and down; it is usually called the y-axis.

x-axis   see *horizontal axis*

x-coordinate   see *coordinates*

y-axis   see *vertical axis*

y-coordinate   see *coordinates*

Bibliography

Brueningsen, Chris, et al. 1997. *Mathematics and Science in Motion: Activities for Middle School*. Austin, TX: Texas Instruments.

Chwast, Seymour. 1993. *The 12 Circus Rings*. New York: Harcourt Brace.

Dickinson, Rebecca. 1996. *The 13 Nights of Halloween*. New York: Scholastic.

Friel, Susan, et al. 2001. *Navigating Through Algebra in Grades 6–8*. Reston, VA: National Council of Teachers of Mathematics.

Grossman, Bill. 1996. *My Little Sister Ate One Hare*. New York: Crown.

Johnson, Iris D. 2000. "Mission Possible! Can You Walk Your Talk?" *Mathematics Teaching in the Middle School* 6(October): 132–34.

McGlone, Chris, and Nieberle McGlone. 2000. "Using Hooke's Law to Explore Linear Functions." *The Mathematics Teacher* 5(May): 391–95.

National Council of Teachers of Mathematics. 2000. *Principles and Standards for School Mathematics*. Reston, VA: National Council of Teachers of Mathematics.

Index